Pragmatism and Pluralism

Harvard Dissertations in Religion

Editors

Bernadette J. Brooten

and

Francis Schüssler Fiorenza

Number 30

Pragmatism and Pluralism:
John Dewey's Significance for Theology

Jerome Paul Soneson

Pragmatism and Pluralism

John Dewey's Significance for Theology

Jerome Paul Soneson

Fortress Press   **Minneapolis**

PRAGMATISM AND PLURALISM
John Dewey's Significance for Theology

Harvard Dissertations in Religion, Number 30

Book design and typesetting at the Harvard Theological Review

Managing Editor: Tamar Duke-Cohan

Editorial Assistants: Ellen B. Aitken and Laura Nasrallah

Library of Congress Cataloging-in-Publication Data

Soneson, Jerome Paul, 1951–
    Pragmatism and pluralism: John Dewey's significance for theology
    / Jerome Paul Soneson.
        p.   cm. — (Harvard dissertations in religion)
    Includes bibliographical references.
    ISBN 0–8006–7086–8 (alk. paper) :
    1. Theology—Methodology. 2. Religious pluralism. 3. Dewey,
    John, 1859–1952. I. Title. II. Series.
    BR118.S65 1992
    230'.01—dc20
                                        92–30396
                                                CIP

Manufactured in the U.S.A.   AF 1–7086
97   96   95   94   93   1   2   3   4   5   6   7   8   9   10

Dedicated to my parents,

Dagmar L. Soneson

and

J. Melburn Soneson

Contents

Short Titles

Information appears here for frequently used works that are cited by short title. A few short titles do not appear in this list, but in each instance full bibliography is given on the page(s) preceding such references.

Alexander, *John Dewey's Theory of Art*
> Thomas M. Alexander, *John Dewey's Theory of Art, Experience, and Nature: The Horizons of Feeling* (Albany, NY: State University of New York Press, 1987).

Boisvert, *Dewey's Metaphysics*
> Raymond D. Boisvert, *Dewey's Metaphysics* (New York: Fordham University Press, 1988).

Dewey, *Art as Experience*
> John Dewey, *Art as Experience* (New York: G. P. Putnam's Sons, 1934).

Dewey, *A Common Faith*
> John Dewey, *A Common Faith* (New Haven: Yale University Press, 1960).

Dewey, "Context and Thought"
> John Dewey, "Context and Thought," in Richard J. Bernstein, ed., *On Experience, Nature and Freedom* (New York: Bobbs-Merrill, 1960).

Dewey, *Democracy and Education*
> John Dewey, *Democracy and Education: An Introduction to the Philosophy of Education* (New York: Macmillan, 1916).

Dewey, *Ethics*
> John Dewey and James H. Tufts, *Ethics* (rev. ed.; New York: Holt, 1932).

Dewey, *Experience and Education*
> John Dewey, *Experience and Education* (New York: Collier, 1938).

Dewey, *Experience and Nature*
> John Dewey, *Experience and Nature* (2d rev. ed.; New York: Dover, 1958).

Dewey, *How We Think*
> John Dewey, *How We Think: A Restatement of the Relation of Reflective Thinking to the Educative Process* (rev. ed.; New York: Heath, 1933).

Dewey, *Human Nature and Conduct*
> John Dewey, *Human Nature and Conduct: An Introduction to Social Psychology* (New York: Holt, 1922).

Dewey, "Interest"
> John Dewey, "Interest in Relation to Training of the Will," in *Second Supplement to the Herbert Year Book for 1895* (Bloomington, IL: National Herbert Society, 1896), reprinted in John J. McDermott, ed., *The Philosophy of John Dewey* (2 vols.; New York: G. P. Putnam's Sons, 1973) 2. 421–42; references are to the reprint.

Dewey, *Logic*
> John Dewey, *Logic: The Theory of Inquiry* (New York: Holt, Rinehart & Winston, 1938).

Dewey, "Philosophy"
> John Dewey, "Philosophy," in Jo Ann Boydston, ed., *John Dewey: The Later Works 1925–1953*, vol. 8: *1933* (Carbondale, IL: Southern Illinois University Press, 1986).

Dewey, "Philosophy and Civilization"
> John Dewey, "Philosophy and Civilization," in idem, *Philosophy and Civilization* (New York: Minton, Blach & Company, 1931).

Dewey, *Quest*
> John Dewey, *The Quest for Certainty* (New York: G. P. Putnam's Sons, 1960).

Dewey, *Reconstruction in Philosophy*
> John Dewey, *Reconstruction in Philosophy* (enl. ed.; Boston: Beacon, 1948).

Dewey, "The Subject Matter of Metaphysical Inquiry"
> John Dewey, "The Subject Matter of Metaphysical Inquiry," in Richard J. Bernstein, ed., *On Experience, Nature and Freedom* (New York: Bobbs-Merrill, 1960).

Dewey, *Theory of Valuation*
> John Dewey, *Theory of Valuation* (Chicago: University of Chicago Press, 1939).

Dewey, "Time and Individuality"
>   John Dewey, "Time and Individuality," in Richard J. Bernstein,
>   ed., *On Experience, Nature and Freedom* (New York: Bobbs-
>   Merrill, 1960).

Dewey, *The Philosophy of John Dewey*
>   Robert E. Dewey, *The Philosophy of John Dewey: A Critical
>   Exposition of His Method, Metaphysics, and Theory of
>   Knowledge* (The Hague: Nijhoff, 1977).

Dicker, *Dewey's Theory of Knowing*
>   Georges Dicker, *Dewey's Theory of Knowing* (Philosophical
>   Monographs; Philadelphia: University City Science Center,
>   1976).

Gouinlock, *John Dewey's Philosophy of Value*
>   James Gouinlock, *John Dewey's Philosophy of Value* (New
>   York: Humanities Press, 1972).

James, *Principles of Psychology*
>   William James, *The Principles of Psychology* (Cambridge, MA:
>   Harvard University Press, 1983).

Kaufman, *Essay on Theological Method*
>   Gordon D. Kaufman, *Essay on Theological Method* (rev. ed.;
>   Missoula, MT: Scholars Press, 1979).

Kaufman, *Theological Imagination*
>   Gordon D. Kaufman, *The Theological Imagination: Con-
>   structing the Concept of God* (Philadelphia: Westminster,
>   1981).

Perry, *Realms of Value*
>   Ralph Barton Perry, *Realms of Value: A Critique of Human
>   Civilization* (Cambridge, MA: Harvard University Press, 1954).

Rorty, "Dewey's Metaphysics"
>   Richard Rorty, "Dewey's Metaphysics," in Stephen Chan, ed.,
>   *New Studies in the Philosophy of John Dewey* (Hanover, NH:
>   University Press of New England, 1977) 45–74, reprinted in
>   Richard Rorty, *Consequences of Pragmatism* (Minneapolis:
>   University of Minnesota Press, 1982) 72–89; references are to
>   the reprint.

Rupp, *Christologies and Cultures*
>   George Rupp, *Christologies and Cultures: Towards a Typol-
>   ogy of Religious Worldviews* (The Hague: Mouton, 1974).

Schilpp, *The Philosophy of John Dewey*
>   Paul Arthur Schilpp, ed., *The Philosophy of John Dewey*
>   (Chicago: Northwestern University Press, 1939).

Sleeper, *The Necessity of Pragmatism*
>R. W. Sleeper, *The Necessity of Pragmatism: John Dewey's Conception of Philosophy* (New Haven: Yale University Press, 1986).

Thayer, *The Logic of Pragmatism*
>H. S. Thayer, *The Logic of Pragmatism: An Examination of John Dewey's Logic* (New York: Humanities Press, 1952).

Tiles, *Dewey*
>J. E. Tiles, *Dewey* (New York: Routledge, 1988).

van Buren, *The Edges of Language*
>Paul van Buren, *The Edges of Language: An Essay in the Logic of a Religion* (New York: Macmillan, 1972).

Wieman, *The Source of Human Good*
>Henry Nelson Wieman, *The Source of Human Good* (Carbondale, IL: Southern Illinois University Press, 1946).

Wittgenstein, *Philosophical Investigations*
>Ludwig Wittgenstein, *Philosophical Investigations* (trans. G. E. M. Anscombe; New York: Macmillan, 1953).

PREFACE

Theological literature over the last several decades has become increasingly confusing. For some time now, the harmony that seemed to mark neo-orthodoxy has been replaced by a cacophony of dissonant voices, each claiming its due attention. No longer are the tools of the trade firmly in place, nor can one with confidence take the tradition as a body of authoritative truths that simply need interpretation for the present generation. Instead, new sources for doing theology have arisen, and the theological task has been defined and redefined in a multitude of different ways. In some circles, orthodoxy has given way to orthopraxis, reflection upon the tradition has been replaced by social and political analysis, and "oppression," "liberation," and "revolution" have become the watchwords of the day. In quite different circles, the later philosophy of Wittgenstein has proved a rich resource for justifying traditional Christian language and for stimulating creative thought upon ecumenism and other matters of interest for the church. In still other circles, Foucault and Derrida are being used to deconstruct theology and its ontological claims and implications. Even the most sacred symbols of the tradition are not left untouched. "God" has been replaced by "Goddess" for some, and the figure of Jesus has been increasingly criticized as too narrow a focus for reflection upon divinity for many of those theologians who still consider divinity worthy of thought.

The theological scene, in short, has become pluralistic. At the same time, the historical analysis of scripture and the Christian tradition that has gone on for almost two centuries has led many to see that the tradition, from its very beginning, has always been pluralistic to some degree, despite the monolithic claims of orthodoxy. This awareness further complicates the confusion of the times and helps to raise a series of important questions for many who wish today to reflect theologically. How is reflection to proceed, we ask, in light of our awareness of the different and conflicting normative claims in the tradition and in contemporary thought? What are or ought to be the sources for theological work? What are or ought to be its central task and function? What, in fact, is theological work all about?

One approach to these problems is to examine the larger problem of religious pluralism. If this problem can be understood and addressed, a significant context will be provided for considering how theologians may best proceed within the pluralistic context of contemporary theological discussion. Of course, the concern to work out a method for theological reflection is not the only important or even the most important reason for considering the problem of religious pluralism. Over the last forty years our world has changed dramatically. Among other things, its various parts have been increasingly knit together by technological advances in travel and communication. Today we live in a world in which men and women from vastly different religious traditions are interacting with increasing interdependence—socially, educationally, politically, and economically. If human life is to continue to develop amid these significant changes, it is important that we come to understand more clearly the nature of religious pluralism and how it is possible to live meaningfully with others who hold profoundly different normative convictions. What we need, in short, is a way to proceed in reflection that will help us to understand and respond creatively to different normative forms of life around us.

This requires a general method for reflection appropriate for guiding human interaction within a context of divergent and conflicting normative interests. Developing such a method, in fact, constitutes the central aim of this book. For this task, I have chosen to use the mature philosophy of John Dewey, his work after 1914, for it is my conviction that this work represents a thorough, creative, and powerful attempt to respond thoughtfully and responsibly to conflict among normative cultural interests. His anthropology, aesthetics, logic, ethics, philosophy of science, philosophy of religion, and metaphysics can all be understood as efforts to address this problem from different angles. To be sure, Dewey does not take up the problem of religious pluralism as such, but as I shall argue, conflict among cultural norms is the same kind of problem as that of religious pluralism. This makes it possible for us to use his philosophy to address the latter problem.

There is a second reason for choosing Dewey for this work. In recent years, philosophers have turned to Dewey with increasing interest, and a number of excellent major pieces on various aspects of his philosophy have been published.[1] While there are many signs that theologians and philosophers of religion are also taking note of Dewey,[2] up to this point there has not been, to my knowledge, a recent major effort by this group to interpret the significance of Dewey's philosophy for theology or for the study of religion. This volume, I hope, will begin to fill that gap.

In particular, I shall use the mature philosophy of John Dewey (1) to show how plural normative interests in human life have emerged and (2) to develop a framework for guiding reflection when normative interests conflict. At the end of the book I shall argue that the direction that Dewey provides can be taken over by theologians as an appropriate method for theological reflection within a pluralistic context, since the concept of God with which theologians are most concerned, when properly understood, helps to bring out and underscore what is significant about Dewey's theory of method within and for a context of competing normative claims. My hope is that this methodology will help theologians better understand and respond to the pluralistic confusion both within Christian theology and among the Christian tradition and other religious traditions.

---

[1]See Gouinlock, *John Dewey's Philosophy of Value*; Dicker, *Dewey's Theory of Knowing*; Sleeper, *The Necessity of Pragmatism*; Alexander, *John Dewey's Theory of Art*; Tiles, *Dewey*; and Boisvert, *Dewey's Metaphysics*.
[2]I make reference to some of these signs in chapter five, n.1.

Writing a book is not unlike taking a journey. As I come to the conclusion of this particular journey, I am deeply conscious of those who have walked with me and made my walking lighter. My father, J. Melburn Soneson, not only guided me on many of my early philosophical journeys, at home and as my teacher at North Park College, but he has also walked with me throughout this particular journey, offering advice and support. M. Thomas Thangaraj, now teaching at Candler School of Theology, joined me while I was in the midst of some particularly difficult terrain. With his usual humor and insight into human affairs, he reminded me of the many journeys I have taken before and helped to restore my confidence in what I was doing. While dean of Harvard Divinity School, George Rupp first introduced me to the problem of religious pluralism, and his significant work in this area set me on the particular path that I have taken. While teaching for a semester at Harvard Divinity School, John Cobb read and criticized an early outline of the argument and one chapter. His interest in and writings on the problem of religious pluralism have provided an important inspiration. Richard R. Niebuhr encouraged and supported my interest in religious pluralism and offered significant advice in the early stages of my work. As one of my professors, he was the first to show me the importance of reflecting upon religion and understanding human life religiously. As I tried to wend my way through the thicket of Dewey's texts, Niebuhr's way of walking with and reflecting responsibly upon the journeys of others proved a significant source of illumination. Gordon Kaufman, my advisor at Harvard Divinity School, has carefully read and criticized each chapter. When Whitehead and James did not prove as helpful as I had hoped as guides for this particular expedition, he advised that I walk for a while with Dewey. Although slowing down my progress, this encounter marked a significant turn of events. More importantly, he has shown me, in word and by example, what it is to take a theological journey, encouraging me to walk courageously and with a full store of creativity and imagination. My deepest gratitude is reserved for MaraBeth Soneson who has been my companion on this and earlier journeys. Without her patience, encouragement, and support, this all-too-lengthy journey would never have been completed.

There are others too numerous to name who have been of assistance in various ways. Yet for graduate students who are forced to live on meager terms, financial assistance is greatly appreciated and cannot go unmentioned. Thus I would like to thank the Harvard Graduate School of Arts and Sciences for granting me a Merit Fellowship, which helped to support my journey for one year, and the Woodrow Wilson National Fellowship Foundation for granting me a Charlotte W. Newcombe Doctoral Dissertation Fellowship, which helped to provide support for another year.

J. P. S.
Watertown, Massachusetts

1

INTRODUCTION: THE PROBLEM OF RELIGIOUS PLURALISM

I n his seminal article, "Historical and Dogmatic Method in Theology," Ernst Troeltsch argues that the method of historical research developed and refined during the nineteenth century presupposes a different set of assumptions about the world than does the old dogmatic and authoritarian method of theology. Among other things, it presupposes "the *interaction* of all phenomena in the history of civilization."[1] This

---

[1]Ernst Troeltsch, "Über historische und dogmatische Methode in der Theologie," in idem, *Gesammelte Schriften* (4 vols.; Tübingen: Mohr/Siebeck, 1913) 2. 733; my emphasis. The translation is by Ephraim Fischoff, revised by Walter Bense, located in the Andover-Harvard Theological Library at Harvard Divinity School, p. 5. Two other fundamental aspects of historical method that Troeltsch discusses are first, a critical attitude toward all historical matters fostered by the effort to judge their probability, and second, the use of analogy in judgment that presupposes that all historical events are similar in kind. See "Über historische und dogmatische Methode," 2. 731–37 (or Fischoff's translation, pp. 3–9).

means that all historical matters, including religious traditions, are taken to emerge out of and to be conditioned by other historical events. It is not difficult to see that the effect of this relatively new method upon the view of religion in the world is at least twofold. First, it relativizes one's own religious tradition. Among other things, men and women who have been influenced by historical method find it increasingly difficult to understand their tradition in the same way it has been understood in the past, as uniquely embodying what is most real and valuable, for all traditions, including their own, are understood in relation to the historical circumstances of their origin and development and are subject to critical appraisal in those terms. Second, it opens up the possibility of appreciating the worth of alternative religious traditions as they are studied within their own historical contexts, a possibility that has been increasingly actualized particularly over the past forty years.

This double effect can be called "pluralistic consciousness," for it constitutes an awareness and growing appreciation of plural historical traditions. The difficulty that this often presents for life is uncertainty and confusion over the fundamental normative ideas and ideals that provide direction in judgment, decision, and conduct. Pluralistic consciousness, in short, constitutes *a practical problem*, making it difficult to understand how to proceed in thought and conduct.

It is least helpful, I suggest, to treat this problem as most fundamentally a conflict of truth claims about ultimate reality as such. At least three options are open to theologians if they choose this direction. First, they may argue that their tradition holds the only and exclusive truth, as do fundamentalists in the Christian and Islamic traditions. For those who have been influenced by the historical method or who have come to appreciate alternative religious traditions, this move appears intellectually arbitrary and morally arrogant.

Second, they may argue that their tradition holds the norm for judging the truth of other religious traditions, as does Karl Barth. Barth's move is complex and sophisticated. It is meant to respond to historical consciousness by positing a dualism between God and the historical world and by arguing that the true religious norm breaks into history, revealing itself definitively in Jesus Christ and from time to time in the church.[2] As Hegel has shown, however, such a move is incoherent; the

---

[2]See Karl Barth, *Church Dogmatics* (4 vols.; trans. G. T. Thomson and Harold Knight; Edinburgh: T. & T. Clark, 1956) 1.2. sec. 17. "No religion is true,"

claim that separates God (that ultimate reality that constitutes the norm for truth) and the historical world presupposes their togetherness in thought—God cannot be conceived apart from the concept of the world.[3]

Third, theologians may argue that all religious claims are equally true, as does John Hick. Hick, like Barth, presupposes an ultimate dualism between God and the world, particularly between our concept of God (or ultimate reality) and what that ultimate reality is in itself.[4] This infinite and unknowable God, Hick claims, has revealed or "impinged" God's own self upon human consciousness in various cultures at different times, and this impingement has been interpreted in alternative ways due to different conceptual categories.[5] Thus we can admit the truth of the convictions of many different religious traditions, Hick argues, while recognizing that each constitutes only a perspective on ultimate reality, not the complete truth.[6] Because of its dualism, however, Hick's program is subject to the same criticism given Barth. Furthermore, what his position ignores is the fact that different ways of conceiving ultimate reality lead to different and often conflicting ways of acting in the world, for they call our attention to different possibilities for conduct and for judging the worth of that action. Hick's response to religious pluralism, consequently, seems to overlook what is most troubling about it, the awareness of many conflicting norms for understanding, judging, and guiding conduct in the world.

One difficulty with treating religious pluralism as most fundamentally an issue of truth, consequently, is the fact that religious thinkers are forced into conceiving a dualism between ultimate and historical reality. Value or worth in life, consequently, is taken as subordinate to truth. Ideas, decisions, and actions are understood to have worth to the extent

---

writes Barth. "It can only become true,. . . and it can become true only in the way in which man is justified, from without. . . . Like justified man, religion is a creature of grace. But grace is the revelation of God. . . . Revelation can adopt religion and mark it off as true religion. . . just as there are justified sinners. If we abide strictly by the analogy. . . we need have no hesitation in saying that the Christian religion is the true religion" (1.2. 325–26).

[3]See G. W. F. Hegel, *Phenomenology of Mind* (trans. J. B. Baillie; New York: Harper & Row, 1967) 593. For a significant discussion of what Hegel calls the spurious infinite, see Rupp, *Christologies and Cultures*, 99–101.

[4]John Hick, *God Has Many Names* (Philadelphia: Westminster, 1982) 92.

[5]Ibid., 71–72.

[6]See ibid., 94.

that they truly correspond to this ahistorical reality. While historically developed ideas and ideals may be taken to be significant, as in the case of both Barth and Hick, their worth is understood to lie not in their development and consequences for human life but in the extent to which they reflect a normative, absolute, and static reality external to history. Because this way of conceiving matters entails incoherent dualism, it is inadequate, deepening, rather than resolving, the problem.

When the conception of an absolute, ahistorical normative reality is understood to be inadequate, a possible alternative is to admit complete relativism or skepticism with respect to norms for understanding and action. Yet this move overlooks the fact that in order for men and women to live, to speak and act in one way rather than another, they must rely upon norms. Normative interests are implicitly operative even in their explicit denial. Even complete inaction or the desperate act of suicide are acts that implicitly affirm their normative worth within the contexts in which they occur. In practice, human interests are not taken to have equal worth, for conduct requires the elevation of some interests over others.

Recognition of this fact opens up an alternative way of considering and responding to the problem of religious pluralism. It suggests that a critical consideration of practice or human interaction in its historical development is the proper framework for understanding and responding to this issue. If norms are required for practice, and if they develop within practice, an interpretation of how this occurs may provide insight as to how pluralistic, normative interests have emerged and how new and more comprehensive norms can be developed that transform those now in conflict so that they become mutually supportive. Such an approach would not require a dualism between ultimate and historical reality, nor would it accept a complete relativism among norms. Rather, it would provide a historical and developing framework for judging the worth of insight by its capacity to promote fulfillment in historical interaction.

This is the approach taken here. I shall proceed by developing an interpretation of human nature, based upon the thought of Dewey, which seeks to account for the emergence, continuity, and critical transformation of normative interests within the historical process of interaction. Such an anthropology, it is hoped, will enable us to see how normative interests are or can be developed that are appropriate and responsible within a given historical context and yet are open to modification and transformation as historical interaction proceeds.

2 ◆

ANTHROPOLOGICAL
BACKGROUND

One of the initially disturbing features of religious pluralism is the realization that other men and women are committed to alternative religious beliefs and values. Human beings, we realize, are capable of developing widely different normative interests. If we are to work out an interpretation of human nature that will help us understand and respond adequately to the problem of religious pluralism, it is important that we are able to account for this diversity of interest at the very outset. One advantage of working with John Dewey is that he is able to help us with this matter. In this chapter, consequently, I argue that human beings, according to Dewey, are distinguishable from other animals by their capacity for a greater number and variety of interests, and that this capacity is actualized by the development and shared use of meanings embodied in language and other cultural institutions.

Human Life in Nature

It can be hardly be disputed that human beings are a part of nature. As living organisms, they are natural products of natural processes. However much men and women wish to distinguish themselves from the rest of nature, they can only live in and by means of the natural processes that surround them, breathing air, digesting food, drawing life-nourishing warmth from the sun and the burning of natural fuels. Almost every human activity, in fact, involves some interchange between human beings and the natural environment. Even distinctively human activity, activity informed by culture, presupposes some interpretation of what the surrounding natural processes mean by way of use and enjoyment for human life, and this interpretation and the activity that proceeds from it deepen and extend the connections between human life and its environment.

An adequate interpretation of human life, consequently, requires at least some preliminary theory of nature which can help clarify how human beings are a part of nature, on the one hand, and how they are yet distinctive within nature, on the other. We shall begin our discussion of human nature, accordingly, by considering two interdependent categories of interpretation central to Dewey's theory of nature: "interaction" and "continuity."

The Categories of "Interaction" and "Continuity"

According to Dewey, "nature is an affair *of* affairs, wherein each one, no matter how linked up with others, has its *own* quality."[1] Dewey's category of *interaction* is implicit in this claim, for it suggests that things that exist, the things of nature, are understood most appropriately not as static and independent substances but as events in interaction or events in a history of interaction with other events that set the conditions for their emergence and determine the kind of change they undergo.[2] Dewey argues that things are best conceived as events in interaction, for

[1]Dewey, *Experience and Nature*, 97.

[2]Gouinlock (*John Dewey's Philosophy of Value*, 8) interprets Dewey's use of "affairs" to mean "human situations." "These 'affairs,'" he says, "Dewey also calls situations or contexts. . . . It must be recognized that 'situation' always implies for Dewey conscious human participation. If there were no human beings (or comparably sentient creatures) there would be no situations [i.e., affairs] in nature." This undocumented claim is puzzling to me in what is otherwise a very helpful book. In effect, it *reduces* nature to human situations. As I read Dewey, he uses the concept of "affair" to interpret something wider than human activities, namely, the happenings in and of the world, whether or not they enter as a factor in human consciousness. The valid insights, I suspect, that prompted Gouinlock's interpretation are (1) that the concept of nature can be used to interpret only that which is capable of entering human situations, and (2) that the

all things that human beings know to exist are also known to be dependent upon other things and therefore subject to change.[3]

It ought to be obvious, however, that nature should not be conceived as mere interdependent change. Events do not interact with every other event, nor is each interaction of the same kind. If this were the case, we would be unable to make distinctions among the various happenings of nature. That we make distinctions means that nature is best understood not as mere events but as qualitatively distinct events. Hence, Dewey writes,

> while there is no isolated occurrence in nature, yet interaction and conjunction are not wholesale and homogeneous. Interacting-events [*sic*] have tighter and looser ties, which qualify them with certain beginnings and endings, and which *mark them off* from other fields of interaction.[4]

Affairs, consequently, can be understood to have a double nature. While they are taken by Dewey to be events interacting with other events and thus in the process of change, he also understands them to be *specific or unique interactions.* "Empirically," Dewey writes,

---

concept of nature is a human concept, a particular way we take the world, our discrimination in our situations of that which enters into them (such discrimination, moreover, not being neutral, but informed by human purposes and interest). Gouinlock would have been more accurate, I believe, if he had said that human situations or affairs constitute not only the means but also the analogue by which Dewey interprets less complex happenings in nature.

[3]Dewey, *Experience and Nature*, 70–71. Dewey's argument can be strengthened somewhat. A condition for knowing something that exists is that the thing in question be in interaction with other things. This is implicit in Dewey's comment, "Everything that exists in so far as it is known and knowable is in interaction with other things" (p. 175). We know a thing not in itself but in the way it functions in its environment, in the kind of connections it has with other things, in the way things make an impact upon it and the way it makes an impact upon them. Consequently, if something existed that was not in interaction with other things, it would not be knowable. To be sure, there may exist some things in isolation. Yet with these things we would have no intercourse, no possible knowledge whatsoever, and hence they could form no part of our concept of nature.

[4]Ibid., 271–72; my emphasis.

> there is a history which is a succession of histories [an affair of
> affairs], and in which any event is at once both beginning of one
> course and close of another; is both transitive and static. The
> phrase. . . "state of affairs" is accurately descriptive. . . . There are
> no changes that do not enter into an affair, *Res*, and there is no affair
> that is not bounded and thereby marked off as a state or condition.[5]

An affair is unique as a specific and emergent result of antecedent affairs. As a specific result, it is bounded by or limited to just what it is
in its particular relations, thus representing a concrete limitation placed
upon further process.[6] This emergence of a qualitatively distinct affair
can be conceived as the emergence of a new order in nature.

> There is in nature, even below the level of life, something more
> than mere flux and change. Form is arrived at whenever a stable,
> even though moving, equilibrium is reached. Changes interlock and
> sustain one another. Whenever there is this coherence there is en-
> durance. Order is not imposed from without but is made out of
> relations of harmonious interactions that energies bear to one an-
> other. Because it is active. . . order itself develops. It comes to
> include within its balanced movement a greater variety of changes.[7]

A qualitatively distinct event or affair emerges, according to this interpretation, when interacting changes interlock and sustain one another in
a new way. Because this ordered condition is active, an interdependent
order of changes, it can be conceived as itself capable of developing, as
it interacts with other conditions, to the point at which it is qualitatively
different from its initial character.

---

[5]Ibid., 100–101.

[6]Ibid., 272. A molecule of water, for example, emerges as a concrete and
unique result of the interaction between hydrogen and oxygen. It is, so to speak,
a new affair bounded in and by its particularity. In its particularity, it begins a
new affair, conditioning further process as it interacts with other affairs that in
turn condition the molecule of water until it eventually becomes qualitatively
different from what it initially was. If it were to interact with iron, for example,
it would result in iron oxide in which new energies would be released and to
which new qualities would appertain.

[7]Dewey, *Art as Experience*, 14.

This concept of the emergence of order within nature is the key to Dewey's principle of continuity. This principle postulates a

> continuity of the lower (less complex) and the higher (more complex) activities and forms. . . . The growth and development of any living organism from seed to maturity illustrates the meaning of continuity. . . . What *is* excluded by the postulate of continuity is the appearance upon the scene of a totally new outside force as a cause of changes that occur.[8]

Central to this principle are two claims: (1) that order in nature consists of interacting events that are interdependent, marking distinctive affairs in nature, and (2) that complex order does not represent a sharp break or separation from less complex fields of interacting order but emerges as their *novel integration*, marking a new and more extensive way in which changes or events are interdependent.

The significance of Dewey's principles of interaction and continuity for our purposes is that it helps us understand the continuity between human life and the rest of nature. Dewey argues that there are three broad levels of order or increasingly complex interaction that can be distinguished in nature: the physical, the psycho-physical (the biological), and the mental (communication, the social). That the relations among these forms of existence are best understood not as different and separate kinds of existence but rather as increasingly complex modes of interaction, Dewey argues, is evident in the fact that biological organisms are adapted to their environment and that human activity responds appropriately to an understanding of the meanings of the events of its environment.[9] In order to understand the way in which the unique form of human interaction, communication, is related to the other two levels of nature, it is appropriate to examine the character of continuity between them.

Continuity Between the Physical and the Biological

In contrast to physical events, biological organisms, Dewey argues, are organized internally in such a way as to preserve or maintain their life processes. Physical things react indifferently to their environments,

---

[8]Dewey, *Logic*, 23–24.
[9]Dewey, *Experience and Nature*, 286.

showing no tendency to maintain their characteristic pattern of activity. For example,

> Iron as such exhibits characteristics of bias or selective reactions, but it shows no bias in favor of remaining simply iron; it had just as soon, so to speak, become iron-oxide. It shows no tendency in its interaction with water to modify the interaction so that consequences will perpetuate the characteristics of pure iron. If it did, it would have the marks of a living body, and would be called an organism.[10]

Unlike physical events, biological organisms are sensitive to surrounding events that are useful and harmful to the continuation of life, and they respond accordingly, adjusting their interaction with the environment. As a result, they demonstrate an "ability to procure a peculiar kind of interactive support of needs from surrounding media" not demonstrated in inanimate events.[11]

This ability is evident in what Dewey takes to be the most obvious difference between living and nonliving things, namely, "the activities of the former are characterized by needs, by efforts which are active demands to satisfy needs, and by satisfactions."[12] Dewey defines these terms in what he calls a "biological sense":

> By need is meant a condition of tensional distribution of energies such that the body is in a condition of uneasy or unstable equilibrium. By demand or effort is meant the fact that this state is manifested in movements which modify environing bodies in ways which react upon the body, so that its characteristic pattern of active equilibrium is restored. By satisfaction is meant this recovery of equilibrium pattern, consequent upon the changes of environment due to interactions with the active demands of the organism.[13]

"Need" and "satisfaction" are defined with respect to the order of interdependent changes *within* the organism. They may be equally described

---

[10]Ibid., 254.
[11]Ibid., 255.
[12]Ibid., 252.
[13]Ibid., 253.

with respect to the order *between* organism and environment.[14] From this perspective, a need is a disturbance in the interdependent balance between organism and environment that threatens the continued existence of the organism, and a satisfaction is the result of an effort by the organism that restores that balance. What distinguishes a living organism, therefore, is that it has and is sensitive to needs, to disturbances in the interactive balance between itself and its environment, and that it is able to modify its action in such a way that a balance is restored.[15]

This means that the kind of interaction between a living organism and its environment is different and more complex than that between a physical event and its environment. An organism represents an order of interdependent changes that is itself intimately coordinated with the order of its environment.[16] So intimate is this interdependence that Dewey, in his later writings, calls it a "transaction,"[17] an exchange of energies or a

[14]Dewey, *Art as Experience*, 13–14. These different ways of interpreting needs and satisfactions can be understood as two ways of talking about the same kind of occurrence in nature. Because the order within the organism is interdependently coordinated with the order of its environment, a disturbance in the equilibrium between organism and environment (whether initiated by some new change in the organism or in the environment) can be equally described as a disturbance within the organism, just as a reestablishment of balance between organism and environment entails the recovery of the equilibrium pattern within the organism. The advantage of interpreting need and satisfactions with respect to a balance between organism and environment is that it underscores the fact that they are not merely subjective or private but are descriptive of an observable and hence public state of affairs.

[15]It should be evident that the restoration of balance between organism and environment is not always a return to the same state, for life not only subsists but also grows and degenerates. "In a growing life, the recovery [of balance] is never mere return to a prior state, for it is enriched by the state of disparity and resistance through which it has successfully passed. If the gap between organism and environment is too wide, the creature [degenerates or] dies. If its activity is not enhanced by the temporary alienation, it merely subsists. Life grows when a temporary falling out is a transition to a more extensive balance of the energies of the organism with those of the conditions under which it lives" (ibid., 14).

[16]Dewey, *Logic*, 25.

[17]"No organism is so isolated that it can be understood apart from the environment in which it lives. Sensory receptors and muscular effectors, the eyes and the hand, have their existence as well as their meaning because of connections with an outer environment. . . . *This interaction is the primary fact and it con-*

mutual adaption that sustains both organism and environment in a continuity of interaction.

Two further points about living organisms are worth consideration. First of all, as animals become more complex, susceptibility to the useful and harmful in the environment is increasingly realized as premonitory feeling. As animals develop distance-receptors (vision, smell, and hearing) and locomotor organs, the period of time between the rise of needs and their satisfaction is increased. Vitally connected with remote events as well as those nearby, responsiveness to the distant in space "becomes increasingly prepotent and equivalent in effect to response to the future in time. A response towards what is distant is in effect an expectation or prediction of a later contact."[18] Responsiveness, consequently, becomes *anticipatory* activity, moved by the feeling associated with later contact.[19]

Secondly, and at the same time, consummatory activities, activities that satisfy anticipatory responsiveness, qualify and reinforce the latter:

> A consummation or satisfaction carries with it the continuation, in allied and reinforcing form, of preparatory or anticipatory activities. It is not only a culmination out of them, but an integrated cumulation, a funded conservation *of* them. Comfort or discomfort, fatigue or exhilaration, implicitly sum up a history.[20]

In the successful capture and consumption of prey, for example, the series of anticipatory activities that led up to it are concretely integrated as a completed unit of behavior. The feeling associated with the consummation, consequently, reinforces the anticipatory responses, qualifying and conditioning their occurrence in similar future circumstances.

---

stitutes a transaction. Only by analyses and selective abstraction can we differentiate the actual occurrence into two factors, one called organism and the other, environment" (my emphasis); see John Dewey, "Conduct and Experience" in Carl Murchison, *Psychologies of 1930* (Worcester, MA: Clark University Press, 1930) 411; cited in H. S. Thayer, *The Logic of Pragmatism,* 29. See also Dewey, *Logic,* 25.

[18]Dewey, *Experience and Nature,* 257.
[19]Ibid.
[20]Ibid.

The consequences of these developments are twofold. On the one hand, they make possible "learning or habit-formation."[21] In more complex animals, this means that organic responses or instincts are capable of being shaped or conditioned by their consequences. Anticipatory responsiveness is moved by the feelings of prior consummations, and behavior is redirected accordingly. On the other hand, the behavior of complex animals can be understood to be responsive to and integrated with a much wider environment:

> [The] organism acts with reference to a time-spread, a serial order of events, as a unit, just as it does in reference to a unified spacial variety. Thus an environment both extensive and enduring is immediately implicated in present behavior. Operatively speaking, the remote and the past are "in" behavior making it what it is.[22]

Living organisms, consequently, represent a further complexification of inanimate bodies. As Dewey says,

> the difference. . . is not that the former has something in addition to physico-chemical energy; it lies in the *way* in which physico-chemical energies are interconnected and operate, whence different *consequences* mark inanimate and animate activity respectively.[23]

Communication, that form of interaction that is represented to a unique degree among human beings, denotes an even further complexification of organic life, constituting a more extensive and intimate interaction between organism and environment. As we shall see, in this form of interaction the living organism responds not only to the feeling of what is useful and harmful in the environment but to an awareness or understanding of what environing events mean with respect to their future consequences in and for a shared or social life.

---

[21]Ibid., 279.
[22]Ibid.
[23]Ibid., 253–54.

Communication as Distinctively Human Interaction

Communication, Dewey writes, is the "heart of language."[24] In making this claim, Dewey states what he takes to be the essential function of language. Indeed, for Dewey, language is any form of interaction that functions to establish communication among people.[25]

[24]Ibid., 179. In claiming that communication is the "heart of language," Dewey explicitly distinguishes his theory of language from a more popular theory that dominated the nineteenth century, namely, that the function of language is the expression of feeling or thought. "The heart of language," he says "is not 'expression' of something antecedent, much less expression of antecedent thought. It is communication" (p. 179). Dewey does not deny that language can be used to express thought, but this is not its essential function. This is evident in the fact that the expression of thought presupposes that the meanings of language are already established. "To say that language is necessary for thinking is to say that signs are necessary. Thought deals not with bare things, but with their *meanings*, their suggestions; and meanings, in order to be apprehended, must be embodied in sensible and particular existences." See Dewey, *How We Think*, 231. Thinking and the expression of thinking presuppose that the meanings of events, sounds, gestures, and other things that take place in the environment are already understood. Because it is in social communication that language meanings are established and shared, Dewey argues, communication is the more essential function of language. For a recent brief although illuminating discussion of these different theories of the function of language, see George A. Lindbeck, *The Nature of Doctrine: Religion and Theology in a Postliberal Age* (Philadelphia: Westminster, 1984) chap. 2.

[25]Language, according to Dewey, is not restricted to spoken and written words, to sounds and marks. It is "wider than oral and written speech. It includes the latter. But it includes also not only gestures but rites, ceremonies, monuments and the products of industrial and fine arts. A tool or machine, for example, is not simply a simple or complex physical object having its own physical properties and effects, but is also a mode of language. For it *says* something, to those who understand it, about operations of use and their consequences. To the members of a primitive community a loom operated by steam or electricity says nothing. It is composed in a foreign language, and so with most of the mechanical devices of modern civilization. In the present cultural setting, these objects are so intimately bound up with interests, occupations and purposes that they have an eloquent voice" (Dewey, *Logic*, 46). Our tendency to reify words makes it difficult for us to recognize the significance of Dewey's more inclusive interpretation of language. When we reify words, we fail to see what we are doing

Communication, broadly stated, is cooperative interaction in which different persons establish and pursue common purposes.[26] When interaction is cooperative, Dewey writes,

> Something is literally made common in. . . different centres of behavior. To understand is to anticipate together, it is to make a cross-reference which, when acted upon, brings about a partaking in a common, inclusive undertaking.[27]

---

when we speak. Words are not hard or eternal things but sounds we make for certain purposes within social situations in order to effect mutual understanding and cooperation. A loom or a painting, although far more complex than sounds, are also things we make for certain purposes that effect mutual understanding and guide social coordination toward ends that are conjointly enjoyed.

[26]Dewey, *Experience and Nature*, 179.

[27]Ibid., 178–79. Dewey's theory of communication is remarkably similar to George Herbert Mead's interpretation of language. Of significance at this point is Mead's insight that the achievement of a common perspective in language, the ability to anticipate together, is made possible by the capacity of human beings to put themselves in the place of other people with whom they are interacting, to take their attitude, and thus to anticipate how the others will respond to their own actions. In contrast to human beings, Mead writes, an animal "does not put himself in the place of another person and say, in effect, 'He will act in such a way and I will act in this way.' If the individual can act in this way, and the attitude which he calls out in himself can become a stimulus to him for another act, we have meaningful conduct. Where the response of the other is called out and becomes a stimulus to control his action, then he has the meaning of the other person's act in his experience." See Mead, *Mind, Self, and Society: From the Standpoint of a Social Behaviorist* (Chicago: University of Chicago Press, 1934) 73. When the meaning of the other person's act is in one's experience, then "he is occupying his [the other person's] perspective" (p. 89). The ability to anticipate another's response, Mead claims, is realized gradually as people come to connect their gestures with the subsequent activities of others as responses to the gestures. As a result, people become aware of what the gestures mean to others, anticipating the responses themselves as they perform the gestures. As Mead says, "We are, especially through the use of the vocal gestures, continually arousing in ourselves those responses which we call out in other persons, so that we are taking the attitudes of the other persons into our own conduct" (p. 69). Communication, as Dewey understands it, involves the mutual anticipation of one another's responses and thus a sharing of a common perspective that is used to guide the conduct of each participant to a shared end.

In communication, therefore, human beings come to share a common perspective that guides their interaction. In becoming mutually aware of the purposes that inform the acts of others in a social activity, they are able to act in concert with one another in order to achieve a common and shared end.

Communication is possible insofar as the meanings of events are established and shared in and by and through the process of communication itself. The mutual awareness of purposes is an awareness of what the activities of others mean, of what others intend by their actions. "Primarily meaning is intent," writes Dewey, but "intent is not personal in a private and exclusive sense."[28] Rather, it is "a property of behavior," that kind of behavior that is "cooperative, in that response to another's act involves contemporaneous response to a thing as entering into the other's behavior, and this on both sides."[29] Human behavior, the sounds and motions of men and women, take on meaning as they are used to communicate and to urge cooperation in the achievement of purpose, of intended consequences. More particularly, the meanings of these activities come to be established in and by the communication process when they function "as a *means* of evoking different activities performed by different persons so as to produce *consequences* that are shared by all the participants in the conjoint undertaking" (my emphasis).[30] When established, consequently, meanings in language are consti-

[28]Dewey, *Experience and Nature*, 180. Ludwig Wittgenstein (*Philosophical Investigations*, sec. 337) writes, "An intention is embedded in its situation, in human customs and institutions. If the technique of the game of chess did not exist, I could not intend to play a game of chess. In so far as I do intend the construction of a sentence in advance, that is made possible by the fact that I can speak the language in question."

[29]Dewey, *Experience and Nature*, 179. By "a thing," Dewey is referring to the intended consequences of the other's action, which the other anticipates and which guides his or her behavior. In the terms used in the following section of this chapter, he is referring to an object of interest.

[30]Dewey, *Logic*, 47. In many respects, Dewey's approach to language is similar to that taken by Ludwig Wittgenstein in his later philosophy. Dewey's claim—that meaning is established when sounds function (or are used intentionally) as means for shared consequences—is reminiscent of Wittgenstein's so-called definition of meaning: "For a *large* class of cases—though not for all—in which we employ the word 'meaning' it can be defined thus: the meaning of a word is its use in the language" (*Philosophical Investigations*, sec. 43). Paul Van Buren

tuted by an awareness or understanding of the connections between events as shared means and events as shared social consequences.

It is important to note that communication confers meanings not only upon sounds and gestures but upon all natural events that enter into it. "Language," writes Dewey,

> is a release and amplification of energies that enter into it, conferring upon them the added quality of meaning. The quality of meaning thus introduced is extended and transferred, actually and potentially, from sounds, gestures and marks, to all other things of nature. Natural events become messages to be enjoyed and administered. . . . Thus events come to possess characters; they are demarcated, and noted.[31]

In communication, men and women not only interact with one another but with the larger environment as well. Sticks and fire, food and clothing, toys and cars and books all enter human purposes and thus take on the meaning of their use and enjoyment in human interaction.

There are several important consequences that mark human life as a distinctive form of interaction in nature, yet one that has emerged in continuity out of the psycho-physical level. In particular, human responsiveness to the environment is radically transformed in three important ways when it is conditioned by communication. First of all, responsive-

---

(*The Edges of Language*, 53–54) correctly points out that this remark is "singularly useless" if it is interpreted as a rule for finding out the meaning of a strange word. "If I do not know the meaning of a word," he writes, "I shall hardly know how to use it. It is therefore no help at all to tell me to look to the use in order to learn the meaning." Van Buren argues persuasively that Wittgenstein probably had something else in mind: "in saying that the meaning of a word is its use in the language, he was inviting us to look at language in a certain way, namely, when it is being put to work. If we accept this invitation, we shall see that the question of what a word means includes also a question about the person who uses that word and about what he intended in speaking as he did. 'Language,' in its normal or paradigmatic sense, refers to human language. Understanding language, therefore, means understanding what is going on when people talk." It is in this larger and humane sense that the understanding of language meaning by Dewey and Wittgenstein have striking similarities.

[31]Dewey, *Experience and Nature*, 174.

ness to the useful and harmful in the environment, organic impulses, are now conditioned by an awareness or understanding of the meanings they have in society. Children, for example, like other complex animals, will respond more cautiously to fire once they are burned. Yet when they enter into the communication of their culture, they also learn a variety of things that people do with fire, passing their fingers through a candle flame without getting burned, cooking with it, lighting the family hearth, and so on, and these meanings significantly qualify the initial negative, shrinking responsiveness to fire.[32]

The second consequence of communication is that human responses become more flexible. Stated in different terms, learning and habit formation become more complex and far reaching. "The very operation of learning," Dewey argues, "sets a limit to itself, and makes subsequent learning more difficult."[33] We have seen in the case of complex animals that, when anticipatory or instinctive responsiveness leads to consummation, the latter reinforces the anticipatory activities, prompting the same activity in similar situations in the future. As a result, "behavior is confined to channels established by prior behavior."[34] The difficulty of learning a new response once a habit is formed, however, is confined to "a habit in isolation, a non-communicating habit," for

> communication not only increases the number and variety of habits, but tends to link them subtly together, and eventually to subject habit-forming in a particular case to the habit of recognizing that new modes of association will exact a new use of it. Thus habit is formed in view of possible future changes and does not harden so

[32]In the same way, our response to someone speaking a foreign language is not much more complex than the response of a family dog. If their voice is harsh, we may respond in a shrinking or protective way, just as our dog may run away or growl. On the other hand, if their voice is pleasant, we may respond expansively, nodding our heads and smiling, while our pet may wag its tail. Yet as we gradually come to understand the foreign language, which we can do only as we learn how different tones and sounds are used for certain social purposes, our response to the same voice becomes increasingly complex—we learn to distinguish the variety of tones and sounds as having stable social meanings, and our response to its harshness or pleasantness is transformed by an understanding of those meanings.

[33]Dewey, *Experience and Nature*, 280.

[34]Ibid.

readily. As soon as a child secretes from others the manifestation of a habit there is proof that he is practically aware that he forms *a* habit subject to the requirements of others as to his further habit formations.[35]

This increased power to learn, Dewey adds, "means increased susceptibility, sensitiveness, responsiveness. . . explosiveness."[36] By coming to understand the meanings of events that enter communication, human beings become consciously aware of and sensitive to their many and often conflicting possible consequences. The result for human life, Dewey concludes, is "instability, novelty, emergence of unexpected and unpredictable combinations," which demand flexibility in responsiveness if present conduct is to reach a successful conclusion.[37]

Finally, human responsiveness shaped by communication is conditioned not only by the past and the remote in space, as in complex animals, but by the experiences of other human beings as well. In Dewey's words:

> Not merely its own distant world of space-time is involved in its conduct but the world of its fellows. When consequences which are unexperienced and future to one agent are experienced and past to another creature with which it is in communication, organic prudence becomes conscious expectation, and future affairs living realities.[38]

When meanings in language have been established, men and women can learn from the experiences of one another even though they have not undergone those experiences themselves. This learning—which can be exceedingly extensive, crossing cultures and historical epochs when translation and written records are available—is, in effect, growth in the understanding of and capacity to respond to the environment. So unique

---

[35]Ibid., 280–81.

[36]Ibid., 281.

[37]Ibid. The seeming paradox, Dewey concludes, is that the "more an organism learns—the more that is, the former terms of a historic process are retained and integrated in this present phase [of activity]—the more it has to learn, in order to keep itself going" (ibid.).

[38]Ibid., 280.

and significant is this dimension of human life, Dewey concludes, that "human learning and habit-forming present thereby an integration of organic-environmental connections so vastly superior to those of animals without language that its experience appears to be super-organic."[39]

It is possible to summarize these three consequences of communication by noting that they constitute mind or mental interaction. The interactions of communication, Dewey claims, while diverse throughout, are marked "by common properties, which define mind as intellect; possession of and response to meanings."[40] Mind, according to Dewey, is not something that is possessed originally or in isolation from the environment. Rather it is a developing product of communication. As Dewey says, "mind can be understood in the concrete only as a system of beliefs, desires and purposes which are formed in the interaction of biological aptitudes with a social environment."[41] As a system of cultural meanings, however, mind is not a collection of data stored in one corner of the brain. It is, more accurately, biological aptitudes (or drives, impulses, responses) shaped and formed by cultural meanings.[42] Consequently, mind is conceived by Dewey as the organized possession and understanding of the meanings of culture (not in a static sense but) as the *capacity*, the dynamic ability, to understand and respond to the meanings of things, that is, to respond to and use natural events intelligently or with purpose.[43] It is a capacity, in short, that "designates an instrumental method of directing natural changes,"[44] a capacity realized in "intelligent or purposeful engagement in a course of action into which things enter."[45]

Dewey's categories of "interaction" and "continuity," consequently, provide significant insight into the ways human beings are a part of

[39]Ibid.

[40]Ibid., 272.

[41]Dewey, *Human Nature and Conduct*, ix.

[42]Dewey, *Experience and Nature*, 303.

[43]"Mind appears in experience as ability to respond to present stimuli on the basis of anticipation of future possible consequences, and with a view to controlling the kind of consequences that are to take place." See Dewey, *Democracy and Education*, 130–31.

[44]Dewey, *Experience and Nature*, 160.

[45]Dewey, *Democracy and Education*, 137.

nature and yet can be distinguished from the rest of nature. With these categories, we can see that communication, the human form of organization and interaction that develops and responds to meanings, is not isolated from the physical and biological, but in specific ways is a more complex form of organization that includes and transforms them, making it possible for human beings to interact with a much wider environment and in new and more consequential ways.

A Theory of Interests

The capacity of human beings for communication is one with their capacity for a greater number and variety of interests than other animals. Stating the matter in this way highlights the fact that human (and other organic) life is not only actively engaged with an environment but that the engagement is *interested* activity, activity in which the organism has a stake in the results of interaction. Because consequences of interaction matter to living organisms, their responses to the environment, at least in more complex creatures, are capable of modification, development, and diversification into what may be called "organized interests." In human life, this concern for or interest in the outcome of various transactions underlies the development of cultural and religious pluralism, of many different and varied interests.

Because the concept of interest is fundamental to the interpretation of human nature proposed in this chapter, it is appropriate to examine it. Unfortunately, this concept is not central to Dewey's anthropology, although he does consider it at several points and often makes rich suggestions about its meaning. The discussion in this section, accordingly, will constitute a constructive development of Dewey's thought on the matter. The significance of developing this concept for the interpretation of human nature, among other things, is that it helps us to bring more clearly into focus the human capacity for the development of pluralism.

The claim that human beings have a capacity for a greater number and variety of interests than other animals presupposes, of course, that other animals have interests. This assumption may seem forced, since the most common uses of the word have reference to human life. Men and women, we say, take interest, and have and pursue interests. While we may speak of dogs and cats as taking interest in their surroundings, it is less clear what we would be saying were we to say that they have an interest in certain proceedings. And what would we mean if we were to say that they pursue certain interests? Indeed, in the two places where Dewey explicitly focuses upon and analyzes the concept of interest, he does so in relation to human life.[46] Nevertheless, the concept can be used to highlight, as Dewey himself occasionally does, certain common features that belong to organic life, if the extension of its use is adequately explained. The advantage of doing this is to highlight the continuity between human interests and the activities of other organisms, adding depth to our understanding of the former.

The word "interest" is a rich and flexible word in the English language. It can be used as a noun, "an interest"; a verb, "to interest"; an adjective, "the interested party" or "the interesting song"; and an adverb, "interestingly." A variety of expressions that use this word, moreover, have been developed over time: "to take interest in something," "to have an interest in something," "to be of interest," "to be interested in," "to pursue an interest," "the interest of a group," and so on. Any attempt to abstract a general meaning from the various nuances of expression, of course, is an exercise in reduction, but in this sense all generalization and scholarship involve reduction. The advantage of such an exercise is that it helps to bring clarity to understanding, drawing together a variety of details into a unified pattern.

Dewey in fact does not reduce the various meanings of this word to one but to three interrelated meanings. The first meaning is embodied in the form of the noun: "an interest" or "the interest of." In general, he suggests, it refers to teleological modes of behavior. The word "interest," he writes, is used to express

> the whole state of active development. . . . An occupation, employment, pursuit, business is often referred to as an interest. Thus we say that a man's interest is politics, or journalism, or philanthropy, or archæology, or collecting Japanese prints, or banking.[47]

Interests such as politics or journalism, whatever else they may be, are organized ways of acting in and with an environment for achieving certain purposes. Dewey makes this explicit at another point. The word "interest," he claims,

---

[46]Dewey, "Interest," 209–46; and Dewey, "Interests and Discipline," chap. 10 of *Democracy and Education*, 124–38.

[47]Dewey, *Democracy and Education*, 126.

names a transaction. It points to an activity which takes effect through the mediation of external conditions. When we think, for example, of the interest of any particular group, say the bankers' interest, the trade-union interest, or the interest of a political machine, we think not of mere states of mind but of the group as a pressure group having organized channels in which it directs action to obtain and make secure conditions that will produce specified consequences. . . . Whenever a person has an interest in something, he has a stake in the course of events and in their final issue—a stake which leads him to take action to bring into existence a particular result rather than some other one.[48]

Understood as a way of acting so as to achieve results beneficial to the one who acts, the concept of interest may be applicable to the activity of living organisms. As we have seen, living things may be distinguished from non-living ones by the fact that the activity of the former results in an interactive support of its needs from the surrounding environment. Functionally speaking, the responses of living organisms to their environment are discriminatory in a way quite different from inorganic responses, being sensitive to the useful and harmful in the environment and aiming at results that support the continued activity of the

[48]Dewey, *Theory of Valuation*, 17. Ralph Barton Perry in *Realms of Value* presents a theory of interest that in many respects is similar to the one offered here. "Interest," according to Perry, "is a *train of events determined by expectation of its outcome*" (p. 3). In my estimation, however, Perry inappropriately excludes for generalization the "use of the word 'interest'. . . in which it refers to the collective, and more or less permanent, interest of a social group, as when one speaks of 'the interest of labor' or 'the interest of the consumer.' The expression '*the* interests,' used in a political context, suggests interest that is both selfish and collective or permanent" (p. 6). While agreeing with Perry that "there is need of another and broader use which makes it possible to speak of interests which are generous, or fleeting and individual" (p. 6), I would argue that the former use highlights something important, namely, that interests are ways of acting, organized channels or means by which a group or individual interacts with the environment for the purpose of achieving certain consequences. Moreover, it is important to acknowledge the former meaning in order to reflect upon the continuity between individual and fleeting interests and the social and more permanent ones. In human life, at least, these different meanings may be distinguished but never separated, for the individual's interests are shaped to a large extent by the wider interests of culture.

organism. "This discrimination," Dewey writes, "is the essence of sensitivity. Thus with organization [i.e., with living organisms], bias [or selective response] becomes interest, and satisfaction a good or value and not a mere satiation of wants or repletion of deficiencies."[49] As particular ways of acting on behalf of results useful to the creature, organic responses can be understood as "interested" responses, similar in function to human interests.

The significance of this insight is that it helps to illuminate human interests. It suggests that human interests, like those of other animals, are based upon organic drives or impulsive responses that give the interests their initial direction and urgency. Dewey, in his early article on interest, in fact makes just this point: "In the selective or preferential quality of impulse, we have the basis of the fact that at any given time, if we are. . . awake at all, we are always interested in one direction rather than another."[50] While organic appetite may account for the initial direction and intensity of interests, however, it is important not to reduce interests to original organic responses, at least with respect to complex animals, especially human beings. For as we have seen, organic responses are modified by their consequences in the case of more com-

[49]Dewey, *Experience and Nature*, 256. Although organic responses are discriminating, they do not necessarily entail consciousness. They are discriminating in their function, leading to ends useful to the creature. In most cases, they represent blind appetite which "is only felt; it is not known. It is not considered from the standpoint of its bearings or relationship. It is not translated over into terms of its result" (Dewey, "Interest," 435). Dewey draws an important distinction, in this respect, between human beings and other animals. "In the animals, while the appetite is not conscious of its own end, it none the less seeks that end by a sort of harmony pre-established in the animal structure. Fear serves the animal as a stimulus to flight or to seeking cover. Anger serves it for purposes of attack or defense. It is a very unusual occurrence when the feeling gets the better of the animal and causes it to waste powers uselessly. But of the blind feelings in the human being, it is to be said that most of them require adjustment before they are of any regular permanent service. There is no doubt that fear and anger may be rendered useful to the man as they are to the animal. But in the former case they have to be trained to this use; in the latter they originally possess it. . . . The [human] agent has to become conscious of the end or object and control his aroused powers by conscious reference to it. . . . [There] must, in other words, be a consciousness of both end and means" (Dewey, "Interest," 435–36).

[50]Dewey, "Interest," 430.

plex creatures and even more radically transformed in human life by communication.

We have been considering what might be understood as the most general interpretation of interest: behavior that is teleological. It has been suggested that this general meaning represents an interpretation of organic behavior in general, the kind of transactions that take place between organisms and their environment. The second and third meanings of interest represent the two sides of this interaction, the subjective and objective poles, if you will. Activity which can be described as an interest always involves subjects who take interest in some object or end. While the subjective and objective meanings of interest cannot be separated, they nevertheless emphasize different aspects of teleological activity.

The subjective side of interest is expressed largely in the form of verbs: "to interest," "to take interest," "to be or become interested." These uses of the word, as Dewey says, express

> the personal emotional inclination. . . . When we speak of a man as interested in this or that the emphasis falls directly upon his personal attitude. To be interested is to be absorbed in, wrapped up in, carried away by, some object. To take an interest is to be on the alert, to care about, to be attentive. We say of an interested person both that he has lost himself in some affair and that he has found himself in it. Both terms express the engrossment of the self in an object.[51]

---

[51]Dewey, *Democracy and Education*, 126. Perry is particularly helpful in characterizing what I have termed the subjective pole of interest. "Interest," he writes, is a name for those "acts or states which have the common characteristic of *being for or against*. The expressions 'motor-affective attitudes' or 'attitudes of favor and disfavor' serve as its best paraphrases. 'Caring' and 'concern' are also convenient synonyms. The absence of interest is indifference. . . . Indifference is to be distinguished from negative interest. . . . It is especially significant to note that the words for which 'interest' is substituted come in pairs of opposites. . . . 'Interest,' then, is to be taken as a class name for such names as 'liking'-'disliking,' 'loving'-'hating,' 'hoping'-'fearing,' 'desiring'-'avoiding,' and countless other kindred names. What they all ostensibly mean is what *it* ostensibly means. It invites attention to that to which they in their severality and community already invite our attention." Perry, *Realms of Value*, 7.

It is helpful to see that the personal interest of a subject is always that of a participant. Unlike mere spectators, participants are engaged in and with an environment, and the outcome of the engagement matters to them; consequently, they do what they can to influence present events in favorable directions.[52] "The attitude of a participant in the course of affairs," Dewey writes, "is thus a double one: there is solicitude, anxiety concerning future consequences, and a tendency to act to assure better, and avert worse, consequences."[53]

The objective side of interest represents that which is of interest. "Interest," as Dewey says, "does not end simply in itself as bare feeling may, but always has some object, end or aim to which it attaches itself."[54] The word "interest" expresses

> the objective results that are foreseen and wanted. . . . By an interest we also mean the point at which an object touches or engages a man; the point at which it influences him. In some legal transactions a man has to prove "interest" in order to have a standing at court. He has to show that some proposed step concerns his affairs. A silent partner has an interest in a business, although he

---

[52]The spectator, Dewey (*Democracy and Education*, 124) writes, "is indifferent to what is going on; one result is just as good as another, since each is just something to look at." The participant, on the other hand, "is bound up with what is going on; its outcome makes a difference to him. His fortunes are more or less at stake in the issue of events. Consequently, he does whatever he can to influence the direction present occurrences take. One is like a man in a prison cell watching the rain out of the window; it is all the same to him. The other is like a man who has planned an outing for the next day which continuing rain will frustrate. He cannot, to be sure, by his present reactions affect to-morrow's [*sic*] weather, but he may take some steps which will influence future happenings, if only to postpone the proposed picnic. If a man sees a carriage coming which may run over him, if he cannot stop its movement, he can at least get out of the way if he foresees the consequence in time."

[53]Ibid., 124–25. The notion of "motor-affective" attitudes captures this double characteristic of the subjective role of interest. Perry (*Realms of Value*, 15) writes, "'Motor-affective' is a loose expression [used in psychology] designed to cover instinct, desire, purpose, will, feeling, emotion, motivation, etc.; whatever, in other words, constitutes man as a being who *acts* in behalf of what *concerns* him. Perhaps the best thing about the expression 'motor-affective' is the hyphen, which suggests, if it does not reveal, the unity of concern and action."

[54]Dewey, "Interest," 429.

takes no active part in its conduct[,] because its prosperity or decline affects his profits and liabilities.[55]

Generally speaking, something becomes an object of interest when it engages or influences us, when it represents consequences of interaction which make a difference to us, leading us to respond or act so as to avoid or maintain them. Our interactions with the environment have a variety of outcomes or results which we undergo, consequences which we enjoy or suffer. Interaction with certain foods, for example, end in our enjoyment of various tastes and of the final satiation of hunger, while other kinds of interaction with our surroundings result in our suffering scraped knees, bumped heads, or unfulfilled hopes. Because we enjoy or suffer the various consequences of our interactions, they prompt our attention and concern and constitute our central objects of interest:

> They alone, as we say, are of interest, and they are the cause of taking interest in other things. For living creatures they form the natural platform for regarding other things. They are the basis, directly and indirectly, of active responses to things. As compared with them, other things are obstacles and means of procuring and avoiding the occurrence of situations having them.[56]

Objects of interest, being consequences, are not directly given to a subject, but emerge within a context of interaction. To be sure, the consequences of interaction often befall us in strange and unexpected ways. Without anticipating it, for example, a child may be pleased by the warmth of the sun or delighted by the first taste of ice cream or suffer the pain of a burnt finger. Yet the warmth and taste and burning sensation are *results* of interaction between organism and environment— the child did something in and with an environment, walking out into a warm spring day, eating the offered ice cream cone, and sticking his or her finger in the bright flame. These activities led to a change in the situation, the set of relations between the child and the environment, which affected the child in various ways.

---

[55]Dewey, *Democracy and Education*, 126.
[56]Dewey, *Experience and Nature*, 104.

Dewey does not adequately discuss or distinguish various meanings of the term "object of interest." As we have seen, the term in general refers to the consequences of interaction between organism and environment about which the organism is concerned and to which it responds. This general meaning, however, can be understood to have at least four interrelated meanings that we can represent as increasing levels of complexity. On the first and least complex level, an object of interest is simply *a concrete end or conclusion* of an affair (a bumped head or the taste of ice cream), consisting of a particular concrete set of relations between organism and environment that the organism undergoes or feels and to which it responds. Such immediately felt ends, Dewey claims, constitute aesthetic objects.[57]

On the second level, objects of interest are *anticipatory ends.* Vital activity, as we have seen, is constituted by responses to felt consequences of prior interaction. The felt quality of consequences serves a double function: (1) it marks the end of an affair, the results of interaction that the organism undergoes, and (2) it prompts new responses, initiating a new affair. This new affair, in its turn, has its own results. As we saw earlier, in complex animals in which an affair becomes extended over a period of time, the second ending reinforces the responsive behavior leading up to it, enabling the animal to learn a habit of response to the initial circumstances, which embodies the anticipation of the coming conclusion. This anticipated end of activity is a complex object of interest. Indeed, it is the complexification of the object of interest to which it initially responds, representing its possible results in

---

[57]Aesthetic objects, Dewey writes, are "all immediately enjoyed and suffered things,. . . things directly possessed" or undergone (ibid., 87). Dewey finds aesthetic objects not in a museum, separated from life, but in "that phase of experience [which] manifests objects which are final [i.e., felt ends or consequences]," claiming the "attitude involved in their appreciation is esthetic" (p. 80). He is highly critical of the interpretations of the so-called cultivated. "Esthetic, fine art, appreciation, drama have an eulogistic flavor. We hesitate to call the penny-dreadful of fiction artistic, so we call it debased fiction or a travesty on art. Most sources of direct enjoyment for the masses are not art to the cultivated, but perverted art, an unworthy indulgence. Thus we miss the point. A passion of anger, a dream, relaxation of the limbs after effort, swapping of jokes, horse-play, beating of drums, blowing of tin whistles, explosion of firecrackers and walking on stilts, have the same quality of immediate and absorbing finality that is possessed by things and acts dignified by the title of esthetic" (p. 80).

the future. Once burned by fire, for example, the sight of fire will function as a more complex object of interest, leading the animal to respond to it more cautiously, that is, in anticipation of what the fire can do to it. In the same way, once an animal has coupled in the sexual act, the scents that led to this act will be qualified forever more by an anticipation of the act itself.

The third meaning of an "object of interest" is a *conscious or foreseen end*. Human behavior, as we have seen, is constituted by responses not just to felt consequences but to an awareness of what the consequences mean with respect to possible future ends. The possible ends of responses to present consequences, so to speak, come into view. Human beings not only anticipate possible results of present states of affairs as animals do but are consciously aware of the connections between the present and its possible future consequences, being able to abstract and reflect upon the connections in and with the use of language. The word "fire," for example, enables us to focus upon the event of fire and to compare and think about the various things we do with it. As a result, the sight of fire is or becomes exceedingly complex, involving conscious awareness of the various ends to which it can lead. These foreseen ends constitute the third meaning of the term "object of interest."

The fourth and most complex meaning of an "object of interest" is an end-in-view. What Dewey calls an end-in-view is not any and every possible end of which one is aware in a given set of circumstances; at its most developed stage, it represents that possible end which is deliberately and reflectively chosen to pursue and which therefore becomes conscious purpose. Because of the awareness of meaning, Dewey writes,

> the initial stage [in developing situation] is capable of being judged in light of its probable course and consequence. . . . The terminal outcome when anticipated [in this way]. . . becomes an end-in-view, an aim, purpose, a prediction usable as a plan in shaping the course of events.[58]

There would be no need for deliberate reflection upon the probable course and consequence of the initial stage of situations unless the situations themselves were troubling in some way. Because of the intricate com-

[58]Ibid., 101.

plexity in the relationship between the interests and abilities of human beings and the powers and energies of the environment, it is often the case that obstruction, conflict, and confusion arise in the situation itself. This is an essential condition for the emergence of an end-in-view. Awareness of the various possible ends of a given situation, no doubt, contributes at times to the confusion and conflict. At the same time, however, this awareness enables men and women to reflect upon the various possible or potential courses of and conclusions to a situation, to trace them out in imagination, and to choose that possible end which they believe will restore unity to the situation. This possible end becomes the end-in-view of the situation, the present object of interest:

> The "object" which. . . presents itself in thought as the goal of desire [in a troubling situation] is the object of the environment *which, if it were present*, would secure a re-unification [*sic*] of activity and the restoration of its ongoing unity. The end-in-view of desire [or interest] is that object which were it present would link into an organized whole activities which are now partial and competing.[59]

Imagine a student, for example, who, working upon a dissertation at home, suddenly smells and then sees a fire burning in the waste paper basket. The fire presents the student with a troubling situation, since he or she is aware that it means the possibility of the loss of home and life. After a moment of reflection, the student decides that the best way to resolve the situation and restore the unity of activity, allowing the student to get on with the dissertation, is to use the fire extinguisher which is in the next room. Thus he or she rushes to get it and sprays the fire.

---

[59]Dewey, *Human Nature and Conduct*, 230. Use of the phrase "object of the environment" in this quotation may be misleading. The object of interest which functions as an end-in-view is not simply some object of the environment but an imagined conclusion of interaction between organism and environment, a particular way of using or acting with objects of the environment that is expected to be consummatory, functioning so as to restore harmony to the situation. To a person with a fever, the mere presence of aspirin will not bring unity to the various factors in the present situation, but the obtaining and taking of aspirin will. It is the latter, when imagined and anticipated, which constitutes an end-in-view.

The imagined use of the fire extinguisher, in this situation, is the developed end-in-view.[60] Believing it to be the best outcome (and thus most appropriate meaning) of the fire in that situation, it constitutes that complex object of interest to which the student responds.[61]

[60]Again, it is not the imagined fire extinguisher, but the imagined use of it which constitutes the end-in-view.

[61]It is helpful to see that the student in this situation responds to a variety of negative and positive meanings. For example, the student responds to those possible courses and consequences of the fire that would mean the loss of the dissertation work, the loss of home, and even the loss of life (his or her own and that of others); or, positively, which would mean decisive and praiseworthy action in an emergency, respect for property, and so on. The fire prompts many concerns and tendencies of responses. These in turn depend upon other factors in the situation, such as the student's past experiences with fires and emergencies and the availability of a fire extinguisher or other implements with which to put out the fire. The chosen end-in-view does not exclude these other meanings and tendencies of response but functions so as to unify or coordinate them: "The *end-in-view*," as Dewey (*Theory of Valuation*, 48–49) says, "is that particular activity which operates as a co-ordinating factor of all other sub-activities involved," as "the means of effecting this co-ordination." The imagined use of the fire extinguisher, consequently, is that meaning of the fire (the possible outcome) which includes other meanings in a unified perspective, allowing it therefore to guide the behavior of the student.

It is to be noted that Perry (*Realms of Value*, 3) restricts the meaning of the term "object of interest" to the last three meanings proposed here, without distinguishing among them. "A thing is an object of interest," he writes, "when its being expected induces actions looking to its realization or non-realization." Without including the first meaning of the term, however, it is not clear how the other types of objects, which are anticipated consequences, are built up. As Dewey (*Experience and Nature*, 104) puts the matter in relation to the fourth meaning, "ends-in-view, aims, are formed from objects taken in their immediate and terminal qualities; objects once having occurred as endings, but which are now not in existence and which are not likely to come into existence save by an action which modifies surroundings." The latter types of objects represent possibilities, but they are possibilities of antecedent consequences (or conditions). The imagined use of the fire extinguisher, for example, represents a possible meaning or end of the sight and smell of the fire. The connection between these two ends (the sight and smell of fire and the imagined use of a fire extinguisher)

It is important to note that in human life objects of interest are capable of developing, given the appropriate conditions, into exceedingly complex ends of highly organized and diverse activities or interests. As we saw in an earlier quotation, the felt quality of consequences is "the cause of taking interest in other things," particularly the *conditions and means* of the consequences which are enjoyed or suffered.[62] A bumped head, for example, leads us to attend more carefully to things round about us so that we may avoid similar accidents in the future. Likewise, the enjoyment of certain tastes or delightful sounds focuses attention upon and prompts concern for activities that contributed to those results so that the consequences may be maintained in the present or repeated in the future. By seeking and incorporating within one's behavior the conditions or means of consequences, initial objects of interest themselves develop around increasingly complex, organized, and varied interests. Given the right conditions, for example, initial interest in certain delightful sounds may eventually lead to an interest in learning how to play one or several instruments in order to reproduce similar sounds. This in turn may lead to an increased appreciation or enjoyment of more complex musical sounds and sequences. In particularly talented people, these more complex objects of interests may eventually lead to other organized interests, such as participation in an orchestra, apprenticeship in the making of musical instruments, the study and teaching of music history, and so on. These complex teleological modes of behavior represent the *historical development of interests* in which initial enjoyment results in increasingly organized and varied interests with their increasingly complex objects of interest.

---

requires a history of circumstances in which the student undergoes at least some of the consequences which fire has, learning at the same time the many ways that others in the culture respond to it. Without ever having seen or heard of the devastating consequences of fire, for example, a young child quite likely would not take any special notice of a fire in the home until it was too late to do anything about it other than run. In this situation, the fire becomes an object of interest, not as an expectation of consequences but as consequences directly suffered that the child seeks to escape. As a result of this experience, in future situations the child will be prepared to respond to a fire more adequately, at that time anticipating its possible consequences.

[62]See above, pp. 27–28, esp. n. 56.

Human Interests and the Meanings of Language

Dewey writes that "an organization of impulse into a working habit forms an interest."[63] The aim of this final section will be to examine what this means for human life. How is it that impulses are organized into working habits in such a way that human interests emerge? I shall argue that this issue is best understood as the need for, and the consequent development of, meanings in human life. The implicit premise of this section, hence, is that interests, on the human level, are to be understood as meanings.

Instincts and Culture

In his pioneering work in psychology, William James was one of the first to treat with any sophistication the insight that the behavior of human beings, unlike that of other animals, is not directed by relatively fixed instincts. In the lower animals, he writes,

> fixed habit is the essential and characteristic law of nervous action. The brain grows to the exact modes in which it has been exercised, and the inheritance of these modes—then called instincts—would have in it nothing surprising. But in man the negation of all fixed modes is the essential characteristic.[64]

This claim is James's attempt to explain why it is that human beings are more flexible in their activities than other animals. In the other animals, he claims, there is widespread evidence for the theory that "what was acquired habit in the ancestor may become congenital tendency [or instinct] in the offspring"; with human life, however, there is little or no evidence for this: "we certainly do not observe," for example, "that a baby whose ancestors have spoken German for thirty generations will, on that account, learn Italian any the less easily from its Italian nurse."[65] This means, James concludes, that human behavior is less determined by genetic inheritance and thus more flexible and open ended in its development. In this matter, Dewey, who learned a great deal from James's *Principles of Psychology*, is in essential agreement: "the human being

[63]Dewey, *Human Nature and Conduct*, 153.
[64]William James, *Principles of Psychology*, 990.
[65]Ibid.

differs from the lower animals," he writes, "in precisely the fact that his native activities [propensities, tendencies, impulses] lack the complex ready-made organization of the animals' original abilities."[66]

That human behavior is not determined by fixed instincts, however, does not mean that human beings are born without instinctive or impulsive drives.[67] Both James and Dewey argue, in fact, that human beings have more instincts than other animals. Indeed, James wants to argue that human instincts are not fixed precisely because they have so many of them:

> Man is born with a tendency to do more things than he has ready-made arrangements for in his nerve-centres. Most of the performances of the other animals are automatic. But in him the number of them is so enormous, that most of them must be the fruit of painful study.[68]

Dewey writes in a similar vein: "Man can progress as beasts cannot, precisely because he has so many 'instincts' that they cut across one another, so that most serviceable actions must be *learned*."[69]

These quotations give rise to tension in the writings of both James and Dewey. There seem to be two different and incompatible answers to the question of why, on the whole, the stimulation of human impulses does not lead to automatic and fixed behavior, particularly in the young,

[66]Dewey, *Human Nature and Conduct*, 102. On the pivotal and enduring influence of James's *Principles of Psychology* upon the thought of Dewey, see Jane M. Dewey, ed., "Biography of John Dewey," in Schilpp, *The Philosophy of John Dewey*, 23; and Sidney Hook, *John Dewey: An Intellectual Portrait* (New York: John Day, 1939) 8.

[67]Both Dewey and James equate instinct and impulse, using them interchangeably. "The use of the words instinct and impulse as practical equivalents is intentional," Dewey (*Human Nature and Conduct*, 99 n.) writes, "even though it may grieve critical readers. The word instinct taken alone is still too laden with the older notion that an instinct is always definitely organized and adapted—which for the most part is just what it is not in human beings. The word impulse suggests something primitive, yet loose, undirected, initial." See also James, *Principles of Psychology*, 1006.

[68]James, *Principles of Psychology*, 118.

[69]Dewey, *Human Nature and Conduct*, 99–100 n.

but requires learning in order for the impulses to be effective. The incompatibility of the answers is most evident in the fact that the answers presuppose a different interpretation of human instincts. The first answer, for example, presupposes that human instincts are very much like the instincts of other animals in the sense that they contain the organizing principles that direct their release in behavior. James writes, for example,

> However uncertain man's reaction upon his environment may sometimes seem in comparison with those of lower creatures, the uncertainty is probably *not due to their possession of any principles of action which he lacks*. On the contrary, man possesses all the impulses that they have, and a great many more besides.[70]

Hesitation, the seeming lack of "'instinctive' demeanor," consequently, is evident in a human being not because impulses lack their own principles of action, but "rather because he has so many that they block each other's path."[71]

While Dewey at times seems to subscribe to this position (as in the quotation in the paragraph preceding the last one), more often he takes another position. According to this second position, human instincts are not principles of action that direct behavior but are inchoate impulses that require direction in order to be effective at all:[72]

> The inchoate and scattered impulses of an infant do not coordinate into serviceable powers except through social dependencies and companionships. His impulses are merely starting points for assimilation of the knowledge and skill of the more matured beings upon whom he depends. They are tentacles sent out to gather that nutri-

---

[70]James, *Principles of Psychology*, 1013; my emphasis; in the text the last sentence is emphasized.

[71]Ibid. According to this point of view, consequently, human instincts are relatively unfixed only in the sense that they are flexible to adjustment and coordination with other instincts, not because they lack an initial principle of action.

[72]Note that James also at times seems to take this second position, as evidenced in his claim, already quoted, that "man is born with a tendency to do more things than he has ready-made arrangements for in his nerve-centres" (ibid., 118).

tion from customs which will in time render the infant capable of
independent action.[73]

In the case of a tiger or eagle, [for example, the impulse of] anger
may be identified with a serviceable life-activity, with attack or
defense. With a human being it is as meaningless as a gust of wind
on a mudpuddle apart from a direction given it by the presence of
other persons, apart from the responses they make to it. It is a
physical spasm, a blind dispersive burst of wasteful energy.[74]

According to this second position, human impulses require learning, not
because the directions they give in response to the same stimuli conflict,
but because they give little or no direction at all. They are merely physical spasms, representing no skills, no modes of effective behavior.

That the second position is more adequate than the first can be seen
in two ways. On the one hand, while both positions are able to account
for flexibility in the development of human behavior, the second one is
able to account more adequately for diversity among human beings and
cultures. If impulses are not already organized, they may by considered,
in their initial appearances, to be more open ended, capable of being
organized into a variety of different concrete modes of behavior. "In the
case of the young," Dewey writes,

it is patent that impulses are highly flexible starting points for
activities which are diversified according to the ways in which they
are used. *Any impulse may become organized into almost any dis-
position according to the way it interacts with surroundings.* Fear
may become abject cowardice, prudent caution, reverence for supe-
riors or respect for equals; an agency for credulous swallowing of
absurd superstitions or for wary skepticism. A man may be chiefly
afraid of the spirits of his ancestors, of officials, of arousing the
disapproval of his associates, of being deceived, of fresh air, or of
Bolshevism.[75]

On the other hand, the second position accounts more adequately for
continuity within a culture. If the directions for impulsive behavior are

[73]Dewey, *Human Nature and Conduct*, 89.
[74]Ibid., 86.
[75]Ibid., 91; my emphasis.

not intrinsic to or inherent in the impulses themselves, the directions must, at least initially, be supplied from without, for example, by the way others respond to the sporadic bursts of energy in infants. Dewey illustrates this with the impulse of anger. In the infant, he writes, the impulse of anger initially appears as a blind burst of energy which is useless. It becomes something more only when it gains significance and direction and thus becomes a specific mode of behavior, "a smoldering sullenness, an annoying interruption, a peevish irritation, a murderous revenge, a blazing indignation." What is of importance is this, that

> although these phenomena which have a meaning spring from original native reactions to stimuli, yet they depend also upon the responsive behavior of others. They and all similar human displays of anger are not pure impulses; they are habits formed under the influence of association with others who have habits already and who show their habits in the treatment which converts a blind physical discharge into a significant anger.[76]

An impulse becomes effective, consequently, only as children learn how to respond in the same way as others who surround them. In this process, the habits and customs of the culture are learned and adopted by children, providing continuity to the culture from generation to generation.

The second position is adopted by the cultural anthropologist Clifford Geertz, who provides a further argument for its support. In his book *The Interpretation of Cultures*, he argues that the evidence of archeology suggests that the process of evolution that resulted in the rise of *Homo sapiens* was not complete before cultural development began. Culture, Geertz argues, is best understood not as customs or habits which constitute tool using, language, moral practices, social organization, and so on, but as the principles that inform them, "as a set of control mechanisms—plans, recipes, rules, instructions (what computer engineers call 'programs')—for the governing of behavior."[77] The evidence that these extrasomatic cultural instructions for directing behavior had begun to

[76]Ibid., 86.
[77]Clifford Geertz, *The Interpretation of Cultures* (New York: Basic Books, 1973) 44.

develop and were effective in the evolutionary stages preceding the rise
of our species means, Geertz claims, that culture became ingredient in
our very production.

> The slow, steady, almost glacial growth of culture through the Ice
> Age altered the balance of selection pressures for the evolving *Homo*
> in such a way as to play a major directive role in his evolution. . . .
> As culture, step by infinitesimal step, accumulated and developed,
> a selective advantage was given to those individuals in the popula-
> tion most able to take advantage of it—the effective hunter, the
> persistent gatherer, the adept toolmaker, the resourceful leader—
> until what had been a small-brained, protohuman *Australopithecus*
> became the large-brained fully human *Homo sapiens*.[78]

The most important evolutionary development, as Geertz indicates, took
place in the central nervous system, particularly the forebrain which
"ballooned into its present top-heavy proportions."[79] The significance of
this development is that the human nervous system now requires the
control mechanisms of culture in order for men and women to act:

> As our central nervous system. . . grew up in great part in inter-
> action with culture, it is incapable of directing our behavior or
> organizing our experience without the guidance provided by sys-
> tems of significant symbols. What happened to us in the Ice Age
> is that we were obliged to abandon the regularity and precision of
> *detailed genetic control over our conduct* for the flexibility and
> adaptability of a more *generalized*, though of course no less real,
> *genetic control over it*. To supply the added information necessary
> to be able to act, we were forced, in turn, to rely more and more
> heavily on cultural sources—the accumulated fund of significant
> symbols.[80]

[78]Ibid., 47–48.

[79]Ibid., 48.

[80]Ibid., 49; my emphasis. This does not means that all human activity is
controlled by culture. "The boundary between what is innately controlled and
what is culturally controlled in human behavior," Geertz (p. 50) writes, "is an ill-
defined and wavering one. Some things are, for all intents and purposes, entirely
controlled intrinsically: we need no more cultural guidance to learn how to breathe

The appropriate conclusion that Geertz draws is that human beings are incomplete or unfinished animals at birth.[81] The importance of this conclusion, for our purposes, is that it adds further support to the second interpretation of the nature of human instincts. In contrast to other animals, as Geertz points out, human instincts or impulses are not relatively detailed "programs" guiding behavior but are general capacities that need shaping.[82] If human instincts are understood as general response capacities, however, in what sense is it meaningful to say, as do James and Dewey, that human beings have more instincts or impulses than other animals? It would be problematic "to try to restrict original activities to a definite number of sharply demarcated classes of instincts,"[83] Dewey argues, for such an approach presupposes that human instincts contain a fixed means of release. This means that human beings do not have more instincts in the sense of having a given and specific number that is greater than the number of instincts in a given animal species. A more adequate way of interpreting this claim is to recognize, as Dewey says, that in human beings "there are as many specific reactions to differing stimulating conditions as there is time for,"[84] or again, that "there are an indefinite number of original or instinctive activities, which are organized into interests and dispositions according to the situations to which they respond."[85] Human instincts have an "indefinite number," I would

---

than a fish needs to learn how to swim. Others are almost certainly largely cultural; we do not attempt to explain on a genetic basis why some men put their trust in centralized planning and others in the free market, though it might be an amusing exercise. Almost all complex human behavior is, of course, the interactive, nonadditive outcome of the two. Our capacity to speak is surely innate; our capacity to speak English is surely cultural. Smiling at pleasing stimuli and frowning at unpleasing ones are surely in some degree genetically determined. . . ; but sardonic smiling and burlesque frowning are equally surely predominantly cultural."

[81]Ibid., 49. Geertz's most concise statement on the matter (p. 46) reads: "man is, in physical terms, an incomplete, an unfinished animal;. . . what sets him off most graphically from nonmen is less his sheer ability to learn (great as that is) than how much and what particular sorts of things he *has* to learn before he is able to function at all."

[82]Ibid., 45–46.

[83]Dewey, *Human Nature and Conduct*, 124.

[84]Ibid., 125.

[85]Ibid., 138.

suggest, in the same sense that they are general. Apart from cultural guidance they can hardly be called instincts at all, for they are not responses but merely unformed bursts of energy. They *become* responses only as they are shaped and guided by cultural modes of response. As these modes over history and across cultures have been widely diverse and often unimaginably complex, human beings, accordingly, can be said to have more instincts than other animals in the sense that they have the *potentiality or capacity* of responding in an indefinite number of specific ways and to an exceedingly wide and complex range of stimuli, a potentiality or capacity that is realized in the concrete in vastly different ways by human beings living at different times and in different places.

Language, Meanings, and the Development of Interest

So far we have attempted to establish the need for human beings to learn cultural modes of response in order for their conduct to have adequate guidance. The most important aspect of culture that meets this need, as we shall see, is the learning of language. Some development apart from learning of language is possible, to be sure, as an infant gradually learns to coordinate its vision with muscular movement to focus upon, grasp, and tinker with things round about. But even here the child lives within a social environment, sustained by other people whose activities and responses gradually become the chief focus of the child's interest and affection. More than anything else, the infant wants to learn to coordinate its body so that it can enter more fully into the life of those to whom its interests and affections cling.

This entry into the social world is made possible by learning language, by learning how to use language as others do so as to participate in shared purposes and activities. We have seen that language is that kind of activity in which men and women cooperate in the pursuit and achievement of common purposes, and that this cooperation is possible insofar as the communication process establishes a common understanding of meanings, of how sounds and motions are used in various contexts to anticipate and promote shared consequences. In particular, by learning the meanings of language a child learns cultural modes of response essential to the possibility of action. This is implicit in Dewey's functional interpretation of the meanings of language, of how they operate or are used in social contexts.

Three interrelated aspects of Dewey's functional interpretation of language help to clarify how meanings are bound up with common ways of responding. First of all, meaning is not directly given in and with the speaking of a word (or the motion of hands or the head), but emerges and is established in historical interaction. Meaning comes into being, if you will, in and with and through human communication. In particular, Dewey writes, it "is established by agreements of different persons in existential activities having reference to existential consequences."[86] Unfortunately, the use of the word "agreement" is easily misunderstood. The agreement of which Dewey writes is not mere convention, the arbitrary assignment of some meaning to some sound; it is, rather, *agreement in practice*, agreement as embodied in the way certain sounds are used in practice to bring about certain consequences. The agreement, to borrow a phrase from Wittgenstein, is "not agreement in opinions but in form of life."[87] To be sure, Dewey writes,

> the particular physical existence [sound] which has meaning is, in the case of speech, a conventional matter. But the convention or common consent which sets it apart as a means of recording and communicating meaning is that of agreement in *action*: of shared modes of responsive behavior and participation in their consequences. The physical sound or mark gets its meaning in and by conjoint community of functional use.[88]

The meanings of language are grounded in human activity, in human interaction, emerging or coming into being insofar as sounds and gestures are used and responded to in similar ways. The meanings of the sound "flowers," for example, are not directly given in and with the sound. Rather, they have come into existence (the word has come to mean what it now in fact does mean) as men and women have discovered and come to share the different sorts of things that they can do with this sound, pointing out flowers, planting and tending flowers, giving and receiving them, preserving them as a memento of a delightful evening, and so on.

Second, this agreement is regulative in and for human interaction. Agreement is stabilized by the regular use of a word, and once estab-

---

[86]Dewey, *Logic*, 47.
[87]Wittgenstein, *Philosophical Investigations*, sec. 241.
[88]Dewey, *Logic*, 46.

lished it becomes prescriptive for future use.[89] "Meanings," Dewey writes, "are rules for using and interpreting things."[90] Such meanings regulate both *understanding*, enabling "interpretation" by "an imputation of potentiality for some consequence,"[91] and *conduct*, providing direction for how to use or respond to some event to bring about certain consequences. When one understands the meanings of "flower," for example, one understands the many consequences to which the different uses of this word have led in the past and thus the various potential consequences to which it might lead in the present or future. This understanding gives direction as to how to use the word in new contexts, opening up possible purposes and means to achieve them.

It is important to recognize that the rules that regulate understanding and conduct are not rigid or fixed in any final way. As Wittgenstein

---

[89]Wittgenstein (*Philosophical Investigations*, sec. 198) suggests a similar connection between the regular use of a thing (a custom) and its regulative character for future use: "Let me ask this: what has the expression of a rule—say a sign-post—got to do with my actions? What sort of connexion is there here?—Well, perhaps this one: I have been trained to react to this sign in a particular way, and now I do so react to it." The interlocutor pushes the point. "But that is only to give a causal connexion; to tell how it has come about that we now go by the sign-post; not what this going-by-the-sign really consists in." And then the response, "On the contrary; I have further indicated that a person goes by a sign-post only in so far as there exists a regular use of sign-posts, a custom." The regular use of the sign-post (or of a sound or gesture) that constitutes a custom is the expression of the sign-post (or sound or gesture) as a rule that regulates future behavior. The regular use of something need not be formulated as a rule in order for it to regulate behavior; one need only to be trained in its use, to learn how to respond to it as others and thus to agree with them in practice. Thus Wittgenstein (sec. 31) writes: "One can. . . imagine someone's having learnt the game [of chess] without ever learning or formulating rules. He might have learnt quite simple board-games first, by watching, and having progressed to more and more complicated ones. He might be given the explanation 'This is a king,'—if, for instance, he were being shown chessmen of a shape he were not used to. This explanation again only tells him the use of the piece because, as we might say, the place for it was already prepared. Or even: we shall only say that it tells him the use, if the place is already prepared. And in his case it is so, not because the person to whom we give the explanation already knows rules [as explicit formulations], but because in another sense he is already master of a game."

[90]Dewey, *Experience and Nature*, 188.

[91]Ibid.

notes, "It is only in normal cases that the use of a word is clearly prescribed; we know, are in no doubt, what to say in this or that case. The more abnormal the case, the more doubtful it becomes what we are to say."[92] This ambiguity in the meaning of words is consistent with the historical or emergent character of meaning. The normal cases in which there is little doubt about how to use a word are those circumstances that are similar to many situations in the past in which the word has been used consistently for the same purposes. When a word is first used within a particular set of circumstances, its use is not clearly prescribed, and thus we use it only gropingly and tentatively. Only gradually, as its use becomes frequent and widespread, when it has been used often in the same way in similar circumstances, does its meaning stabilize and thus lose doubt. In most cases now, for example, we do not hesitate to call roses and daffodils "flowers," to grow them in our garden, to buy them for our spouse, and to put them in vases and upon the dinner table to enjoy and share. Nevertheless, even now there are new or unusual circumstances in which the established meanings of the word are unable to regulate behavior precisely, in which several different kinds of meanings or rules might apply, making the situation ambiguous for us. If our young child or grandchild were to offer us a handful of dandelions with a smiling face, what are we to say and what are we to do with them? We might exclaim, "What pretty flowers!" Yet, is it clear we ought to call them flowers? Should we tell the child that these things are usually considered weeds and are bad for the lawn and garden, or would that simply spoil their delight? And when the child leaves, do we throw them in the waste basket or do we put them in a vase? While giving some direction for understanding and conduct in this unusual case, it is clear that the meanings of the words "flowers" and "weeds" do not rigidly regulate how we are to treat the child's gift. There is, in other words, a certain openness to the meanings of our words that becomes apparent in unusual circumstances, reminding us of their historical character. Emerging and developing in historical interaction, consequently, the meanings of words are regulative insofar as they have been used regularly in the past and insofar as the present context is similar to situations in the past in which the words have been so used. Insofar as the situation is unusual, however, the meanings that have already been developed are not able to regulate behavior in a precise way, and thus men and women

---

[92]Wittgenstein, *Philosophical Investigations*, sec. 142.

have to discover, work out or grope towards new ways of responding to it. Insofar as these new modes of response become widespread, they in turn become established meanings and are grafted onto the common stock of meanings already operative in the culture.

Third, the regulative character of a meaning makes it possible for us to call it a *method for social action*. "A word," Dewey writes, is "a mode of social action with which to realize the ends of association."[93] More particularly, "a meaning is a method of action, a way of using things as a means to a shared consummation."[94] Meanings, in other words, give direction for how to proceed in the world, how to respond. It is in learning the meanings of language, consequently, that the need for guidance in the responsive activity of children is met. In learning how to use the word "flowers," for example, children learn how to respond to flowers, what to do with them. More generally, in learning how to use words, children learn how to participate in the social forms or modes of life present in their culture. They learn how to build with toys and later with bricks and cement; they learn how to cook and to eat properly, to tell stories and to joke, to ask questions, to organize their thoughts, to state claims, to decide, to make love and war, to pray, and to do all those other sorts of things that constitute distinctively human activities.[95] Stated more generally, when children learn to use words, they learn to understand the kind of situations in which they find themselves, and they are capable of envisioning and projecting a wide variety of purposes, of communicating those purposes, and of urging cooperation in their achievement.

As a method for action, meaning is a behavioral characteristic. More specifically, to have and to understand a meaning is to be prepared to act or respond in a certain way when the right situation arises.[96] When meaning is understood, Dewey writes, "an attitude is formed which is a preparatory readiness to act in a responsive way when the conditions in question [i.e., in which the meaning was formed] or others similar to them actually present themselves."[97] It is the forming of such behavioral attitudes in and through the learning of language meanings which trans-

---

[93]Dewey, *Experience and Nature*, 184.
[94]Ibid., 187.
[95]See Van Buren, *The Edges of Language*, chap. 3; 45–60.
[96]See Gouinlock, *John Dewey's Philosophy of Value*, 87.
[97]Dewey, *Logic*, 48–49.

forms the general impulses of infants into working habits, concrete modes of response.

As we have seen, meanings arise as the connections inherent in purposes, as the way certain events (such as sounds) are used to bring about other events (shared consequences). In this process, as Dewey notes, brute events cease to be mere happenings; they are transformed by becoming associated with other events, understood or perceived in terms of their potential consequences:

> What a physical event immediately is, and what it *can* do or [what] its relationship [is to other things, are matters which] are distinct and incommensurable. But when an event has meaning, its potential consequences become its integral and funded feature. When the potential consequences are important and repeated, they form the very nature and essence of a thing, its defining, identifying, and distinguishing form. To recognize the thing is to grasp its definition. Thus we become capable of perceiving things instead of merely feeling and having them. To *perceive* is to acknowledge unattained possibilities; it is to refer the present to consequences, apparition to issue, and thereby to behave in deference to the *connections* of events. As an attitude, perception or awareness is predictive expectancy, wariness.[98]

When events come to be associated with their potential consequences, they are capable of perception. Perception, according to Dewey, is never of isolated sense data, as the positivists would have it, but always consciousness or awareness of meanings, of "actual events. . . *in* their meanings."[99] Perception is never merely given, consequently, but is always an active taking of some event in some way, an active and alert expectation of its potential consequences.

Objects, in contrast to mere events, are to be understood by Dewey in relation to perception, the awareness of connections among events. Perception, Dewey writes, is always perception of objects, of events in relation to other events:

[98]Dewey, *Experience and Nature*, 182.
[99]Ibid., 303.

What is perceived are meanings, rather than just events or existence. . . . When it is denied that we are conscious of *events* as such
it is not meant that we are not aware of *objects*. Objects are precisely what we are aware of. For objects are events *with* meaning;
tables, the Milky Way, chairs, stars, cats, dogs, electrons, ghosts,
centaurs, historic epochs and all the infinitely multifarious subject-
matter of discourse designated by common nouns, verbs and their
qualifiers.[100]

Events become objects when they take on meaning, when we know what
to expect from them, how to use them, how to respond to them. This
does not mean that the meanings of events need to be fully established
or certain in order for the events to be objects perceived. Indeed, to the
extent that each perceived event is unique, it is perceived as a "this," as
an object marking the transition between established meanings and meanings adequate for understanding and behavior in the present:

"This," whatever *this* may be, always implies a system of meanings
focussed at a point of stress, uncertainty, and need of regulation. It
sums up history, and at the same time opens a new page; it is
record and promise in one; a fulfillment and an opportunity. It is
a fruition of what has happened and a transitive agency of what is
to happen.[101]

Even a relatively unique event, such as "that" over which we stumble in
the dark, is perceived as an object, as an event-with-meaning. The meaning in this case is "relatively unknown meaning," or "meaning yet to be
discovered," a meaning that prompts us to seek and confirm a more
precise meaning.

We can see at this point that meanings can be understood as human
interests. On the one hand, meanings represent methods of action that
are teleological modes of behavior, organized ways of acting for certain
purposes. The emphasis here is upon meanings as means to the satisfaction of interest. On the other hand, meanings represent objects that are
of interest, events that embody foreseen consequences and general purposes or ends-in-view. The emphasis in this case is upon meanings as

[100]Ibid., 317–18.
[101]Ibid., 352.

objects of interest which determine the ends of human activity. The development of meanings constitute the coordination of means and ends in interests which guide impulsive activity, providing understanding and direction. Without this coordination in meanings, there could be no interests. If means, a particular way of acting, did not have some end that was envisioned and desired, it would lose its reason to be in its dull routine. On the other hand, if one desired some end and yet lacked means to realize it even partially, the end would eventually lose interest. Meanings emerge as interests because they are particular means of guiding behavior to ends that are enjoyed.

In interpreting meanings as human interests, it is helpful to emphasize what has only been implied, namely, that learning language meanings is not only an intellectual and practical process but one infused with affections, feelings of quality, that underlie it and develop within it. This is important, for it is our affections that prompt and sustain interest. We have seen that we are affected by the results of our interactions and that these enjoyed or suffered consequences stimulate impulsive energy. Children learn the meanings of the events that prompt these organic drives as their energy is directed by cultural modes of response, resulting in further events (consequences) that are also enjoyed or suffered. Representing the particular connections among these events, each of which has its own quality that is felt in a particular way, a meaning accrues from the felt qualities of the events it relates. As James Gouinlock writes:

> The meaning of an object is funded with all these various immediate values [the felt qualities of the events it relates]. . . . [A] meaning is an amalgam of immediate values. To put the matter in more precise terminology: The meaning of an object is a complex of prizings (and/or rejections) [enjoyments and/or sufferings, likings and/or dislikings] presumed to exist in certain unified relations contingent upon specified forms of action with that object.[102]

At the same time, and as a result, when they come to have meaning, the immediate felt qualities of events change; the events as objects become marked or qualified by the felt qualities of the other events with which they are connected. How a person feels about an event, the worth it has for him or her, consequently, depends upon the meanings of that event

---

[102]Gouinlock, *John Dewey's Philosophy of Value*, 155–56.

which have developed for that person and are presently associated with it.[103]

We can summarize this discussion by noting that the development of meanings is the development of interests, a process which proceeds upon the basis of affections, of liking and disliking certain conditions and consequences that are enjoyed or suffered, and of desiring to maintain or avoid them. Even though it is initially felt in only a vague way by an infant, an event that is enjoyed or suffered forms that which is of interest to the infant, prompting attention and stimulating general impulsive responses. At the same time, it constitutes the ground for the infant gradually to take interest in other things, in the means by which it is repeated, sustained, or avoided. This eventual coordination of means and ends is learned as the child gradually learns the meanings of language. When this happens, the initial and vague object of interest is transformed into an organized interest with a discriminated object or end that is understood in relation to, and that takes on the qualities of, those events with which it is connected.

The continual development of interests is made possible by the fact that any physical event (including a sound) is capable of innumerable meanings.

> The same existential events are capable of an infinite number of meanings. Thus an existence identified as "paper," because the meaning uppermost at the moment is "something to be written upon," has as many other explicit meanings as it has important consequences recognized in the various connective interactions into which it enters. Since possibilities of conjunction are endless, and since the consequences of any of them may at some time be significant, its potential meanings are endless. It signifies something to start a fire with; something like snow; made of wood-pulp; manufactured for profit; property in a legal sense; a definite combination illustrative of certain principles of chemical science; an article the inven-

---

[103]Gouinlock (ibid.) writes, "the value of any object or event [once it comes to have meaning] will be a function of its meanings—of its existential relations to other objects and events of value. That is, the actual felt value [or qualities] of an object for an individual depends upon the meaning with which the object is funded for that individual." Hence, just as a meaning is an amalgam of immediate values, so "anything possessing value of any kind beyond its sheer immediacy is an amalgam of qualitative meanings."

tion of which has made a tremendous difference in human history, and so on indefinitely.[104]

In the course of living, men and women have discovered, through trial and error, a variety of uses to which a particular kind of occurrence can be put. As different uses and consequences are discovered, its meanings grow and the event becomes a highly complex object, connected with a variety of different events. Because events are capable of a wide variety of meanings, this process of discovery is indefinitely open and capable of enormous refinement. As this occurs, the world is opened up to men and women who are now capable of extending themselves in the world in all sorts of ways. The world, in short, becomes humanized, full of complex and interrelated objects of interest.

We can see, now, how human beings are capable of a greater number and variety of interests than other animals and how this capacity is realized in human experience. Born without the relatively fixed instincts that shape the interests and direct the activities of other animals, human infants are, in comparison, exceedingly plastic and open ended, capable of development in a variety of different directions. This development is initially achieved through socialization, the process of learning how to participate in social communication. In this process, children learn to share the meanings or interests that have been developed and refined in their culture over many generations. When they come to master the range of meanings in their culture, they gain practical freedom and are in a position to continue to expand, refine, and transform the meanings or interests they have inherited. Such a continual process of expansion and transformation is necessary, as we saw in the first section of this chapter. As meanings multiply, men and women are exposed to wider and more complex environments in which meanings or interests conflict, requiring the development of meanings if understanding and action is to occur. While these developed meanings or interests must be initially conceived in the imagination and usually by an individual, they gain significance and stability only as they become widely shared in social interaction. In this historical and dialectical process that moves from the social to the individual to the social, the human capacity for an increased number and variety of interests is realized in human life.

---

[104]Dewey, *Experience and Nature*, 319–20.

3

ART AND THE
TRANSFORMATION
OF INTERESTS

I argued in the last chapter that human beings, according to Dewey, can be distinguished from other animals by their capacity for a greater number and variety of interests. The development of these interests, we saw, not only shapes impulsive desires but also illuminates their meaning. When established, consequently, these interests come to function normatively in human life, regulating understanding and conduct.

It should come as no surprise, consequently, that confusion, ambiguity, and uncertainty arise when interests come into conflict, when the purposes and ends that inform them exclude one another. The normative character of two different interests, truth telling and care for the neighbor, for example, is called into question and leads to confusion in those situations in that it becomes clear that to tell the truth to the neighbor about some particular matter at issue would be cruel and destructive to their well-being, and yet failure to tell the truth would jeopardize trust essential for the continuity of the relationship. This kind of problem arises from time to time in any context that admits a pluralism of normative interests. It arises on a more comprehensive scale between different religious traditions, a matter that this work addresses as the problem of religious pluralism.

The present chapter constitutes the first step in addressing this problem. When established normative interests conflict, what is needed is their development and transformation so that they can again provide understanding and meaningful orientation. This development and transformation, Dewey argues, occurs by means of art. This chapter, consequently, will focus upon Dewey's concept of art. The thesis is as follows: According to Dewey, art is that dynamic process by which established normative interests are subject to continual growth and transformation so that human beings are able to respond more appropriately to the increasingly complex, ambiguous, and novel contexts of their lives. This means that art is capable of functioning as the formal norm for judgment of interests and their development.

Discussion in this chapter is divided into two parts. In order to understand Dewey's concept of art, we must first look at his concept of "context" as the framework within which interest and art occur and have meaning. Secondly, we shall examine more directly several central features of Dewey's concept of "art."

Contexts, Ends, and Means

Dewey's notion of "context" is rich but peculiar. It is equivalent in meaning to a number of other words he often uses: "situation," "interaction," "affair," "event," and "history." On one level, it represents the central metaphysical concept by which he draws together his vision of nature as temporal and emergent. On another level, it is that meaning by which one is reminded that all meanings, including this one, are human meanings emergent in natural and social contexts which have histories. This concept, consequently, affirms a metaphysical vision of the kind of world in which we live and, at the same time, qualifies that vision by placing it in a human and historical perspective.

We considered Dewey's concept of context in the last chapter when we discussed his notions of "interaction" and "continuity." In order to understand his discussion of the function of art, we must consider the concept of context further, this time focusing more directly upon what Dewey calls "ends" and "means." Before we address this matter, however, it may be helpful to ask what Dewey has in mind when he calls the notion of context "metaphysical." We can anticipate some of our discussion in chapter six by noting that Dewey's metaphysics is an attempt to understand the conditions for the possibility of the use and development of meanings in human life. His metaphysical use of language can be taken as an effort not to describe the structures of reality as such, but to put together a picture of the kind of world in which human beings can be understood as historical creatures who use and develop interests and meanings in communication and the thinking process. His project, therefore, is not directly empirical but rather imaginative and speculative, a creative investigation of the implications of the human use of meanings. This somewhat controversial claim about Dewey's metaphysics will be argued in some detail in chapter six. It is important to keep it in mind, however, for the way Dewey uses language metaphysically makes it sometimes appear as though he thought he were looking directly at reality or existence and describing it as such.

The Nature of Contexts

I have suggested that Dewey's notion of "context" is the fundamental metaphysical concept that he uses to draw together his vision of nature as temporal and emergent. Although our aim in this discussion is to consider contexts with respect to means and ends, we should begin by recalling a point made in the last chapter, namely, that nature is best understood as being constituted, not by substances that undergo change, but by changes themselves, by events in interaction with other events. This is to understand that the fundamental units of reality, according to Dewey, not only are but become. In Dewey's words, "existence consists of events,. . . possessed of temporal quality, characterized by beginning, process and ending."[1]

The use of the word "context," as an alternative for event or affair, helps to bring out the idea that whatever occurs in nature never occurs as a self-enclosed happening but always in relation to other occurrences:

> That all existences are *also* events I do not doubt. For they are qualified by temporal transition. But that existences as such are *only* events strikes me as a proposition that can be maintained in no way except by a wholesale ignoring of context. For. . . every oc-

[1]Dewey, *Experience and Nature*, 110.

currence is a concurrence. An event is not a self-enclosed, self-executing affair.[2]

Dewey's concept of an event is a concept of what is understood to happen when various events come into contact, qualifying each other in a new way. This means that any new event is taken by Dewey to be *a context of interacting events*, for each event of the context can be understood to be what it is in its functional relationship to the other events of that context.[3]

[2]Dewey, "Context and Thought," 96.

[3]This notion of event as *a context of interdependent and mutually qualifying events* can be contrasted with older metaphysical positions in which change was not seen as a development or a genuinely temporal qualification, a change in the quality of what was. Atoms, as they were classically conceived, Dewey argues, "do not have careers; they simply change their relations in space. . . . The Newtonian atom, for example, moved and was moved, thus changing its position in space, but it was unchangeable in its own being. What it was at the beginning or without any beginning it is always and forever. Owing to the impact of other things it changes its direction and velocity of motion so that it comes closer and further away from other things. But all this was believed to be external to its own substantial being. It had no development, no history, because it had no potentialities. . . . Time did not enter into its being either to corrode or to develop it" (Dewey, "Time and Individuality," 231). While Hobbes and other philosophers conceive of life according to this billiard ball model of reality, many others were struck by the uniqueness and apparent qualitative change of human historical events and were content to acknowledge a dualism between physical matter (called "nature") and human life. It was not until the nineteenth century that Hegel and others began to conceive reality as a whole on the model of history. Dewey's attempt to establish a continuity between nature and human life by historicizing nature, reconceiving it as a developing and emergent process, is one aspect of his philosophy that he shares with Hegel. By interpreting the fundamental units of reality as *contexts*, however, Dewey's metaphysics is far more pluralistic and open ended than is Hegel's vision of reality as the unfolding of *Geist*. There are, however, contemporary Hegelians who have attempted to reconstruct Hegel in a more pluralistic and open ended fashion. See, for example, Rupp, *Christologies and Cultures*, 85–158. When Hegel's philosophy is reconstructed in this way, it has much in common with Dewey's work. The point is of some importance for theologians who wish to work out the theological significance of Dewey's philosophy, for they can learn much from Hegel who thought more extensively about religious and theological matters.

Several important consequences follow from this concept of a context. First of all, a context or an affair can be taken to represent a unique or distinctive qualitative change in the world. "Every event in the world," as Dewey says, "marks a difference made to one existence in active conjunction with some other existence."[4] The mutual qualification of events that constitute a context is understood to result in a qualitative change, or a difference made to, those events as they were when they initially came into conjunction, for what was occurring before the context emerged has now become qualified in a new and distinctive way.[5]

Second, it follows that contexts not only become; more appropriately, they can be taken as events which grow together into organic wholes of mutually interdependent changes. To use Whitehead's term, they concresce.[6] This is to take contexts as *becoming* distinctive qualitative

---

[4]John Dewey, "The Need for a Recovery of Philosophy," in Bernstein, *On Experience, Nature, and Freedom*, 51.

[5]"Since every event is also an interaction of different things, it is inherently characterized by something from which and to which. . . . The 'from which' and 'to which' qualify the event and make it, concretely, the distinctive event which it is" (Dewey, "Context and Thought," 97).

"An 'affair,' *Res*, is always at issue whether it concerns chemical change, the emergence of life, language, mind or the episodes that compose human history. Each [event or affair] comes from something else and each when it comes has its own initial, unpredictable, immediate qualities, and its own similar terminal qualities. The later is never just resolved into the earlier. What we call such resolution is merely a statement of the order by means of which we regulate the passage of an earlier into the later" (Dewey, *Experience and Nature*, 111).

[6]See Alexander, *John Dewey's Theory of Art*, 104. The continuity between the metaphysics of Whitehead and Dewey at several key points, such as the present one, is remarkable. There are, however, several important differences between Whitehead's actual occasions and Dewey's contexts. While actual occasions, for example, are self-enclosed processes of subjectivity, cut off from their contemporaries, contexts are open ended and do not necessarily have subjective feelings. Such feelings arise only with biological interactions. Also, while actual occasions are microscopic units of reality, the fundamental building blocks, as it were, for "societies," the larger things familiar to human beings, contexts, in being open ended, are not exclusively microscopic but also include the macroscopic objects and events of ordinary human experience. Interestingly enough, the fact that contexts are open ended means that Dewey is able to articulate and interpret more adequately than Whitehead the interactional (transactional) and mutually participatory (intersubjective) character of human relationships.

wholes to the extent that the events that constitute them come to condition and qualify one another and thus become events of that context, parts of that whole. A context forms a whole not only spatially, with respect to concurrent events, but also temporally. As Dewey says, "Every event as such is passing into other things, in such a way that a later occurrence is an integral part of the *character* or *nature* of present existence."[7] Later events of a context are taken to represent possibilities of earlier events that are inherent in (or belong to) that context, qualifying the earlier events and making them what they are, just as later events in a context are understood to be qualified by the earlier events, by what has taken place.[8]

---

[7]Dewey, *Experience and Nature*, 111.

[8]Later in his life, Dewey was quite insistent that situations or contexts are best conceived as wholes which have their own immediate qualitative unity (see especially his *Logic*, 65–71). As Alexander (*John Dewey's Theory of Art*, 60; see also xv–xii, 2–13, 62–69) points out, this claim has been the occasion of the most persistent criticism of Dewey. "The nature of this problem," he avers, "is described differently by different critics at various times, but I believe that the essence of it lies in the claimed opposition of Dewey's statements about the immediate qualitative nature of experience and the naturalistic and instrumental interpretation of experience." One difficulty with the notion of immediate qualitative unity, surely, is that it seems to suggest that quality is a vague something-or-other that is simply and mysteriously (unaccountably) given *to* a context (as discrete sensations are understood by the British empiricists to be given to a self), and this in turn seems to undercut Dewey's naturalistic claims regarding the development and emergence of qualities, the fact that they constitute the results of interactions and can therefore be accounted for with respect to (or understood to be mediated by) the specific ways that the events of a particular context interact. Although there is not time to address this issue fully, the present discussion in which quality is understood functionally rather than statically (as something simply given to a context) is helpful in order to gain some perspective on this matter. If quality is understood as the "qualification of," as the way things are qualified, then the quality of a context can be understood to belong both to the result and to the context as a whole, as that which unifies the whole. Because a context is conceived as a progressive qualification of events, its quality cannot be taken to be fully actual and determinate until the process has been completed, until the change has taken place. It is in the results, therefore, that any particular context shows itself as being just that particular qualitative change. This does not mean, however, that there is no quality in the initial events of a context. The quality they have is a result (1) of past events coming together in

Third, this interpretation of the mutual conditioning of the events of a context means that a context, as a concrete change, is at one and the same time both a result and a process.[9] Any context, according to this way of understanding matters, is a result as that concrete qualitative change, marking a distinctive state or condition. And yet it is not separated from other changes. Because contexts are taken to be active processes, they are also understood to be ongoing and therefore open ended, capable of further changes as they interact with other contexts.

The claim that contexts are at once ends and processes is an exceedingly important claim not only for Dewey's principle of continuity but also for his theory of means and ends. We shall consider this matter in some detail, but we can already see that Dewey's concept of a context or an affair means that it can be taken as an end to the extent that it represents qualitative change that results from the conjunction of prior changes. At the same time, because it is understood as a change or process, it can also be taken to condition or cause what follows, qualifying other changes that lead to further results. This means that any end

a new way and (2) of the fact that this novel coming-together is not yet fully determinant—it is changing in a way yet to be determined. The point of interest is that the context as a whole can be understood as unified by the progressive development of the relatively indeterminant quality of the initial events as it changes and becomes fully determinant. This means that the quality of the context belongs to the whole context as a dynamic, temporal, progressively emergent qualification. The quality becomes fully determinant in the result, to be sure, but the result is the end term of that particular progressive and dynamic qualification. Take, for example, the process of listening to a musical composition. A whole range of events come together at the beginning of the piece. This initial qualification of events represents quality in the making. That quality, of course, changes as the piece proceeds, but it is always a progressive determination of the initial, relatively indeterminate events. That dynamic qualification is not fully determinate until the conclusion. It is at that point that the quality of the piece as a whole is rendered distinct—as that particular affair or piece of music. Again, what is rendered distinct is not the result (the last note) as such but the dynamic quality of the whole process. It is this progressively emergent quality which Dewey understands to unify the whole context and to mark it as *that* and not some other context. What Dewey terms the "immediate" quality of a context as a whole, consequently, is not a static something simply and mysteriously given to a context but rather a dynamically emergent and developing qualification of events that becomes increasingly determinant over time.

[9]Dewey, *Experience and Nature*, 100–101; see above, pp. 7–8.

is capable of being understood and therefore used instrumentally or as a means for the ends that follow.

Finally, the notion that a context is both an end and a process is helpful for understanding Dewey's claim that existence is both stable and unstable (precarious). This claim is the topic of chapter two in *Experience and Nature* and constitutes what Dewey calls the "starting point" of his metaphysics.[10] Although much could be said about this matter, we shall limit our discussion by considering it in relation to what we have already said about contexts. The instability of nature is best understood by Dewey's notion of the open ended character of contexts, for this means contexts will inevitably come into contact with other events, and thus their unique qualities are ineluctably subject to further qualification. In this sense all concrete contexts are unstable. This instability, Dewey argues, is a fundamental and irreducible feature of nature.[11]

Nature, however, can also be understood to have its stability and order. "Unless nature had regular habits, persistent ways, so compacted

---

[10]Dewey, *Experience and Nature*, x.

[11]Dewey's metaphysics of contexts is an attempt, among other things, to take change seriously as a fundamental feature of reality. He argues that most historical philosophies, while recognizing change and the precariousness and contingency which it entails, have attributed full reality only to the complete, finished and reliable. In fact, he argues (*Experience and Nature*, 46–47), they can all be seen "as different ways of supplying recipes for denying to the universe the character of contingency which it possesses so integrally that its denial leaves the reflecting mind without a clew [*sic*], and puts subsequent philosophising at the mercy of temperament, interest and local surrounding." Even the so-called philosophies of change, "from Heraclitus to Bergson," Dewey writes, have failed in this way, for they "also indicate the intensity of the craving for the sure and fixed. They have deified change by making it universal, regular, sure" (p. 50). For this reason Dewey wants to begin his metaphysics by proclaiming the precariousness and contingency of life: "Man finds himself living in an aleatory world; his existence involves, to put it baldly, a gamble. The world is a scene of risk; it is uncertain, unstable, uncannily unstable. Its dangers are irregular, inconstant, not to be counted upon as to their times and seasons. . . . Plague, famine, failure of crops, disease, death, defeat in battle, are always just around the corner, and so are abundance, strength, victory, festival and song. . . . The world of empirical things includes the uncertain, unpredictable, uncontrollable, and hazardous. . . . Man fears because he exists in a fearful, an awful world. The *world* is precarious and perilous" (pp. 41–42).

that they time, measure and give rhythm and recurrence to transitive flux," Dewey argues, "meanings, recognizable characters, could not be."[12] Such stability and order that the world possesses, as we saw in the previous chapter, however, is taken by Dewey not to be imposed from without but to be emergent from within: it emerges, as he says, "whenever a stable, even though moving, equilibrium is reached. Changes interlock and sustain one another."[13] Just as all contexts are unstable, so do they exhibit some order or pattern, for the events of a context can be understood to interlock and sustain one another to the extent that they grow together in mutual interdependence.

Two things are worth noting about this matter. On the one hand, the order exhibited by contexts can be understood as active rather than static; it consists of the way the events come together. Because it is active, Dewey points out, it is capable of development, of coming to include "within its balanced movement a greater variety of changes."[14] On the other hand, not all existential order can be taken as conducive to stability or endurance. Indeed, the more complex the order is, the less likely it will be to endure, to be repeated exactly. The successive physical interactions among the atoms of a rock, for example, have much greater similarity and thus endurance than do the successive biological interactions of a tree and its environment or the successive social interactions among human beings. Yet, because order is understood as active and thus capable of development, it is possible to conceive of an order be-

---

[12]Ibid., 351. That nature has regular habits is so taken for granted by human beings that Dewey hardly ever argues the matter. In this quotation, of course, he is presenting an argument; yet he quickly adds the following: "But also without an interplay of these patient, slow-moving, not easily stirred systems of action with swift-moving, unstable, unsubstantial events, nature would be a routine unmarked by ideas" (p. 351). What Dewey in fact wants to argue is that the world is constituted by a mix of the stable and unstable, the reliable and the precarious, and he does this by arguing that without this mix we would not even be conscious, for it is the combination of these traits that creates suspense so necessary for attention; nor would we ever experience satisfaction or fulfillment in life: "The union of the hazardous and the stable, of the incomplete and the recurrent, . . . is the source of the delight which fulfillments bring. For if there were nothing in the way, if there were no deviations and resistances, fulfillment would be at once, and in so being would fulfill nothing, but merely be" (p. 62).

[13]Dewey, *Art as Experience*, 14.

[14]Ibid.

longing to the development of order, an order of development, if you
will. We can understand this order as the creative adjustment to changing and novel circumstances that transforms established forms of activity, making possible stability and endurance when established order is
threatened and disturbed. This order of adjustment, of course, happens
most frequently on the biological and especially on the social level of
interaction. Dewey calls it *"growth"* or *"growing,"* a concept that, as we
shall see at the end of this chapter, is central to his interpretation of
behavior as art.

The Ends of Contexts

We are now in a position to look more carefully at the character of
what Dewey takes to be "ends" in nature. We have seen that an end, as
Dewey understands it, is the end of a context, the result of what happens
when events come to qualify one another. Furthermore, we have seen
that, as the result of the mutual qualification of events, ends are taken
to constitute the emergence of quality in nature, the completion or actualization of qualitative change. In the last chapter, we argued that
these qualitative ends are central to the concept of interest. On the human level, they represent the felt quality which results from interaction
and to which men and women respond.[15] Having this connection with

---

[15]Gouinlock criticizes Sidney Hook for arguing that Dewey's metaphysics is
really philosophical anthropology. "This contention," he claims, "so far as it is
not merely a dispute about the meaning of 'metaphysics,' could be interpreted in
a most unhappy way. That is, it could be taken to mean that when Dewey speaks
of traits of experience he is *not* thereby speaking of traits of nature. This would
clearly be a fatal misinterpretation; for it contradicts Dewey's most crucial assumption: the continuity of experience [human interaction] and nature." See
Gouinlock, *John Dewey's Philosophy of Value*, 56. Gouinlock's point, I believe,
is well made. It is therefore all the more puzzling that he should at a later point
seem to attribute ends to human experience alone: "Of the physical universe as
it is described in physics alone, the notion of endings could have no meaning. An
ending is only what is distinguished as such in experience; and what is thus
distinguished is some event that for some purpose is marked off qualitatively
from other events" (p. 81). Gouinlock's claim can be supported readily by quotations in Dewey's works. Unfortunately, Dewey's writing on this issue is vague
and inconsistent. What he does say clearly, however, is that physical science, as
a science, is not interested in qualities or ends which mark *individual* contexts
and interactions; the interest of physicists, rather, is in statistical probabilities,

the concept of interest in mind, several important things about Dewey's interpretation of ends and their felt qualities are to be noted.

We can begin by considering Dewey's claim that "the realm of immediate quality contains everything of worth and significance."[16] What we attend to and care about, Dewey is suggesting, are things having qualities, for it is qualities we like and dislike and thus want to preserve or avoid. Qualities, in short, are the goods and bads of our lives in which we take interest and which shape our purposes.[17]

---

and for this reason ends are not considered. This is quite a different matter from saying that ends or qualities should not be conceived to exist on the physical level. In point of fact, the burden of one of Dewey's later essays, "Time and Individuality," (see esp. pp. 231–36) is to argue that inanimate elements as individuals, as continuous contexts of interacting elements, undergo qualitative change with their own distinctive qualitative results. If one reduces quality to felt quality or to what is felt, one is forced to agree with Gouinlock that physical events have no ends or qualities. Yet if quality is understood functionally as a mutual qualification of events, then one can acknowledge ends or qualities (concrete individual qualitative change) on the physical level that allows for a continuity between physical existence and human experience. In particular, ends, that appear in experience as felt qualities to which human beings respond, can be seen in continuity with, or as a development of, physical ends—neither as identical with them, nor as something which mysteriously and therefore unaccountable appears in nature when human beings arise, but rather as more complex results of more complex interactions. If this kind of continuity is not maintained, it is difficult to understand how human experience is part of nature (a more complex development of physical and biological interactions) and therefore how knowledge is of and about nature.

[16]Dewey, *Experience and Nature*, 114.

[17]In Dewey's words (ibid., 104), ends or qualities "alone. . . are of interest, and they are the cause of taking interest in other things. . . . They are the basis, directly and indirectly, of active response to things. As compared with them, other things are obstacles and means of procuring and avoiding the occurrence of situations having them." As the basis of the development of interest, it is important adequately to interpret the status of quality in nature. It was an unfortunate occurrence in the history of thought, for example, when the concept of nature was gradually reduced to the extensive relations among things with which science is concerned, for qualities came to be conceived as "secondary" and subjective, an attribution of the mind. This move did not undercut the possibility of the use, enjoyment, and suffering of qualities, but it did mean that thinking about relations could not be used to guide responses to qualities, for qualities

Because contexts are understood to be unique and novel, never precisely duplicated in their full concreteness, ends in nature, as the concrete results of the qualitative changes, are understood by Dewey to be unique and novel as well. This means two things. On the one hand, it means that anticipation and prediction are never certain but always, as Dewey puts its, experimental and hypothetical:

> The richer and fuller are the terminal qualities of an object the more precarious is the latter, because of its dependence upon a greater diversity of events. At the best, therefore, control is partial and experimental. All prediction is abstract and hypothetical. Given the stability of other events, and it follows that certain conditions, selected in thought, determine the predictability of the occurrence of say, red. But since the other conditions do not remain unalterably put, what actually occurs is never just what happens in thought; the thing of mere redness does not happen, but some thing with just this shade and tinge of red, in just this unduplicable content. Thus something unpredictable, spontaneous, unformulable and ineffable is found in any terminal object.[18]

On the other hand, that terminal qualities are taken to constitute unique and novel results means that nature can be understood to harbor novel possibilities that belong to specific contexts as the unique possibilities of those contexts. The significance of this cannot be over estimated. In Dewey's words, it means that "potentiality is a category of existence."[19] In making this claim, Dewey wants to distinguish his notion of potentiality from the Aristotelian doctrine of fixed ends, the notion that an individual has only one end toward which it moves. In contrast, poten-

---

were not taken to be the result of the way things were related. Dewey's metaphysics of contexts is a deliberate attempt to establish the continuity between the relations-among-things and qualities by arguing that qualities are not subjective but rather constituent traits of nature that result from the way things come into relationship and qualify one another. Qualities and relations-among-things, as Dewey conceives the matter, represent different emphases or phases of a continuous context rather than different kinds of being. Dewey's interest in making this point, in part, is so that thinking that is concerned with the relations among things, can be taken seriously as a means for guiding our responses to qualities.

[18]Ibid., 117.

[19]Dewey, "Time and Individuality," 237.

tiality with respect to any individual, according to Dewey, is better conceived as consisting of an indeterminate range of novel possibilities:

> Potentialities must be thought of in terms of consequences of interactions with other things. Hence potentialities cannot be *known* till *after* the interactions have occurred. There are at a given time unactualized potentialities in an individual because and in so far as there are in existence other things with which it has not yet interacted. Potentialities of milk are known today, for example, that were not known a generation ago, because milk has been brought into interaction with things other than organisms, and hence now has other than furnishing[-]nutriment consequence. . . . When the only possible use of milk was as an article of food, it was "natural" to suppose that it had an inherent tendency to serve that particular end. With the use of milk as a plastic, and with no one able to tell what future consequences may be produced by new techniques which bring it into new interactions, the only reasonable conclusion is that potentialities are not fixed and intrinsic, but are a matter of an indefinite range of interactions in which the individual may engage.[20]

The concept of an indeterminate range of potentiality as a trait of existence constitutes a notion of the world as a place in which genuinely new things happen—in which there takes place, if you will, a qualitative development and transformation of what already exists. This matter has direct bearing upon the burden of my argument. To conceive potentiality as a genuine feature of our world is at one and the same time to take seriously the historical and progressively developmental character of our interests. When religious interests conflict, consequently, it makes some difference whether the participants acknowledge potentiality as a genuine trait of existence, for this acknowledgment makes it possible for men and women to be open to the development and transformation of their interests.

We have considered to some extent the notion that contexts are at once a result and an ongoing process which leads to further results. This means that qualitative ends suffered and enjoyed are more ambiguous than one might think at first. While ends can be understood to sum up

---

[20]Ibid., 238–39.

an affair, they nevertheless remain open, leading out to the future, and this means, at least in human affairs, that ends are often qualified by a vague presentiment, a sense of potentiality yet to be determined. This can be conceived as qualitative *telos* (or felt possibility) inherent in the ensuing affair or context. Dewey talks about this sense of finality qualified by vague presentiment in the following terms:

> Although there is a bounding horizon, it moves as we move. We are never wholly free from the sense of something that lies beyond. . . . About every explicit and focal object there is a recession into the implicit which is not intellectually grasped. In reflection we call it dim and vague. But in the original experience it is not identified as the vague. It is a function of the whole situation, and not an element in it, as it would have to be in order to be apprehended *as* vague.[21]

This vague "sense of something that lies beyond" the discrimination of quality can be understood as the dynamic sense of quality in the making that draws us out and is central in guiding the kinds of responses we make in the gradual development and discrimination of newly emergent quality.

This understanding of the dual function of ends makes ends problematic or "tensive,"[22] prompting further interaction. The tensive quality of

[21]Dewey, *Art as Experience*, 193–94. See also Dewey, *Quest*, 236.

[22]The word "tensive" is borrowed from Thomas Alexander who suggests it as more appropriate than the word "problematical." Noting that Dewey early in his career used the former word as descriptive of situations, he adds, "It is a pity Dewey did not retain the use of the term 'tensive' instead of relying upon 'problematical,' since the latter inevitably makes one focus on simple practical 'problem-solving,' like fixing a tire. . . . Situations are always tensional because there is always a certain amount of disequilibrium" (see Alexander, *John Dewey's Theory of Art*, 301 n. 32). The difficulty of conceiving the ambiguity of ends as a matter of problem solving, I believe, is that it leads one to think that the ambiguity of human contexts can be cleared up or solved, and then conduct can be carried on "as usual." One consequently misses the crucial insight that ambiguity is a constant feature of human contexts that underlies and prompts the continuous development of reflection and conduct. Dewey, of course, is guilty of not stating this matter more clearly himself. In particular, he does in fact sometimes talk about reflection in a misleading way as simple problem solving

ends and the contexts of which they are a part, of course, is a matter of degrees, of more or less, rather than a difference of kind, of either-or.[23] On the biological level, the tensive quality of ends represents need that drives effort seeking satisfaction or fulfillment. On the human level, it often emerges as a conflict of interests. As meanings develop in life, any given end comes to embody an anticipated range of potential outcomes, many of which are desired but are seen as incompatible with one another. This is evident particularly in social interactions as the meaning of any potential act comes to be qualified by an anticipation of different kinds of responses by different people, only some of which would be welcome.

Our discussion of ends has three important consequences for our understanding of interests in human life. First of all, the peculiar teleological quality that marks any new context or situation is a result of the dual character of ends that function both to conclude one affair and to initiate a new affair. As we have seen, this quality underlies the emergence and development of interests. What is crucial to note is that interests are, consequently, context bound, and that their fulfillment, which Dewey calls the consummatory phase of experience, is always relative to the needs of the particular situations of which they are a part.

Second, we should qualify this contextual relativity of interests to distinguish it from utter relativism. While contexts are themselves individualized, they are in fact never cut off from other contexts. Hence, when any single context interacts significantly with other contexts, it

---

that interrupts the continuity of conduct. Because of this, Israel Scheffeler criticizes what he takes to be a central problem in Dewey's thought: "There seems to me to be. . . [a] conflict between the discontinuity of the problem-theory of reflective thought, and the continuity of critical thinking that seems to be required by Dewey's interpretation of ends and means." See Israel Scheffeler, *Four Pragmatists: A Critical Introduction to Peirce, James, Mead and Dewey* (New York: Humanities Press, 1974) 237. Had Dewey stated his position more clearly, perhaps by avoiding the word "problem" altogether, he would not be subject to this kind of misunderstanding.

[23] As Alexander (*Dewey's Theory of Art*, 148) points out in this connection, "lying down after a heavy meal is hardly the problematic situation that the lean hunter faces trying to snare today's food. It is for convenience that we call the latter problematic and not the former, but both are [teleological] modes of adjustment. . . . [S]ituations are more or less secure or precarious rather than absolutely one or the other."

does not become something utterly different but rather develops. In short, it has continuity with what came before. This continuity, in fact, emerges from the dual function of ends that simultaneously conclude an event and initiate another. At most, therefore, the theory of interests proposed in this work represents a qualified relativism that recognizes that interests and their fulfillment are always relative to particular contexts but that individual contexts and the tensions inherent in them are continuous with one another.[24]

Third, fulfillment of an interest is not guaranteed. Indeed, because it represents the establishment of a new order of interaction, fulfillment is possible only as effort is exerted to remake the environment of which we are a part. We can deny needs, the tensions inherent in human life, by ignoring them or by creating a fantasy world in which there are no resistances to our desires. On the other hand, we can attempt to discriminate the meaning of the context of our conduct and to direct our behav-

---

[24]Dewey never explicitly states this issue in the terms I have used. Most often, when he addresses this matter, he overemphasizes the uniqueness of contexts and their needs. In *Human Nature and Conduct*, for example, he writes, "In quality, the good is never twice alike. It never copies itself. It is new every morning, fresh every evening. It is unique in its every presentation. For it marks the resolution of a distinctive complication of competing habits and impulses which can never repeat itself" (p. 197). At the time that he wrote, it can be argued, he needed to press home this point, which was completely missed by most of his generation who maintained static and absolute goods, laws, and principles. Yet, at the same time, Dewey should have also stressed the continuity among contexts for which he argues so well in *Experience and Nature*. Only in this way, it seems to me, can he make his second point, namely, that "*Because* situations. . . are new, and therefore unique, general principles are needed" (p. 225). These principles emerge as hypotheses that are capable of guiding discrimination and conduct and are themselves subject to further development, for principles can be established and have significance only if there is continuity among contexts. Had Dewey been more careful in his expressions on this matter, philosophers such as Hilary Putnam would not be as likely to accuse Dewey of a kind of moral relativism that would make it impossible reasonably ("rationally" is Putnam's word) to criticize a Nazi. See Hilary Putnam, *Reason, Truth and History* (Cambridge: Cambridge University Press, 1981) 162, 167–69. For an excellent analysis of how one might reasonably and justifiably criticize and argue against a Nazi from a Deweyan perspective, see Gouinlock, *John Dewey's Philosophy of Value*, 202–3.

ior so as to remake or reorder the context of which we are a part.[25] At its optimum this process, as we shall see, represents the transformation of normative interests and constitutes what Dewey calls "art."

The Means of Contexts

This takes us to Dewey's concept of "means." According to Dewey, means can be understood to have their basis in the causal relations of nature, in the way contexts or affairs proceed. "Causality," he writes, "is another name for the sequential order itself;. . . this is an order of a history having a beginning and end."[26] When this connection between the beginning and ending of a context is recognized and understood, and when it is used deliberately, Dewey argues, the cause and effect relation becomes a means and end relation:

> Means are always at least causal conditions; but causal conditions are means only when they possess an added qualification; that, namely, of being freely used, because of perceived connection with chosen consequences. . . . Similarly, consequences, ends, are at least effects; but effects are not ends unless thought has perceived and freely chosen the conditions and processes that are their conditions.[27]

In the early months of an infant's life, for example, its cries draw the attention and care of its parents. A sequential order or pattern is operative on these occasions. When the infant comes to understand this order, its cry is capable of becoming a means that it can use for the purpose of calling the attention of its parents.

Means, consequently, are tools or instruments that can be used to mediate between the felt qualities of the beginning and ending of affairs. The mediating connection, in particular, consists of a way, mode or

---

[25]"The individual that finds a gap between its distinctive bias and the operations of the things through which alone its need can be satisfied. . . either surrenders, conforms, and for the sake of peace becomes a parasitical subordinate, indulg[ing] in egotistical solitude; or its activities set out to remake conditions in accord with desire. In the latter process, intelligence is born" (Dewey, *Experience and Nature*, 245).

[26]Ibid., 100.

[27]Ibid., 366–37.

method of proceeding from beginning to end. This can be understood by considering the nature of tools. Anything that functions as a tool is not important in and of itself, Dewey claims. This is because "it possesses an objective relation as its own defining property. Its perception as well as its actual use takes the mind to other things. . . as the hammer to the nail, and the plow to the soil."[28] When we recognize the objective relation embodied in a hammer (or an infant's cry), for example, that something becomes a tool, for this recognition in fact constitutes an idea of what it can do or what we can do with it. Consequently, tools represent modes of proceeding that can be used to discriminate various possible ways to respond to initial quality and anticipate the various consequences of those responses.

Among other things, means can be understood as purposes, aims or what Dewey calls "ends-in-view." In the last chapter we saw that Dewey makes a distinction between the end of an interaction and an end-in-view. The latter is an object of interest that represents that activity or human doing which, if actualized, would so coordinate the other subactivities of a context that the context itself would become unified, while an end constitutes the conclusion of a context, in this case the unification of all the subactivities. Ends-in-view, in short, are aims of behavior which, if actualized, function as means for the ends of interactions, their unification.

Dewey makes a further distinction. He argues that in anything other than relatively habitual conduct, the projection of an end-in-view, in order to be a concrete idea rather than an abstract dream, must be worked out as a *series* of means:

> As soon as we have projected [our end-in-view], we must begin to work backwards in thought. We must change *what* is to be done into a *how*, the means whereby. The end [-in-view] thus re-appears as a series of "what nexts," and the what next of chief importance is the one nearest the present state of the one acting. Only as the end [-in-view] is converted into a means is it definitely conceived, or intellectually defined, to say nothing of executable. Just as end [-in-view], it is vague, cloudy, impressionistic. We do not *know*

[28]Ibid., 122–23.

what we are really after until a *course* of action is mentally worked out.[29]

This is a distinction between what is needed in a particular context and how to achieve it or a plan. When we have a headache, for example, we may recognize that what is needed is an aspirin. As an end-in-view, "taking an aspirin," would be that means that would resolve the present tension. "Taking an aspirin," however, is only the end act of a longer series of acts: going to the cabinet to get the aspirin, or getting into the car to drive to the store to buy some if none is found in the cabinet. These other acts are additional or intermediate means that give concrete shape to the initially conceived end-in-view. In point of fact, by their connection to the end-in-view as intermediate means to that final means, the whole series of acts *become* the end-in-view. "Walking down the stairs and getting into the car" constitutes the initial stage of a connected series that concludes with "taking an aspirin."

There are, of course, a vast multitude of means established in culture, but each means, according to Dewey's point of view, has arisen genetically within an unstable or indeterminate context, a context in which tension is sufficiently prominent that conduct requires further discrimination and guidance. We shall examine how they emerge in some detail in the next chapter. At present, the point of interest is that if the means are adequate, i.e., if they discriminate possibilities of a context and guide conduct to a meaningful and unified end, then the means that emerge can be understood to be related organically with the ends that they condition.

This point has two significant implications that we shall mention now but shall discuss to a greater extent in the next section. On the one hand, it means that the entire process of interaction becomes a unified whole with its own distinctive and unified quality. As Dewey puts it:

> The beginning not only *is* the initial term in a *series* (as distinct from a *succession*), but it gains the *meaning* of subsequent activity moving toward a consequence of which it is the first member. The

---

[29]Dewey, *Human Nature and Conduct*, 36.

concluding term conserves within itself the meaning of the entire preparatory process.[30]

The point is not difficult to see. When we do something on purpose—when we go to the store in order to get aspirin and when we take aspirin in order to relieve our headache—our doing is informed by our purpose. In short, it means the end we seek and takes on the quality of that end in the present activity. "An active process," as Dewey says, "is strung out temporarily [sic], but there is a deposit at each stage and point entering cumulatively and constitutively into the outcome."[31] The felt quality of the anticipated consummation enters integrally into preparatory activities, and in this way gives to the process as a whole qualitative meaning that has intrinsic worth in that situation.[32]

On the other hand, the establishment of an organic relation among means and ends within a context results not only in a unity of that context but also in an understood and felt continuity among contexts. It is important to recall that, according to Dewey's interpretation, contexts are not isolated but each conditions those that follow. This means that the understood and felt unity of a context is always qualified by (or contingent upon) an anticipation of what is to follow, upon whether or not there is also an understood and felt continuity among contexts. As a result, the establishment of the means-end relation within a context must also be seen in relation to the contexts that follow. Failure to keep this in mind has disastrous results. Dewey illustrates the problem by repeating Charles Lamb's story about the origin of roast pork:

> The story. . . is that roast pork was first enjoyed when a house in which pigs were confined was accidentally burned down. While

[30]Dewey, *Experience and Nature*, 270.
[31]Ibid., 368.

[32]This is not to argue that the quality of an affair is the same throughout. One would misstate the matter were one to claim that the quality of preparing a complicated dinner is the same as eating that dinner. Dewey does not insist that the difficulty, strain, and boredom often associated with labor are completely overcome when the purpose for which one labors is understood. His point, rather, is that the strenuous quality of labor is qualified by the anticipation of the enjoyment of its results. We might add that it often becomes increasingly qualified in this way (and thus develops) the closer one approaches the end.

searching in the ruins, the owners touched the pigs that had been roasted in the fire and scorched their fingers. Impulsively bringing their fingers to their mouths to cool them, they experienced a new taste. Enjoying the taste, they henceforth set themselves to building houses, inclosing pigs in them, and then burning the houses down.[33]

The obvious problem in this story is not that the people did not have means for their end but that the means and end were not understood in connection with other ends that they also prized. As soon as one recognizes this in any context, the organic relatedness of the means-end connection within that context is called into question, disturbing its unity: we are compelled to ask, for example, is all this labor really worth the enjoyment of pork? If the means-end relation is to be organically unified, it must itself be understood as effectively conditioning other ends that are also of interest. "A genuine instrumentality *for*," Dewey writes, "is always an organ *of* an end. It confers continued efficacy upon the object in which it is embodied."[34]

The way in which Dewey understands an end to become efficacious when organically related to means require some elaboration. How, we might ask, does going to the store to buy aspirin confer efficacy upon relief of a headache? It is important to note two things at this point. First, if every end is at once a conclusion and a continuing process, then the relief of a headache is itself a causal condition of further events so that it would have some efficacy no matter how it is brought about. Second, no context, according to Dewey's view of things, exists in isolation. A headache, for example, arises in the midst of pursuing other purposes, such as making a quilt. We want relief of a headache, not just for its own sake, although that is important too, but also for the sake of being able to concentrate better on the quilt. Going to the store to buy aspirin, consequently, confers efficacy upon the relief of a headache in this way: if the connection is understood between (1) the series of means that results in the relief of a headache, and (2) the ability to concentrate on the quilt that results from the relief of the headache, then going to the store and taking aspirin becomes connected with the relief of the headache as a continuous series of means which, as a whole, is pursued with the intention of being able to concentrate upon the quilt once again.

---

[33]Dewey, *Theory of Valuation*, 40.
[34]Dewey, *Experience and Nature*, 368.

In this kind of situation, therefore, an end (such as the relief of a headache) itself becomes a deliberate means (organically connected with other means) pursued for the sake of further ends. This kind of end, consequently, not only has intrinsic worth, as the unification of a context, but also instrumental worth, marking the understood and felt continuity among contexts.

We began our discussion of means by arguing that the means-end relation is based upon the cause-effect relation, and we have concluded by noting the importance of an organic integration of means-end for the unity and continuity of conduct. According to Dewey, this establishment of the means-end relation represents *the central problem and task of human life*. Among other things, it is the most significant way to keep our interests flexible and capable of development and transformation. What we need to see now is that conduct that is informed and guided by a continual insight into means-end relations is the kind of behavior that Dewey calls art:

> It would. . . seem almost self-evident that the distinction between the instrumental and the final adopted in philosophic tradition as a solving word presents in truth a problem, a problem so deep-seated and far-reaching that it may be said to be *the* problem of experience. For all the intelligent activities of men, no matter whether expressed in science, fine arts, or social relationships, have for their task the conversion of causal bonds, relations of succession, into a connection of means-consequence, into meanings. When the task is achieved the result is art: and in art everything is common between means and ends.[35]

We can see by this quotation that our discussion of contexts—and the means and ends that constitute them—serves not only as a framework for understanding, but also as an introduction to, Dewey's concept of art. We are in a position now to examine this concept more explicitly.

Art as Normative Behavior

It may seem odd that Dewey considers behavior art and that he understands this kind of behavior to be normative for the development of interests. We need to recall, however, that one of the fundamental in-

---

[35]Ibid., 369–70.

sights informing all of his work is that human beings are active creatures seeking meaning and fulfillment. Unlike the mere activity of physical existence, human interaction has a teleological thrust, seeking ends that fulfill the needs characteristic of (increasingly) novel contexts. This thrust marks human life as interested and its development as a development of interests. Dewey's whole philosophy, I suggest, can be interpreted as an effort to illuminate this matter so that the human attempt to find meaning and fulfillment will be given better and more reliable direction. What Dewey sees in art, when it is viewed as a function of human life, is the effort to respond to the tensions inherent in novel contexts in such a way as to bring unity, continuity, and qualitative meaning to those affairs. Dewey's reflection upon art, consequently, is in fact an examination of how interests in human life are developed and transformed. It is this crucial behavioral process in particular that Dewey hopes to illuminate in his discussion of art.[36]

The Extremes of Behavior

It is helpful to begin our discussion by considering what Dewey calls the limiting terms of art: (1) routine or ordered interaction when it has become mechanical and thus separated from meaning, and (2) capricious impulse or inchoate response when that is uninformed by meaning or an understanding of context. As Dewey says,

[36]In this chapter I presuppose that Dewey's concept of art is the central and unifying concept of his mature philosophy. In this matter, I stand within a tradition of interpretation that extends at least as far back as George Geiger's *John Dewey in Perspective: A Reassessment* (New York: McGraw-Hill, 1958). Geiger argues that "experience," which he calls the fundamental and distinguishing concept in Dewey's philosophy, is best understood as "art." This same thesis has been picked up recently (1987) by Thomas Alexander in *John Dewey's Theory of Art*. Earlier, Robert J. Roth, in *John Dewey and Self-Realization* (Westport, CT: Greenwood, 1962) argues that when experience becomes art human beings achieve self-realization. Influenced to some extent by Roth, Gouinlock, in *John Dewey's Philosophy of Value* (1972), argues that value, according to Dewey, constitutes consummatory experience, and that this occurs when experience becomes art. My own work has been shaped most by Gouinlock. Nevertheless, my concern is not simply with value and evaluation but rather with the normative character of interests and their evaluation for the transformation of interests within a context of social interaction. In focusing upon interests and their transformation, consequently, my work has a different emphasis, making it more conducive for addressing the problem of religious pluralism.

The limiting terms that define art are routine at one extreme and capricious impulse at the other. It is hardly worth while to oppose science and art sharply to one another, when the deficiencies and troubles of life are so evidently due to separation between art and blind routine and blind impulse. . . . The idea that work, productive activity, signifies action carried on for merely extraneous ends, and the idea that happiness signifies surrender of mind to the thrills and excitations of the body are one and the same idea. The first notion marks the separation of activity from meaning, and the second marks the separation of receptivity from meaning. Both separations are inevitable as far as experience fails to be art:—when the regular, repetitious, and the novel, contingent in nature fail to sustain and inform each other in a productive activity possessed of immanent and directly enjoyed meaning.[37]

Both of these extremes of conduct represent fundamental discontinuities in human life. It is easier to see this with regard to impulsive behavior. Human activity is often broken apart by the presence of many inchoate desires drawing it in different directions at once with their promises of immediate and novel excitement. We are often reluctant to think about each stimulating desire or irritation long enough to imagine what they really have in store for us. Instead, we act upon them immediately and blindly, flying from one to another, and find that our lives lack wholeness and continuity.

It might seem that routine would provide the very continuity our lives so often lack. Indeed, if it is to survive at all, human life does require routine patterns of habits and customs that provide continuity and stability. Yet when they become fixed and rigid, as they all too often do, we are rendered incapable of understanding or responding to the novel needs of changing contexts. By ending in consequences that fail to meet the novel needs and have little or no meaning, routine conduct becomes both frustrating and dulling, and thus often prompts impulsive, blind behavior which craves release from routine in novelty, difference, and variety.[38]

[37]Dewey, *Experience and Nature*, 360–61.
[38]See Dewey, *Human Nature and Conduct*, 157–58. Among the uncivilized, Dewey notes, "enslavement to custom and license of impulse exist side by side. Strict conformity and unrestrained wildness intensify each other. This picture of life shows us in an exaggerated form the psychology current in civilized life whenever customs harden and hold individuals enmeshed. Within civilization,

Above we noted what Dewey considers to be the central human task, the problem of turning cause-effect relations into means-end relations, into meanings. Both routine and capricious impulse, Dewey argues, are modes of activity that fail in this regard.[39] The reasons for the prevalence of routine and capricious behavior, for the fact that the central problem of life is not often solved, are, no doubt, many, but among them, Dewey insists, is the rigid separation of interests in human life:

> Life is compartmentalized and the institutionalized compartments are classified as high and as low; their values as profane and spiritual, as material and ideal. Interests are related to one another externally and mechanically through a system of checks and balances. Since religion, morals, politics, business has each its own compartment, within which it is fitting each should remain, art, too, must have its peculiar and private realm. Compartmentalization of occupations and interests brings about separation of that mode of activity commonly called "practice" from insight, of imagination from executive doing, of significant purpose from work, of emotion from thought and doing. Each of these has, too, its own place in which it must abide. Those who write the anatomy of experience then suppose that these divisions inhere in the very constitution of human nature.[40]

_____

the savage still exists. Heis known in his degree by oscillation between loose indulgence and stiff habit" (p. 99). This is a profound insight into life. Among other things, it helps to account for the "unrestrained wildness" inherent in the warrior tendencies of the German Nazis and other totalitarian societies. Even in the so-called democratic societies, the occasional cry for war rather than for negotiations can be understood in part as a desperate attempt to escape the boredom of routine. Paradoxically, these particular impulsive cravings for something new are intensified when normative customs are not only hardened but also taken as absolute, as unquestionable. "Nations and races face one another," Dewey writes, "each with its own immutable standards. . . . Never before have there been such occasions for conflict which are the more significant because each side feels that it is supported by moral principles. Customs relating to what has been [normative routines] and emotions referring to what may come to be [novel impulses] go their independent ways. The demand of each side treats its opponent as a wilful violator of moral principles, an expression of self-interest or superior might" (p. 77).

[39]Dewey, *Experience and Nature*, 370.
[40]Dewey, *Art as Experience*, 20–21.

When interests are not organically related, it is impossible to get a perspective upon them in order to see how they bear upon one another. When they conflict, consequently, the issue at stake is rarely more momentous than proportioning an appropriate amount of time to each; almost never does it become a matter of how they can be changed and integrated so that they mutually support and enhance one another. In particular, failure to see how interests bear upon one another is at once failure to see how they function as conditions that have decided consequences for each other, for example, how the way one conducts business has various effects upon one's other concerns for justice, peaceful social relations, democratic participation, or ecology. When the interests of life are (dis)organized in this disconnected way, consequently, people are not able fully to understand (the consequences of) what they are doing, and this in turn means that they are not in a position to use that understanding to criticize, develop, and transform their interests.

Among other things, art is that kind of behavior that is prompted and continually informed by a resolute refusal to let interests remain fixed in different compartments. In particular, it often emerges in and through sensitivity to the potential consequences of various ways of acting and by the use of this as means for transforming established interests. This is possible insofar as art is that kind of behavior in which there takes place the establishment of the means-end relation in conduct. When this happens, behavior takes on three important characteristics: it becomes marked by (1) unity, (2) continuity, and (3) growth. We turn now to examine the normative character of art by considering these three traits of art.

The Integration of Behavior

We begin our discussion of the integration of behavior by looking at how art functions in human life. The first thing to say is that a work of art provides an immediate enjoyment of quality; it grabs us, attracts our attention, and we become absorbed by and in it. In Dewey's words, "artist and perceiver alike begin with what may be called a total seizure, an inclusive qualitative whole not yet articulated, not distinguished into members."[41] When we discussed the nature of contexts, we saw that this initial sense of an inclusive qualitative whole is itself a sense of destabilizing possibility, of qualitative meanings capable of being discrimi-

[41]Ibid., 191.

nated and developed. It is this promise of fulfillment that initially grabs us in a work of art.

As interaction with a work of art proceeds, Dewey argues, the initial enjoyment intensifies and eventually becomes consummatory. Dewey's use of the word "consummatory" is carefully chosen, meaning an end of an affair in which there is an actualization or fruition of possibilities or tendencies. In one sense, the consummatory quality of a work of art, Dewey claims, is "gratuitous, not purchased by endeavor."[42] Yet this does not mean that the one who enjoys is passive; rather, the enjoyment is a result of interaction. Not only must we walk into a room to look at a painting, open a book to read, and sit down to a concert, but our gazing, reading, and listening constitute active responses to quality that we attend to and select.[43] What is gratuitous is the fact that in a work of art the elements of which it is composed have already been so organized that we are led very rapidly from a disclosure of novel possibilities to an appreciation of their actualizations.

A work of art, consequently, conditions the consummatory quality of behavior to the extent that one perceives it to be a dynamic or dramatic whole that moves between tension and resolution, possibility and actualization, need and fulfillment, incompletion and completion, instability and stability. According to Dewey, we see this movement in all art works, in paintings and sculpture as well as in novels and music. This is not difficult to understand, for interest and attention emerge only with suspense which is conditioned by instability, incompletion, and novelty. Yet interest and attention, in order to be maintained, require movement toward fulfillment that is conditioned by stable order.

This aesthetically perceived movement that integrates the unstable and stable in a work of art can be understood as *the integration of means and end in the situation which produced the work*. The end, as a structured novelty, is a result of a deliberate and creative (imaginative) uti-

---

[42]Dewey, *Experience and Nature*, 63.

[43]"The esthetic or undergoing phase of experience is receptive. It involves surrender. But adequate yielding of the self is possible only through a controlled [responsive] activity that may well be intense. . . . Perception is an act of the going-out of energy in order to receive, not a withholding of energy. To steep ourselves in a subject-matter we have first to plunge into it. When we are only passive to a scene, it overwhelms us and, for lack of answering activity, we do not perceive that which bears us down. We must summon energy and pitch it at a responsive key in order to *take* in" (Dewey, *Art as Experience*, 53).

lization of unstable conditions for a consummatory end. "Objects are actually esthetic," Dewey writes, "when they turn hazard and defeat to an issue that is above and beyond trouble and vicissitude."[44] Aesthetic perception is the awareness of this creative use of tension in the life of the artist, the sense that destabilizing possibilities or tendencies have been deliberately turned to good account in and by novel structuring of the various elements and functions of the artist's context. What is witnessed in aesthetic perception, consequently, is the result of the history of a development and transformation of interests in which the different phases of that history (the unstable and the stable) stand together in an organic whole of means-end.

Aesthetic perception, consequently, is perception of the meaning of the behavior of the artist. This provides a key for understanding the nature of behavior as art: behavior becomes art and its result a product of art when the unstable conditions of a context no longer inhibit activity and meaning but are deliberately used as means for a (novel) consummatory end that restores unity and meaning to activity. When this happens, behavior in the whole of its context or history, and in each phase of that history, achieves integration, for what is discriminated and pursued as a means for an end is a vivid anticipation of that end, just as an experienced end that was deliberately pursued is a recollection or funded memory of the means used to achieve it. In this kind of history, the various elements, functions, and phases of the context no longer work against one another by dulling, distracting, or confusing behavior, but in fact sustain and enhance each other in their progressive integration.

The Continuity of Behavior

When behavior becomes art, it is marked not only by integration but also by continuity. It is helpful to begin our discussion of this second trait of behavior as art by once again considering the function of art in human life, especially that which makes works of art great or fine or excellent. Works of art are excellent, Dewey claims, when interest in them is never exhausted. As Dewey puts it, excellence in art "occurs when activity is productive of an object that affords continuously renewed delight. This condition requires that the object be, with its suc-

[44]Dewey, *Experience and Nature*, 90.

cessive consequences, indefinitely instrumental to *new* satisfying events."[45]
Excellence, consequently, is not understood by the intensity or even the
enjoyment of quality in its immediacy but by the fact that it has an
extensive horizon, i.e., that it reverberates with an intimation of novel
possibility that draws attention, prompts exploration and reflection, and
yields to further significant interaction that results in further perceptions
of meaning. This means that the initial result of interaction with a great
work of art is qualified by an anticipation of further consummation, and
thus it functions not only as an end but also as a constantly renewable
means that can be deliberately used for further ends. As Dewey says,

> Anyone, who reflects upon the commonplace that a measure of arti-
> stic products is their capacity to attract and retain observation with
> satisfaction under whatever conditions they are approached, while
> things of less quality soon lose capacity to hold attention[,] be-
> coming indifferent or repellent upon subsequent approach, has a
> sure demonstration that a genuinely esthetic object is not exclu-
> sively consummatory but is causally productive as well. A consum-
> matory object that is not also instrumental turns in time to the dust
> and ashes of boredom. The "eternal" quality of great art is its re-
> newed instrumentality for further consummatory experiences.[46]

Dewey calls this function *artistic* perception and distinguishes it from
aesthetic perception. The latter grasps meaning with an emphasis upon
the completion of tendencies or possibilities while the former grasps it
with an emphasis upon the tendencies or possibilities that await fulfillment.[47] The difference is a matter of degree. Aesthetic perception, for
example, becomes artistic when a means-end relation perceived as completed prompts further exploration of meaning.[48] What Dewey wants to

[45]Ibid., 364–65.
[46]Ibid., 365.
[47]Ibid., 374–75.
[48]"While the means-consequence relationship is directly sensed, felt, in both
appreciation and artistic production, in the former the scale descends upon the
side of the attained; in the latter there predominates the invitation of an existent
consummation to bring into existence further perceptions. Art [,] in being. . . the
active productive process, may thus be defined as an esthetic perception together
with an *operative* perception of the efficiencies of the esthetic object" (ibid.,
375).

highlight by the distinction, however, is the observation that men and women, from time to time, become sensitive to a wide range of possibilities in the enjoyment of an end so that the meaning of the end functions as a means to other ends.

This insight into the way enjoyed ends can be used for further consummations, Dewey argues, is particularly characteristic of artists.[49] We can understand the dynamic character of artistic perception in the way that artists, for example, learn to participate in their tradition. The understood and enjoyed meanings of established works of art function as stimuli for new works that, in turn, extend and transform the meanings and interests of the tradition, not by rejecting the tradition but by building upon it, using it as a means for envisioning novel and more complex ways of acting with new and more interesting results.

The crucial point to note in our discussion is that when ends come to function as means in the way just described, conduct is rendered continuous, i.e., one affair is understood and felt and functions as the condition and foundation for further affairs. This kind of continuity, Dewey claims, is not confined to the behavior of artists alone. What we see in their behavior represents what any mode of behavior undertaken by anyone can become. "Any activity," Dewey insists,

> that is productive of objects whose perception is an immediate good, and whose operation is a continual source of enjoyable perception

[49]See ibid., 375–76. I think it particularly crucial that a hard and sharp line not be drawn between artists and others. Dewey himself insists upon the difference being one of degree (p. 376). If it were not a matter of degree, then art would have no educative effect upon others, and the conduct of others could not become art. What is crucial to see is that, while some seem naturally gifted in discriminating novel possibilities in enjoyed ends, others are capable of cultivating this kind of discrimination or taste. Indeed, even artists, Dewey argues, need to cultivate their gifts: "Continued perception, except when it has been cultivated through prior criticism, dulls itself; it is soon satiated, exhausted, blasé. Cultivated taste alone is capable of prolonged appreciation of the same object; and it is capable of it because it has been trained to a discriminating procedure which constantly uncovers in the object new meanings to be perceived and enjoyed" (ibid., 399). I risk exposing the depth to which Dewey has influenced me when I say that in my estimation it is the fundamental purpose of education—even and perhaps especially religious and theological education—to cultivate this kind of critical taste.

of other events exhibits fineness of art. There are acts of all kinds that directly refresh and enlarge the spirit and that are instrumental to the production of new objects and dispositions that are in turn productive of further refinements and replenishments.[50]

The study of history and the sciences no less than the pursuit of the professions (such as teaching, ministry, law, or medicine) and the crafts (such as carpentry, plumbing, sewing) are all capable of becoming art when their particular modes of activity become continuous.

Thus far we have been considering art largely as something that occurs in the life of an individual. This is not surprising, for art embodies the individual phase of existence, the spontaneous, novel, and unique, which is then used to transform established social meanings. Art as a process and a result, consequently, bears an unmistakable mark of individuality. Nevertheless, it also has a social phase and function: among other things, it can be seen as one of the most significant ways of establishing communication and community. We have seen that conduct often becomes routine and capricious. When this happens, human interaction loses its capacity for communication. This is evident in the compartmentalization of interests, not only within the individual whose interests are shaped by unrelated social organizations, but also among different social groups, each with its own interests, such as the various social classes, men and women, adults and children, different nations, races, religions and so on. When interests are unrelated, there can be no real communication. What passes for communication is either compulsion or trivialities. Art, in effect, is a refusal to be content with this. It is a decided attempt to break out of the fixed boundaries of established tradition and establish communication by reorganizing interests in such away that they are capable of being shared meaningfully by those who have been separated in and by their interests.

This point can be supported by considering the continuity of behavior that we have established as a significant dimension of art. Behavior, as Dewey points out, is never isolated: as interaction, our behavior results in consequences that condition the response of others which in turn affects us:

We live in a world where other persons live too. Our acts affect them. They perceive these effects, and react upon us in consequence. Because they are living beings they make demands upon us for certain things from us. They approve and condemn—not in abstract theory but in what they do to us.[51]

If conduct is to become continuous, consequently, then interests need to be so reconstructed that one's behavior conditions the kinds of responses from others that support and enhance continued behavior. This reconstruction is in effect a critical protest of the established separation of interests; but when it is art, it is a protest that does not compel or coerce change in others. Rather, it is most appropriately understood as a kind of protest that draws men and women into new ways of perceiving things and new ways of organizing their interests—new ways, therefore, of responding. This is made possible by the immediately attractive qualities of art that draw attention and disclose novel possibilities and their actualization. In doing this, it creates objects of interest that are shareable and shared and hence establishes communication and a new sense of community. Dewey is unreservedly explicit about this reconstructive social function of art:

> The saying of Matthew Arnold that poetry is a criticism of life sounds harsh to the ears of some persons of strong esthetic bent; it seems to give poetry a moral and instrumental function. But while poetry is not a criticism of life in intent, it is in effect [i.e., in its consequences], and so is all art. For art fixes those standards of enjoyment and appreciation [ideals] with which other things are compared; it selects the objects of future desires; it stimulates effort. . . . The level and style of the arts of literature, poetry, ceremony, amusement, and recreation which obtain in a community, furnish the staple objects of enjoyment in that community, and do more than all else to determine the current direction of ideas and endeavors in the community. They supply the meanings in terms of which life is judged, esteemed, and criticized.[52]

---

[51]Dewey, *Human Nature and Conduct*, 297.

[52]Dewey, *Experience and Nature*, 204. Works of art, Dewey writes, "are their own excuses for being just because they are charged with an office in quickening apprehension, enlarging the horizon of vision, refining discrimination, creating

We can begin to see, now, how art functions to promote the development and transformation of established interests in society. In examining Dewey's concept of art, we have in fact presented an ideal limit of behavior.[53] No person's life is ever perfectly unified or continuous. Still, there are degrees to which behavior approaches this ideal, and the more it does, the more it exhibits the qualities of art. Significant for our purposes is that when this happens, and to the extent to which it happens, men and women in fact are criticizing, developing, and transforming social meanings and interests with the consequence that social interaction becomes capable of a greater degree of unity and continuity.

The Growth of Behavior

When conduct becomes unified and continuous in this way, we can also say that it is marked by *growth*. This is the third trait of art. Growth, of course, is characteristic of all of life. It consists in the achievement of more complex forms of interaction with an environment after an organism finds itself out of step with its surroundings. "As long as it endures," Dewey writes,

> [life] struggles to use surrounding energies in its own behalf. It uses light, air, moisture, and the material of soil. To say that it uses them is to say that it turns them into means of its own conservation. As long as it is growing, the energy it expends in thus turning the environment to account is more than compensated for by the return it gets: it grows.[54]

In learning how to use environmental energies for is own continued life, biological organisms develop capacities not only for survival but also for

---

standards of appreciation that are confirmed and deepened by further experiences" (p. 366). This is a statement of what we have been arguing in this section, that *art is at once instrumental and consummatory*, that it is in fact the process by which the instrumental and consummatory, means and ends, are integrated in conduct. Although Dewey does not explicitly make the point argued in the last two paragraphs, that art establishes communication, he talks about communication in such a way that it becomes apparent that it represents behavior as art (pp. 204–5).

[53]The use of the term "ideal limit" is borrowed from Gouinlock, *Dewey's Philosophy of Value*, 259.

[54]Dewey, *Democracy and Education*, 1.

their own continued development. What Dewey means by growth is this process of developing in tensive situations habits or capacities that can be utilized in developing other capacities as the environment continues to change. In human life, as we have seen in this and the previous chapter, growth in human capacities occurs most significantly in and through the development of meanings and interests. Our discussion of the integration and continuity of conduct in which development of meanings and interests takes place, therefore, has been an analysis not only of art but of growth.[55]

The concept of "growth" or "growing" helps to bring out the normative character of art. Growth of interests is required because contexts change. Interests established in one context, consequently, not only become routine but pointless and even dangerous in different contexts if they are held in a rigid way, for they fail to provide insight and direction; thus conduct is readily subject to frustration and discontinuity. The same point can be stated in another way. Contexts are always to some extent unique, having their own difficulties, possibilities and opportunities. A rigid imposition of established norms upon a relatively novel situation, consequently, can only lead to a failure to understand and respond appropriately to the unique difficulties and opportunities of that situation.

To say this, of course, is not to dismiss established normative interests as useless in guiding conduct in a new situation, for contexts have similarities as well as differences. Furthermore, without traditions of established interests, habits, customs, and meanings, human beings would be utterly helpless. Established normative interests are meaningful and must be relied upon for understanding and direction, but because contexts change and are unique, established interests must also be criticized and developed. Dewey states the matter as follows:

> Similar situations recur; desires and interests are carried over from one situation to another and progressively consolidated. A schedule of general ends results, the involved values being "abstract" in the

---

[55]"A skilled and intelligent art," Dewey (*Experience and Nature*, 389) writes, deals "with natural things for the sake of intensifying, purifying, prolonging and deepening the satisfactions which they spontaneously afford. That, in this process, new meanings develop, and that these afford uniquely new traits and modes of enjoyment is but what happens everywhere in emergent growths."

sense of not being directly connected with any particular existing case but not in the sense of independence of all empirically existent cases. As with general ideas in the conduct of any natural science, these general ideas are used as intellectual instrumentalities in judgment of particular cases as the latter arise; they are, in effect, tools that direct and facilitate examination of things in the concrete while *they are also developed and tested by the results of their application in these cases.*[56]

Art or growth is normative for the judgment and transformation of other normative interests precisely because it is that process by which the other interests are subjected to the criticism and development necessary for those interests to continue to provide understanding and direction as circumstances change. These other interests can be taken as normative, to be sure, but their normativeness must always be qualified by the recognition that they are subject to growth.

This leads us to a troubling question. Is it not the case that growth or behavior as art is itself an interest subject to the same criticism given other established interests? It is not difficult to see that growth, when it comes to function normatively, is an interest or meaning that, like any other interest or meaning, has emerged in human life. As such, does it not also require criticism and transformation as contexts change?

This kind of question has been raised from time to time,[57] and when Dewey directly addresses it he is, unfortunately, not very convincing.[58] Nevertheless, the question we have raised is of utmost importance, since reflection upon it illuminates a crucially significant trait of the meaning of growth. We can approach this matter by considering the following quotation from Dewey:

> Perhaps the most striking difference between immediate sensitiveness, or "intuition," and "conscientiousness" as reflective interest, is that the former tends to rest upon the plane of achieved goods, while the latter is on the lookout for something *better*. The truly

[56]Dewey, *Theory of Valuation*, 44; my emphasis.

[57]See George Raymond Geiger, "Dewey's Social and Political Philosophy," in Schilpp, *The Philosophy of John Dewey*, 366–37.

[58]See John Dewey, "Experience, Knowledge and Value: A Rejoinder," in Schilpp, *The Philosophy of John Dewey*, 594.

conscientious person not only uses a standard in judging, but is concerned to revise and improve his standard. He realizes that the value resident in acts goes beyond anything that he has already apprehended, and that therefore there must be something inadequate in any standard which has been definitely formulated. He is on the *lookout* for good not already achieved. Only by thoughtfulness does one become sensitive to the far-reaching implications of an act; apart from continual reflection we are at best sensitive only to the value of special and limited ends.[59]

Interest in growth is what Dewey calls "conscientiousness" or continued thoughtfulness, always being on the lookout for something better. Recognizing that we can never understand the full range of the future consequences of any act, Dewey concludes that there must be something inadequate in any established standard used to understand and guide conduct in a particular context. If we are honest, this attitude must include the standard of growth itself. The result is not nihilism, the loss of all standards. A critical interpretation of history allows us to affirm the importance of the concept of growth for interpreting the development and transformation of interests in the past and therefore as normative for men and women now. This affirmation, of course, recognizes that interest in growth has been developed *by human beings* in a history that continues to change in all sorts of unexpected ways. This means that this interest, as we presently conceive it, including the anthropology and metaphysics it presupposes, may be misleading and require revision, and that it must therefore never be taken as absolute but always used, tested, criticized, and developed in the concrete circumstances of human life.

The interest in growth, consequently, is a very peculiar concept, holding together, as it does, the affirmation and negation of its own normativeness. This dialectical character of the concept of growth makes interest in growth relatively unique: it is an interest critical of itself, but critical in such a way that it does not simply undercut itself but is self-correcting in and through its critical application to the ongoing and changing circumstances of life.[60]

[59]Dewey, *Ethics*, 307.

[60]It could be argued that the meaning of growth has been implicit in the highly (and similarly) dialectical concepts of "God," "truth," and "goodness." These are also self-correcting meanings that at once affirm our claims and negate them, relativizing them with the sense that there is "something more" than our present

It may seem that growth is an ambiguous norm, a mixed blessing. The meaning of growth does not specify its own direction or end in the way other interests do, such as honesty, justice, or peace. Consequently, might it not be used for evil as well as good? Is it not the case that a deceitful politician or a burglar can grow in their skills, just as a minister, teacher or nurse can? If this is true, is not the concept of growth misleading for judging and developing other interests?

This kind of question can arise only by a misunderstanding of growth. As we saw earlier, the end of growth is more growth. What Dewey means by this point is that growing occurs when the interests that are pursued establish conditions that make possible more growth.[61] This is not possible when the interests that are pursued are irrelevant to or destructive of the interests of those with whom one interacts, as in the case of a deceitful politician. The compartmentalization of interests inherent in the case of the politician or the burglar means that the adjustments made in the course of interaction are narrow and meager; hence they do not support further growth. Genuine growth is possible, Dewey argues, only as the compartmentalization of interests is broken down in the establishment of shared interests in a community:

> The extension in space of the number of individuals who participate in an interest so that each has to refer his own action to that of others, and to consider the actions of others to give point and direction to his own, is equivalent to the breaking down of those barriers of class, race, and national territory which kept men from perceiving the full import of their activity. These more numerous and more varied points of contact denote a greater diversity of stimuli to which an individual has to respond; they consequently put a premium on variation in his action. They secure a liberation of powers which remain suppressed as long as the incitations to action are partial, as they must be in a group which in its exclusiveness shuts out many interests.[62]

Implicit in the concept of growth, consequently, is *a principle of inclusivity.* This means two interrelated things. On the one hand, growth

---

positing that stands over against it, qualifying it with the sense of possibility not yet discriminated.

[61]See Dewey, *Experience and Education*, 36.

[62]Dewey, *Democracy and Education*, 87.

occurs only as a self has many different and varied interests and as these
are included in an act in the sense that pursuit of one interest supports
and enhances the eventual realization of other interests. In Dewey's words,
"the better is that which will do more in the way of security, liberation
and fecundity for other likings and values."[63] On the other hand, it
means at the same time that the interests organized and pursued must be
capable of being shared by others so that other men and women and
their interests are included in one's own interests.

What is meant by interests that are capable of being shared needs to
be carefully specified. In particular, the capacity of an interest to be
shared does not mean that everyone involved does or even likes the
same thing. That I like the music of J. S. Bach does not mean that
everyone should like and listen to it, nor does it mean that I must
become an automobile mechanic because some of my friends are me-
chanics. Rather, it means that we so modify our interests and activities
that they support and enhance the interests and activities of others. It
means also that we are able to understand and appreciate this connection—a fundamental matter that adds depth, meaning, and the sense of
common purpose or community to our efforts. Dewey's lengthy statement summarizing this point is worthy of being quoted in full:

> Sharing a good or value in a way which makes it social in quality
> is. . . to *take* part, to *play* a role. It is something active, something
> which engages the desires and aims of each contributing member.
> Its proper analogue is not physical division but taking part in a
> game, in conversation, in a drama, in family life. It involves diver-
> sification, not sameness and repetition. There would be no commu-
> nication of feeling and idea in a conversation if each one parrot-
> like said the same sentence over and over, and there could be no
> game played if all made the same motions at the same time. Each
> contributes something distinctive from his own store of knowledge,
> ability, taste, while receiving at the same time elements of value
> contributed by others. What is contributed to each is, first, a sup-
> port, a reenforcement, of his own action; thereby each receives
> from others the factors that give his own position greater *secu-
> rity*. . . . In the second place what is contributed is enjoyment of
> new meanings, new values. In a debate each debater on the same
> "side" tries to strengthen or reenforce the position of every other

[63]Dewey, *Experience and Nature*, 430.

one on that side. But in a genuine conversation the ideas of one are corrected and changed by what others say; what is confirmed is not his previous notions, which may have been narrow and ill-informed, but his capacity to judge wisely. What he gains is an expansion of experience; he learns; even if previous ideas are in the main confirmed, yet in the degree in which there is genuine mutual give and take they are seen in a new light, deepened and extended in meaning, and there is the enjoyment of enlargement of experience, of growth of capacity.[64]

A final point needs to be made. When growth becomes the normative interest for judgment and development of other interests, it makes possible fulfillment even in the midst of failure. We can hardly deny that the world is often unyielding to our interests and ideals, from something personal such as attempting to write a scholarly work in a timely fashion to such momentous concerns as social justice and reconciliation among divergent political and religious groups. What we aim at often fails to materialize. This can and often does lead to bitterness, frustration, and loss of meaning. It is not surprising that many turn to trivial pursuits to distract themselves from the burden of frustration.

The failure of the world to yield to many of our interests means that the world in which we live has a dimension of mystery, a dimension not subject to our control. Recognition of this fact underlies the development of the great religious traditions in which men and women ask and seek to understand answers to the big questions of life, those questions having to do with the meaning of life in the face of this ultimate mystery. Some of Dewey's otherwise competent interpreters fail to understand the depth to which Dewey recognizes this mystery of life. His constant use of the word "control" as that which intelligence seeks to do seems to underscore this reading.[65] Yet this is seriously to misunderstand Dewey. Note his statement of the irresolvably precarious character of life:

[64]Dewey, *Ethics*, 383–84.

[65]For example, John Herman Randall, Jr., a widely respected interpreter of Dewey, writes the following in his discussion of Dewey's understanding of religion: "Human experience is in itself potentially 'divine': man's natural intelligence and moral power, sufficiently developed and educated, are the resources for realizing that potentiality. . . . For Barthian theology or any of its diluted 'neo-orthodox' versions, with their despair of the resources of human nature,. . . Dewey has short shrift. It is rather to the passionate faith in intelligence that we

> Through science we have secured a degree of power of prediction and of control; through tools, machinery and an accompanying technique we have made the world more conformable to our needs, a more secure abode. We have heaped up riches and means of comfort between ourselves and the risks of the world. We have professionalized amusement as an agency of escape and forgetfulness. But when all is said and done, the fundamentally hazardous character of the world is not seriously modified, much less eliminated. Such an incident as the last war and preparations for a future war remind us that it is easy to overlook the extent to which, after all, our attainments are only devices for blurring the disagreeable recognition of a fact, instead of means of altering the fact itself.[66]

Interest in growth has its significance, among other things, in the fact that it allows us to understand and respond meaningfully to the mystery that characterizes and surrounds and undergirds our lives. In particular, it allows us to find meaning and fulfillment even when we meet failure and loss. When all our interests are qualified by the interest in growth, failure to achieve those interests does not end in mere failure but also represents an opportunity for growth. Dewey does not himself specify how this opportunity for growth may come about, but it is not difficult to recognize at least two possibilities. First, we can learn just what those

---

must look to make radical changes in human relationships." See John Herman Randall, Jr., "The Religion of Shared Experience," in *The Philosophers of the Common Man: Essays in Honor of John Dewey to Celebrate His 80th Birthday* (New York: G.P. Putnam's Sons, 1940) 131–32. What I am arguing is that Dewey has far greater sympathy than what Randall indicates for what Barthian theology and its "diluted" neo-orthodox versions articulated as the ultimate mystery that shades, surrounds, and confronts all we do. Even our greatest triumphs are riddled with contingency, uncertainty, inscrutability, and the fact that we often fail to see this makes our triumphs all the more uncertain, inscrutable, and precarious. What Dewey insists upon recognizing and claiming is the fact that we must at all times rely upon powers beyond ourselves over which we have no control. Our achievements, consequently, are never simply our own doings but are made possible by the cooperation and support of the forces that surround us and that can change at any time. This combined sense of mystery and indebtedness is one thing that characterizes the religious quality of experience for Dewey. For a fairly competent but brief reading of this matter, see Sidney Hook, *John Dewey: An Intellectual Portrait*, 212–14.

[66]Dewey, *Experience and Nature*, 44–45.

failed interests mean, the fact that in certain circumstances they end in a specific kind of failure. This enlarges the understanding of our context and makes it possible for better discernment and choice in future circumstances. Second, interest in growth makes us sensitive to the possibilities inherent in failure for modifying and transforming our interests so that they become more inclusive. The loss of a child to illness or in a car accident, for example, can lead to bitterness and withdrawal, but it also can be an occasion for recognizing not only the depth of relationship that might have been developed with the child but also the same kind of relationship which can still be developed with other family members and people around us. When failure is used as a means in these ways, it becomes qualified by a sense of hope, understanding, meaning, and fulfillment. Interest in growth, therefore, results, as Dewey puts it, in "an indestructible union of the instrumental and final. For *this* bias can be satisfied no matter what the frustration of other desires and endeavors."[67]

Much more needs to be said, but we are already in a position to begin to see the significance of Dewey's concept of art as normative behavior for the problem of divergent interests among different religious traditions. The problem we are addressing is that which results when the worth of alternative religious interests is recognized: this represents a conflict of interests, attended by confusion, ambiguity, and uncertainty. Dewey's concept of art, as we have discussed it, allows us to see that this is a normal part of life, something we ought not reject. Among other things, it marks the opportunity for the growth of our own interests. When interests conflict, what is needed is critical inquiry into the given situation, an enlargement of perspective, and a subsequent creative transformation of established interests so that the interests of different traditions, rather than standing in conflict, become integrated in a mutually supportive framework.

The likelihood that this integration will take place in the present context is increased to the extent that men and women are able to see the interests of their traditions as historical, developed by men and women in history, rather than as absolute and final, sanctioned by some unquestionable authority. When it is seen that the authority traditional interests possess is not a priori but historical, found in their capacity to provide for the flourishing human life, then men and women become free to appraise such interests critically and to reconstruct or transform them when they realize they no longer function as they ought.

[67]Ibid., 246.

4 ◈

THINKING AND THE TRANSFORMATION OF INTERESTS

We have had several occasions now to consider the fact that human life does not run an even course. From our earliest years our impulses and desires pull us in different directions. In all sorts of ways, we bump up against things that intrude upon our conduct and refuse to bend to our will. As we mature, we find ourselves engaged in various corporate enterprises, the worth and meaning of which we do not fully understand and which take sudden and seemingly unaccountable turns. Moreover, we live with companions who have their own dreams, desires, purposes, and interests often running counter to ours.

Yet this is not the whole story of human life. Without the nurturing of family and community from which we receive encouragement, companionship, food, shelter, and other forms of care, human life would be so severely impoverished that it could hardly continue. Attention to this pervasive and underlying character of human life as mutually supportive helps us understand in part the nature of the difficulties we often face. In point of fact, difficulties seem to stem not so much from sheer lack of goods, although they occasionally take this form. More often, they result from an abundance of things that we prize but that seem intolerant of each other's company. The issue of how Christians and Muslims are to respond to each other, for example, becomes a far greater problem when they understand one another as friends with quite different but yet meaningful interests than when they see one another as enemies. The result is not dismissal but a *conflict of normative interests*, of things that we care about but that severely impinge on one another in uncomfortable ways.

The attempt to find guidance in the resolution of these kinds of conflicts constitutes a central aim of this work. In the last chapter, we discussed Dewey's concept of conduct as art and proposed it as a normative concept for guiding judgment and conduct in these kinds of situations. We saw that to the extent to which behavior becomes art, conflicting interests are transformed and become unified and continuous. This chapter carries the argument one step further. It examines in some detail what Dewey considers to be the means for this transformation: reflective thinking or inquiry.

The significance of thinking can be stated more precisely. When normative interests become confusing, ambiguous, and conflicting, as in the context of religious pluralism, the establishment of art in human life is no easy matter, since the ambiguity and conflict mean that established means for proceeding in conduct have become ineffective for directing behavior. Men and women have become disoriented and do not know how to proceed. It is at this point that reflective thinking has meaning and importance, according to Dewey, for thinking or inquiry constitutes a significant way of proceeding in conduct when other ways have lost their capacity for orientation. At these moments, of course, conduct does not necessarily become reflective but can, and often does, become impulsive or habitual. If conduct is to become fulfilling, however, men and women need to find some way to proceed intelligently, some way, in short, to develop their interests that have become ineffective. The effective means for this, Dewey argues, is reflective thinking.

Because of its usefulness as a tool in and for the consummation of interaction in the midst of the ambiguity and conflict of normative interests, we turn in this chapter to a discussion of the nature and function of thinking. Our thesis is as follows: while art provides the norm for judging and developing interests, thinking or inquiry, according to Dewey, represents that function in and of conduct that is the most reliable means or method for discrimination of those novel possibilities for developing interests that will transform a context of conflicting plural interests.

We should clarify two points, however, before beginning our discussion. First, this chapter is not meant to cover all that Dewey has to say on the matter of thinking. Our interest is more limited. Our attempt is to provide an interpretation of Dewey's understanding of thinking to the extent that we can show how thinking is able to discover and utilize novel possibilities in and for the transformation of interests, therefore making it possible for behavior to become art. Second, the extent to which we develop Dewey's theory of thinking in this chapter will not yet allow us adequately to address the problem of religious pluralism. Before we can do that, we must first consider the nature and function of religious interests and the particular character of the problem that results from an awareness and appreciation of their diversity. This will be the task of chapter five. We shall then be prepared to discuss how Dewey's interpretation of philosophical thinking, which Dewey takes to be the most comprehensive form of thinking, makes it possible for us to address this particular problem. The latter will be taken up in chapter six.

The Context and Task of Thinking

If we take Dewey's concept of art as the center of his philosophy, it is not surprising to find that he has a particular view of thinking. In *Experience and Nature* he states the matter in this way:

> Art—the mode of activity that is charged with meanings capable of immediately enjoyed possession—is the complete culmination of nature, and. . . "science" is properly a handmaiden that conducts natural events to this happy issue.[1]

"Science" is most consistently used by Dewey to mean the method of thinking used in science as well as in other common sense activities.[2]

---

[1]Dewey, *Experience and Nature*, 358.

[2]Dewey no doubt uses the word "science" as a summary word for his interpretation of inquiry because the natural sciences so obviously illustrate the kind of thinking which Dewey considers good thinking. John Randall ("Dewey's Interpretation of the History of Philosophy," in Schilpp, *The Philosophy of John*

What Dewey is saying in this quotation, consequently, is that thinking is that means or method for proceeding that makes it possible for behavior to become art. As a means for consummation and fulfillment in conduct, thinking is egregiously misunderstood when taken as a spectator's sport, something supposedly effective in the isolation of an ivory tower.[3] Rather, thinking, effective thinking, thinking worthy of note, if you will, is a phase of behavior that seeks to direct conduct so as to establish unity and continuity in the interactive contexts of human life.[4] This notion of thinking is clearly stated in Dewey's formal definition: thinking, or inquiry, he writes,

---

Dewey, 82), however, makes a significant point: "despite all his analysis of the procedure of the natural sciences, Dewey's experimentalism is not primarily based on the methods of the laboratory. It is at once the experimentalism of practical common sense, and the coming to self-awareness of the best and most critical techniques and concepts of the social sciences. In the broadest sense, it is the experimentalism of the anthropologist, of the student of human institutions and cultures, impressed by the fundamental role of habit in men and societies and by the manner in which those habits are altered and changed."

[3]Dewey strongly opposes what he calls the "spectator" theory of knowledge, which he considers to be the dominant epistemology throughout the history of Western philosophy. For a succinct analysis of Dewey's interpretation of this matter, see Dicker, *Dewey's Theory of Knowing*, 3–6. See also Dewey, *The Philosophy of John Dewey*, 142–50.

[4]Dewey never seems to tire of proclaiming thinking as an experimental doing. "Inquiry," he says, "proceeds by reflection, by thinking; but *not.* . . by thinking as. . . something cooped up within 'mind.' For experimental inquiry or thinking signifies *directed activity*, doing something which varies the conditions under which objects are observed and directly had and by instituting new arrangements among them" (Dewey, *Quest*, 123). The "rudimentary prototype" of thinking as directed activity, Dewey writes, "is found in ordinary procedures. When we are trying to make out the nature of a confused and unfamiliar object, we perform various acts with a view to establishing a new relationship to it, such as will bring to light qualities which will aid in understanding it. We turn it over, bring it into a better light, rattle and shake it, thump, push and press it, and so on. The object as it is experienced prior to the introduction of these changes baffles us; the intent of these acts is to make changes which will elicit some previously unperceived qualities, and by varying conditions of perception shake loose some property which as it stands blinds or misleads us" (p. 87); see also pp. 189–90; Dewey, *Reconstruction in Philosophy*, 112–15; and idem, *Logic*, 159–62.

is the controlled or directed transformation of an indeterminate situation into one that is so determinate in its constituent distinctions and relations as to convert the elements of the original situation into a unified whole.[5]

When we understand what Dewey takes to be the function and general aim of thinking, namely, "the reconstructive transformation of antecedent problematic subject-matter,"[6] as he says elsewhere, it becomes clear why he stresses the importance of understanding what he calls the antecedent conditions of thinking. It is the context of thought, its particular and unique indeterminate character, that prompts thinking and that thinking seeks to transform. With this matter, therefore, we shall begin our discussion of reflection.

We have seen that, according to Dewey's interpretation, all contexts are indeterminate and tensive to some degree, since they are all moving into a future that is not fully determinate but open ended, extending out into an extensive horizon of possibilities. When the indeterminate and tensive character of contexts is heightened in human interaction, the contexts become "uncertain, unsettled, disturbed,. . . troubled, ambiguous, confused, full of conflicting tendencies, obscure, etc."[7] These qualities make it difficult for interaction to proceed with business as usual. They represent in human interaction what we earlier identified on the biological level of interaction as need, an imbalance among the elements of the interaction that prompts desire and interest and demands effort, a change in behavior, in order to restore balance or equilibrium.[8]

The first thing we need to say about an indeterminate context, consequently, is that it has a teleological character. Having temporal quality, it moves toward an end. When human beings are involved, there is an urge or desire to move toward a *unified* end, a restoration of balance. What an adequate unified end looks like as well as how it is to be achieved in any indeterminate situation, however, is not something initially understood. At first it is felt as no more than a vague sense of

---

[5]Dewey, *Logic*, 104–5; emphasis in text. For a brief discussion of Dewey's use of the word "control," see below, n. 32.

[6]Ibid., 492.

[7]Ibid., 105.

[8]See ibid., chap. 2, in which Dewey discusses the biological matrix of inquiry, esp. pp. 25–32.

possibility that draws us on. Thinking, if it should begin at this point, consists of the further discrimination of this possibility, a construction and clarification of what this could be in and for the present context. We mentioned that thinking functions to transform an indeterminate context into one that is unified and continuous. In making this claim Dewey is denying that thinking is something that merely goes on in one's head. This is why he makes the somewhat controversial claim that the qualities that prompt thinking are not merely subjective but belong to the context. It is the context that is uncertain, unsettled, disturbed, troubled, and ambiguous. "It is the *situation* that has these traits," he writes. "*We* are doubtful because the situation is inherently doubtful."[9] If these qualities belonged merely to us, we could possibly change them "by manipulation of our personal states of mind" without changing the larger context.[10] This would presuppose, however, a metaphysical dualism between mind and nature, leaving unexplained whether and how our meanings are *of* the world. Meanings that designate qualities such as doubt and uncertainty, if they are to be common at all, must be *of* something more than private feelings. "If what is designated by. . . doubt. . . is to have any objective meaning, to say nothing of public verifiability," Dewey argues, "it must be located and described as behavior in which organism and environment act together, or *inter*-act."[11] Quali-

---

[9]Ibid., 105–6.

[10]Ibid., 106.

[11]Ibid., 33. H. S. Thayer (*The Logic of Pragmatism*, 80) criticizes Dewey for attributing qualities such as doubt, ambiguity, being troubled, which he recognizes as perfectly understandable modes of *human* behavior, to nature or to the context as a whole, accusing him of "animism." He distinguishes between "physical" terms and "behavioral" terms and concedes that physical terms such as "indeterminate," "imbalance," and "unsettled" sufficiently convey what Dewey has in mind, while behavioral terms such as "doubtful" and "troubled" merely confuse the issue, for these are terms that presuppose and apply to an agent, not to an entire context. To illustrate his case he asks: in what sense would it be meaningful to say that the *context* is troubled, confused, and perplexed when a child is placed in an unfamiliar maze? "Only in one clear sense," he responds, "we observe that the child exhibits these characteristics and with respect to *his* relation to the maze, *he* is troubled, confused, perplexed" (ibid., 83).

Thayer is quite willing to admit Dewey's point that "doubt" and "troubled" are not merely subjective phenomena but are what they are in and because of a context, appearing publicly in the way a human agent behaves in that context. Restricting these terms to human behavior would avoid the difficulties of apply-

ties such as doubt are not mere private feelings but constitute the way the elements of a context qualify one another. Consequently, Dewey concludes, "Restoration of integration can be effected. . . only by operations that actually modify existing conditions, not by merely 'mental' processes."[12]

---

ing these terms (that normally apply to humans) to nature and would certainly add clarity to understanding. At the same time, however, I can not help thinking that Thayer has missed something important in what Dewey is trying to say. From time to time we do use the word "troubled" more widely than Thayer suggests. We say, for example, that the sixties in the United States were "troubled times" and even that the skies look "troubled." I think it would be a mistake to say that the transfer of a behavioral trait to social or natural contexts is blind and incoherent, for the word "troubled" in these cases functions as a metaphor that brings out important connections and continuities between human behavior and what Dewey calls a context. Dewey of course realizes that he is stretching the normal use of these words when he applies them to a context, but he wants to say something relatively new and is engaged in trying to find a way to say it. Among other things, he wants to say that we are not the sole masters of our lives but are connected to and dependent upon a multitude of events that qualify everything we do and to which we respond. He says this by purposely stretching the use of words, saying that we are troubled *because* the times are troubled, that we doubt *because* the context in which we live is doubtful. Similarly, when we say that the situation of the child in Thayer's maze is troubled, confused, and perplexed, it is possible to mean more than the fact that the child exhibits these characteristics. What we can also mean is that the habits, meanings, and interests of the child have come together with the powers and energies of the environment in such a way that the result is a kind of interaction in which the environment does not give way to the desires of the child to move freely and confidently. What is emphasized here is the way the elements of the context interact and depend upon one another.

[12]Dewey, *Logic*, 106. Some controversy has been generated by this and similar claims in Dewey's *Logic* (see pp. 34, 159–62). The difficulty, even for sympathetic interpreters, is accepting the comprehensiveness of Dewey's claim that "inquiry effects *existential* transformation and reconstruction of the material with which it deals" (p. 159). Writers such as Thayer (*The Logic of Pragmatism*, 168–97) and Robert E. Dewey (*The Philosophy of John Dewey*, 155–63) affirm that in some and perhaps even most cases of thinking existential material is acted upon and transformed, but they question whether this is a necessary and therefore comprehensive condition of inquiry. Does a historian or literary critic, for example, bring about changes in existential material? To take an even more extreme example, does one who simply reads history or literary criticism in their living room chair and "thinks" about what has been said effect such a change?

Dewey's claim is that thinking is capable of changing the world, or patterns of interaction in and of the world, for the better. This claim

---

It is important to see that at issue is Dewey's view of thinking as a practical activity, a doing. This is integral to Dewey's whole program and centers around his view of art. According to Dewey, conduct becomes art when it becomes consummatory, and this happens most effectively when things are understood and used as means to ends. Thinking is that doing (1) by which one so interacts with the environment that one is able to see possibilities of using things as means for ends, and (2) that completes itself in the actualization of those possibilities in conduct. This is in brief what Dewey has in mind when he claims that inquiry modifies existing conditions.

It would be impractical for the purposes of this work to respond in full to the criticism made of this position. Still, several things can be said. First, it is helpful to recall Dewey's theory of meanings in that meanings are understood to emerge as one learns how to respond to felt qualities. To learn the meaning of something is to anticipate consequences and to be prepared to act accordingly. Understood meaning, in short, is a behavioral characteristic, a habit, if you will. Second, it should be evident that thinking is not always a direct manipulation of things in the environment but a manipulation of things as understood, a manipulation of meanings or symbols. We play with things in the imagination (not unlike the way we play with them physically) in order to see what consequences are likely to come about. Dewey explicitly uses mathematics as an example of meanings or symbols that are manipulated in this way (see Dewey, *Quest*, 150, 159–60; idem, *Logic*, 371–418). Third, it is possible to see how this counts for Dewey as a doing that modifies environmental conditions. We can manipulate meanings in the imagination because we first have learned to manipulate things in the environment and because our meanings are constituted by our understanding of such interaction and what we can reasonably expect. Manipulation of meanings in the imagination, consequently, is not simply a shifting around of subjective states. Rather, it has public force, for when we become aware of potential consequences as a result of our imaginative reflections, we are willing to act in a different way in regard to things as the occasion arises. To realign meanings, in short, is to realign ways in which human beings and their environments interact. One, of course, might still wish to accuse Dewey of the fact that manipulation of meanings simply constitutes a subjective change, since nothing in the environment has in fact been changed (as when one "thinks" about the argument of a literary critic). Finally, therefore, it is important to see what Dewey is denying when he claims that thinking does not merely involve subjective changes—namely, a spectator theory of knowledge in which knowledge is understood to be had intuitively and passively by a special faculty of the mind. If this theory were true, nothing in the environment would have to be changed

presupposes a metaphysics in which the world is understood to change, willy-nilly, and recognition that this change is often a source of tension and conflict. Thinking, according to this perspective, is not a private phenomenon but an active doing, a particular change among other changes that, when effective, is capable of directing the other changes so that life takes on meaning and becomes more fulfilling. It does so, in particular, in and through the modification of conditions that cause the tensions and conflicts of life.

We can pause for a moment to consider what all this means for the understanding of and response to the problem of religious pluralism. Among other things, it helps to locate the tensions and conflicts inherent in this issue in the specific set of ways in which elements (the energies, aims, interests, actions, and so on) of the contexts in which we live qualify one another. This means that the tensions and conflicts that constitute this problem can be resolved only by the reconstitution and transformation of these elements and their qualifications. Consequently, thinking can be understood as an important tool in and for this transformation insofar as it becomes effective not simply in the writing and reading of an overambitious book but only as it helps to transform meanings, habits, and interests constitutive of, alive in, and directive of human interactions.[13]

---

as an essential condition for knowing. "What Dewey sees as the alternative to his thesis that inquiry essentially involves physical manipulation or changes," writes Dicker (*Dewey's Theory of Knowing*, 13), is that understanding "requires some special power or intuition of the mind, such as would indeed be needed if just contemplating the unfamiliar object in my room could enable me to know what it was or how it got into the room." Dewey sees a continuity between physical and imaginative manipulations because he contrasts thinking—as an active process of interaction and manipulation constituting an essential condition of understanding—with the idea of understanding which (mysteriously) happens to us as spectators. When thinking is done in and through the manipulation of meanings in the imagination, consequently, it may be true that environmental conditions are not modified in any visible way—and to this extent some of Dewey's claims might seem misleading. Nevertheless, it represents doings in and of the imagination that are credible and viable as thinking to the extent that they are symbolic of potential doings and changes.

[13]This does not mean that the writing of a book on the problem of religious pluralism is not an important and worthy task. In chapter six, however, I argue that a theory of thinking can be adequate for this problem only as it points out

To return to the argument, it is helpful to see that the indeterminate character of a context is not something at large but rather located at a particular point. It is felt and understood by human beings, Dewey argues, with respect to the anticipated consequences of the interaction of events that constitute the context:

> Interaction is a temporal process, not a momentary cross-sectional occurrence. The situation in which it occurs is indeterminate, therefore, with respect to its *issue*. If we call it *confused*, then it is meant that its outcome cannot be anticipated. It is called *obscure* when its course of movement permits of final consequences that cannot be clearly made out. It is called *conflicting* when it tends to evoke discordant responses. Even were existential conditions unqualifiedly determinate in and of themselves, they are indeterminate in *significance*; that is, in what they import and portend in their interaction with the organism.[14]

We can state this matter in a different way. Earlier we saw that human beings live out of an understanding of meanings. More specifically, they anticipate the qualitative results of their responses to qualities, and these expectations are crucial for guiding their responses. When expectations became obscure, ambiguous, and conflicting, consequently, men and women fail to understand not only the significance of what is occurring but also how to respond appropriately. Hence Dewey writes, "The immediate *locus* of the problem concerns. . . what kind of responses the organism shall make."[15]

When men and women fail to understand how to respond, it is not the case, of course, that they fail to have ends-in-view. Rather, the aims and purposes that they have are confused, ambiguous, and conflicting. This helps us see that the immediate task of thinking is to reconstruct these ends-in-view so that the more ultimate task of thinking, the transformation of the situation itself, can be accomplished.

---

the direction for further reflection, discussion, and conduct. If this problem is to be resolved, it is to be resolved in the concrete affairs of human interaction. See below, pp. 187–89.

[14]Dewey, *Logic*, 106–7.

[15]Ibid., 107.

We should return to a point made at the beginning of this section. We argued that an indeterminate context embodies a vague sense of possible novel unification and that the task of thinking is to discriminate this possibility. This might seem to be a different and even contradictory claim to what was just said, but both are important for an adequate interpretation of the context and task of thinking. Together they represent a creative tension between *what is*, namely, confusing, ambiguous, conflicting ends-in-view, and *what might be*, the sense of a better possibility.[16] There is, after all, no need to think unless understanding and direction become obscure and confusing, and yet there is no interest or desire to think unless we have some sense of a possible better understanding and direction, however vague that may be. Putting these two matters together, we can conclude that the task of thinking is to reconstruct ambiguous and conflicting ends-in-view that are qualified by the sense of the possible so that they come to be the better—adequate, that is, for guiding responses that result in the unification of that context. This is what it means for thinking to discriminate novel possibilities of unity and transform established normative interests. How this happens is something we must now examine.

The Process of Thinking

Thinking is a dynamic, developmental process, according to Dewey, the very heart of which involves two interrelated functions or operations and their results. In a tensive situation, what we need to understand are two sets of issues: (1) what is going on, or what is at issue, and (2) what possible responses can be made, what to expect from the responses, and which response is the better, allowing for the reunification of the present

---

[16]Dewey never states the matter in precisely these terms. The claim I make here represents an attempt to integrate Dewey's discussion of an object of desire in *Human Nature and Conduct*, his interpretation of the function of possibilities in his discussion of art in *Experience and Nature* and *Art as Experience*, and his understanding of an indeterminate context in his *Logic*. Anticipating material considered in the following section, this contrast between "what is" and "what might be" can be used as an interpretive framework for understanding what Dewey considers to be the two sides of thinking: understanding of the "facts of the case" in and through observation, and constructing an appropriate response in and through an imaginative and synthetic consideration of the implications of meanings.

context. The first represents the reduction of the initial indeterminate quality of the context to the discrimination of *a problem* by observing and analyzing the conditions of the situation. The second matter represents an understanding of *a solution* to the problem, the construction of an idea or meaning made possible by the creative functions of imagining, criticizing, developing, and synthesizing the understanding of various possible responses to the interpretation of the present conditions.

In attempting to understand the meaning of these two sides of thinking and their interdependence, it may be helpful to keep a concrete context in mind. Imagine parents working at night in one room and suddenly hearing the moans of their child in the next room. These noises, under normal circumstances, would break the parents' concentration with an unsettling, disturbing, and confusing quality. Something seems to be wrong, but what? The quality calls for some change in the parents' activity, but it is initially unclear what they are to do.[17]

The first thing to see about this kind of situation is the crucial role played by the identification of a problem, a specification of what is wrong, what the change in the quality of the context means. "It is a familiar and significant saying," Dewey writes,

> that a problem well put is half-solved. To find out *what* the problem and problems are which a problematic situation presents to be inquired into, is to be well along in inquiry. To mistake the problem involved is to cause subsequent inquiry to be irrelevant or to go astray. Without a problem, there is blind groping in the dark. The way in which the problem is conceived decides what specific suggestions are entertained and which are dismissed; what data are selected and which rejected; it is the criterion for relevancy and irrelevancy of hypotheses and conceptual structures.[18]

[17]The example I have chosen constitutes a practical, even an emergency, problem. Unfortunately, the choice of any particular kind of problem to illustrate Dewey's theory is likely to lead a reader to think that his theory is appropriate only for that kind of problem. I have chosen a practical problem, which I will use throughout this chapter, in part because I think it better illustrates the effort of thinking to seek an adequate response to a particular tension, but Dewey's theory is meant as a general description of thinking applicable to theoretical problems as well. For a fine account of Dewey's theory of thinking using a theoretical problem as an illustration, see Dicker, *Dewey's Theory of Knowing*, chaps. 1–3.

[18]Dewey, *Logic*, 108.

In a highly indeterminate context we want and need understanding of the tension of the context for adequate guidance in our responses. If we misunderstand this matter, thinking might continue but its results, which are meant to guide interaction, would in fact confuse the interaction further. If the moans of a child at night are thought to be a result of the flu, for example, one might give the child some medication and leave it at that. It could be, however, that the child has appendicitis. Mistaking the conditions of tension in this case could have seriously disturbing consequences.

There are, of course, many different things that go on in any tensive context of which human beings are a part, and one central difficulty for thinking is that it is not immediately apparent which conditions constitute the tension of a context. Often, we are quick to seize upon the more intense conditions, such as the moaning and fever of the child, and prematurely and mistakenly assume what the problem is.[19] For this reason, Dewey insists that the determination of "a genuine problem is a *progressive* inquiry."[20] Indeed, as Dewey notes elsewhere, the complete determination of the problem cannot be specified until the tension of the context is resolved. "Up to that point, our grasp of the problem has been more or less vague and tentative,"[21] for until we adequately respond to and resolve the tension we are unable to affirm that we have correctly understood what is at issue.

We have been arguing that an interpretation of the tension of a context, a statement of the problem, determines and guides the process of thinking. Yet if one's understanding of the tension remains indeterminate until the tension is resolved, where does one begin reflecting and how does one proceed? It is important to recognize that if a context were completely indeterminate, it would be impossible to reduce it to a problem with distinguishable conditions. There are, of course, occasions that approach this indeterminacy, when the structures of meaning upon which we have come to rely all seem to have disappeared, such as when one is suddenly, unexpectedly, and unaccountably fired from a position of employment held for many years. On such occasions, notes Dewey, "we are overwhelmed. We do not think, but give way to depression."[22] One

---

[19]Dewey, *How We Think*, 122.
[20]Dewey, *Logic*, 108.
[21]Dewey, *How We Think*, 108; see also 122–23.
[22]Dewey, *Reconstruction in Philosophy*, 142.

condition for the ability to think, therefore, is the existence of determinate conditions. "Since they are settled or determinate in *existence*," Dewey concludes, "the first step in institution of a problem is to settle them in *observation*."[23]

The dynamic of thinking begins, consequently, with initial observations of determinate conditions of the context. The aim of observation, of course, is not simply to state what is already determinate but to clarify the tension of the context. This includes more than stating what is wrong, that is, which conditions obstruct our activity. More broadly and more importantly, it is to discriminate the "conditions that must be reckoned with or taken account of in any relevant solution that is proposed."[24] These include, therefore, conditions that are obstacles to the unification of the context as well as resources, anything about the context, that is, which is relevant, which we need to understand, for working out an adequate response.[25] Such conditions, consequently, can be meaningfully called "facts of the case" or "terms of the problem."[26]

That observation in thinking seeks to identify relevant conditions means that it has an aim, that it is a purposeful activity and not the passive reception of sense data. It constitutes, if you will, analysis, not in the sense of breaking apart a whole into its elements but in the sense of selection or emphasis of detail, individualizing or discriminating something as important for the purpose of understanding what is happening.[27] Observation and analysis, consequently, involve implicit evaluation or judgment of the worth of what is observed as means for resolving the context. When the concentration of the parents is interrupted by a disturbing and confusing quality, for example, to observe that there is noise going on and that this noise means their child is moaning is at once to select those meanings out of the sense that they are important and relevant for clearing up the present difficulty. Precisely because purpose informs observation in this way, making observation a means-end matter, we are able explicitly to judge our implicit judgments and continue to refine and develop our initial observations. What we need further

[23]Dewey, *Logic*, 109.
[24]Ibid.
[25]Dewey, *How We Think*, 102.
[26]Dewey, *Logic*, 109.
[27]See Dewey, *How We Think*, 126–30.

judgment on is whether and to what extent our observations in fact function well as means for our ends.

We can be more specific in stating how observation constitutes judgment of what is relevant for working out an adequate understanding and response. In particular, they serve as signs, clues, and evidence for what is possibly at issue and in doing so they prompt suggestions, Dewey argues, of how best to proceed in those circumstances and what to expect from that doing:

> A *possible* relevant solution is. . . suggested by the determination
> of factual conditions which are secured by observation. The pos-
> sible solution presents itself, therefore, as an *idea*. . . . Ideas are
> anticipated consequences (forecasts) of what will happen when
> certain operations are executed under and with respect to observed
> conditions.[28]

A child's moan at night, for example, is a sign for or evidence of various possible things—a nightmare, loneliness, the flu, a cold, appendicitis— and hearing a child moan, under normal circumstances, suggests these possibilities. Awareness of these as possible meanings, moreover, indicates (1) further things to do (operations to execute) and (2) what consequences to expect from the doing. For example, they would suggest to any caring parent to go into the child's room and examine the child. One would expect to see the child asleep, tossing and turning in bed, if the child is having a nightmare and is not merely lonely. Again, one would expect the child to have a fever and to complain of discomfort if the child has the flu or some other illness.

The suggestions that are prompted constitute the initiation of the second side of thinking, the solution, an understanding of how to resolve the tensive conditions. In any complex situation, of course, anything that we would call "the solution," meaning by this an act that finally resolves the tension, may be a long way off. This calls for an interpretation of what Dewey means by "solution" and how initial suggestions can constitute the "solution" side of the thinking process. We must be careful not to reify a so-called final act, cutting it off from the reflective process, for thinking has its own continuity. If it were not in continuous

---

[28]Dewey, *Logic*, 109; see also idem, *How We Think*, 15.

development, it would be impossible to understand how the tensions of a context are ever resolved—in particular, how the process of thinking contributes to that resolution. Positively stated, things are cleared up and unified progressively and cumulatively, not all at once, so to speak. This means that the "solution" side of thinking is constituted by this cumulative clearing up and unifying activity; any so-called final act is simply the end point of a gradually transformed context.

Let us imagine, for example, that the context of which we have been speaking concludes with an appendectomy. We could specify that as the final act that resolves the tension of that context. Yet that solution, if I may put it this way, has been in the making in and through the whole of the thinking process. What is wanted as a solution is an understanding of how to respond, what to do, in order to bring about the resolution of a context. Thinking proceeds not by conjuring up some final end-in-view but by making decisions and acting on a number of more modest ends-in-view, ideas, that is, of what to do next, that gradually bring about the resolution. The idea of an appendectomy is only the last in a series of these ends-in-view. The possible ways of responding indicated by the suggestions of loneliness and illness, consequently, represent ideas of the solution of the context at that point in the thinking process, concrete ideas, that is, of what to do next to bring about the resolution of the context. Conduct directed by these aims, moreover, conditions the gradual transformation of the context, for the responses result in a changed relationship among the events of the context clarifying the facts of the case. The changed relationship in turn leads to further suggestions of how to respond appropriately, what to do next to continue to bring the context to its final resolution.

Recognition of the progressive development of the solution side of thinking is central for understanding not only that thinking is an interactive temporal process, a doing over time, but that the doing of thinking is constitutive of the end result, not merely preparatory and therefore external to it. This is to take suggested meanings in the thinking process, when they are appropriately developed, as having the unity of means and ends that characterizes art. In particular, the use of suggested meanings as means for proceeding in uncertain circumstances, as ends-in-view, that become constitutive of a progressive unification or consummation, at once gives the whole process of thinking a felt and understood continuity and unity. Each result that clarifies meaning is understood at once (1) as the result of prior insight and response-as-means-for-that-end and (2) as constituting means for insight into further possibilities that contribute constitutively to the eventual unification of the context. Dewey puts the matter this way:

> To be conscious of meanings or to have an idea, marks a fruction, an enjoyed or suffered arrest of the flux of events. But there are all kinds of ways of perceiving meanings, all kinds of ideas. Meaning may be determined [capriciously] in terms of consequences hastily snatched at and torn loose from their connections. . . . Or, we may be aware of meanings. . . that unite wide and enduring scope with richness of distinctions. The latter sort of consciousness is more than a passing and superficial consummation or end. . . . It marks the conclusion of long continued endeavor; of patient and indefatigable search and test. The idea is, in short, art and a work of art. As a work of art, it directly liberates subsequent action and makes it more fruitful in a creation of more meanings and more perceptions.[29]

When the thinking process produces these latter kinds of meanings, behavior itself becomes art, marked by the sense of continuity and unity in each of its phases.

In the above quotation, Dewey makes an important distinction between ideas "hastily snatched at" and those that are the result of "patient and indefatigable search and test." This distinction pertains to how we treat suggestions when they occur to us. The worth of Dewey's theory of thinking, for our purposes, pivots upon his understanding of suggested responses and how best to treat them. It is important, therefore, that we consider this matter in more detail.

Suggested Meanings: Their Criticism and Transformation

The occurrence of initial suggestions, Dewey claims, is something over which we have no control. It "pops into the mind"; "it is something that happens to us."[30] To be sure, *what* is suggested depends upon "past [analogous] experience and a fund of relevant knowledge at one's command,"[31] such as a general understanding in our case of illness and the susceptibility of a particular child to nightmares and loneliness. Never-

---

[29]Dewey, *Experience and Nature*, 371.
[30]Dewey, *How We Think*, 42, 109.
[31]Ibid., 15.

theless, the occurrence of suggestions is gratuitous. This important acknowledgment by Dewey counterbalances his claim that thinking aims to "control" conduct. Here he acknowledges the contingency and mystery at the very foundation of thinking. To be sure, we can respond to and use suggestions in a thoughtful and intelligent way; this is what makes conduct intelligent rather than capricious or routine. Still, this responsive activity constitutes a response to something that is not our own doing.[32]

[32]Use of the word "control" has recently become suspect because of its patriarchical connotations. The difficulty of using this word to describe thinking, it seems to me, is that it implies that the purpose of thinking is to mold the world to our wishes and desires regardless of what is already there. This denies or at least downplays an understanding of thinking as being responsive and as conditioning cooperation and our own transformation. It should be clear by now that this is not what Dewey has in mind. Indeed, what we have just discussed is Dewey's conviction that thinking cannot proceed at all unless men and women are open and receptive to the possibility of meanings that they cannot control but that come to them serendipitously.

It is hard to explain away altogether Dewey's use of the word "control," not only because he uses it in his definition of inquiry but also because he uses it so frequently. We can grant Dewey the gratuitous nature of initial suggestions, but he constantly reminds us that thinking seeks "to control" the development of these ideas in and through criticism, observation, experiment, testing and so on; in this way it "controls" conduct or the development of a context. It is important, however, that we avoid the extreme connotations of the word "control." At least three things can be noted. First, what Dewey means by "control" is responsibility for our ideas, for their consequences (see Dewey, *Experience and Nature*, 230–34; idem, *How We Think*, 42). As we shall see, Dewey is aware of the fact that ideas as they occur are often either capricious or routine. Stated more strongly, they are often harmful, either avoiding what needs to be attended to for the good of the self and others or inflicting suffering upon the self and others. Consequently, it would be irresponsible to leave our ideas alone and simply act upon them. When Dewey says that we need "to control" our suggestions by criticizing, refining, and testing them, he is in fact calling us to take responsibility for the meanings out of which we live. Secondly, responsibility is not an unilateral activity but includes being receptive and open. According to Dewey, we cannot be critical unless we question, and to question is to be receptive and open to new and alternative meanings. Finally, I think it possible to conclude that for Dewey even the development of initial suggestions never excludes the element of the gratuitous. This is a dialectical point. On the one hand, thinking is something we do—we observe, criticize, and experiment with our environment and our meanings in order to get ourselves in a better position to understand. On the other

The second thing we need to say is that a suggestion prompted by observation is an inference that runs beyond observation to general possibilities and therefore "involves a *jump from the known into the unknown.*"[33] One may know, for example, that a child is moaning and infer that the child may be ill, lonely, or having a nightmare. Yet it is not initially known of which, if any, of the various general possibilities this relatively unique moaning is in fact a sign.

The likelihood that any one initial inference is misleading is enhanced by two human tendencies. On the one hand, there is a tendency, as Dewey puts it, "to believe that which is in harmony with desire. We take that to be true which we should like to have so, and ideas that go contrary to our hopes and wishes have difficulty in getting lodgment."[34] This tendency should not be surprising, for we have seen that when we find ourselves in a tensive context, desire and its object, an initial end-in-view, emerge. This constitutes an initial suggestion. But unless this object of desire is shaped by further understanding of the present context, by its relatively unique needs and demands, it is unlikely that it will adequately guide conduct and expectation in that context. It is more likely to prompt capricious behavior. On the other hand, there is a strong tendency to infer and accept as true those meanings that others hold to be true out of reverence for the authority of others and the desire to be in harmony with them. Respect for those in authority and the desire for harmony are important traits, notes Dewey, yet they "may lead a person too readily to fall in with the prejudices of others and may weaken his independence of judgment."[35] Again, this tendency is quite understandable, for we enter and mature as members of a social group only as we

---

hand, we must also remain constantly open to the occurrence of both new and modified ideas. The fact that we sometimes "rack our brains" to no avail should indicate the gratuitous nature of the actual occurrence of ideas. We work for them, to be sure, but that they come at all is a mystery for which we cannot finally take credit.

[33]Dewey, *How We Think*, 96; emphasis in text.

[34]Ibid., 28. It should be evident from this that Dewey does not subscribe to what is often attributed to pragmatists, namely, that a true idea is what we find satisfying, what we like or want to believe. He does not deny that we find certain ideas satisfying, but this constitutes a starting point rather than the conclusion of the thinking process. Thinking consists of a critical examination, refinement, and testing of these ideas.

[35]Ibid., 29.

learn how to share and cooperate in established and common purposes, which consequently come to shape and constitute the aims and interests out of which we live. Nevertheless, the blind adherence to such purposes in a highly tensive situation, apart from their proper qualification by an understanding of the relatively unique needs and demands of that context, will most likely form inadequate expectation and direction, resulting in inflexible and routine conduct.

At this point we can see the significance of two interrelated ways by which initial suggestions are criticized, refined, and tested. We have already examined one way by which this occurs, namely, in the interaction among observations and suggested hypotheses. In point of fact, we test suggestions when we respond according to the expected consequences that constitute the suggestion. For example, a high fever and acute abdominal pain suggest appendicitis, and this constitutes the expectation of an elevated white blood cell count. Examination of this matter tests the hypothetical suggestion. Observation of an abnormally high count would (in most circumstances) confirm the hypothesis and indicate further responsive conduct, an appendectomy. Not all is lost, however, if the count turns out normal and thus falsifies the hypothesis, for one learns something important, namely, that the child does not have appendicitis. Moreover, one is now in a better position to refine the initial hypothesis.

What is tested in this and other cases is the reliability of suggested ideas to indicate or specify a "connection between the object seen and the object suggested."[36] The connection of which Dewey speaks here is that among events themselves as conditions and consequences. What we need to find out is whether and to what extent "existing [observed] data *really* point to the idea that is suggested in such a way as to *justify* acceptance of the latter,"[37] and we do this by looking for the consequences suggested. Consequently, the grounds for judging the worth of ideas, their warrants, if you will, lie in the results of acting upon the ideas and observing the consequences—or, more particularly, in the extent to which the observed consequences correspond to what was anticipated. This is the specific point of reference that makes it possible for us to distinguish reliable and trustworthy suggestions from those constructed by capricious desire or habitual routine alone.

[36]Dewey, *How We Think*, 10; emphasis in text.
[37]Ibid., 11.

The first way to criticize, refine, and test suggestions that initially occur, consequently, is to act upon them and observe the consequences. In the end, this constitutes the final test of any idea, according to Dewey.[38] It is important that we recognize, however, that in most situations it would be unwise for us to act on suggestions as they first occur, for these, as we have seen, are often the result of what we want to be the case, whether that be a matter of capricious desire or habitual norms. Having a pressing need to meet an urgent deadline, for example, the parent who hears his or her child moan may jump to the conclusion that the child has the flu in part because it allows him or her to dismiss the matter by simply giving the child medication. If the moan were a result of appendicitis, this act could be disastrous. What we need, then, is judgment of suggestions before we act upon them. In particular, we need to judge whether an idea will guide conduct to results that resolve (or contribute to the resolution of) tensive conditions.

This issue leads Dewey to make an important distinction between spontaneous likings, what is desired, and judgment or appraisal of their worth:

> There is a difference between esteem and estimation, between prizing and appraising. To esteem is to prize, hold dear, admire, approve; to estimate is to measure in intellectual fashion. One is direct, spontaneous; the other is reflex, reflective. We esteem before we estimate, and estimation comes in to consider whether and to what extent something is *worthy* of esteem.[39]

The prizings of which Dewey speaks are objects of desire or interest, things that matter, however vague they may be, that emerge in a tensive situation. They constitute emerging ends-in-view, spontaneous initial suggestions of what is wanted. This prized and desired sense of what is wanted, we have seen, is at the basis of conduct, drawing us on. This is just as much the case whether the context in which this occurs is primarily practical or theoretical.[40] Dewey calls these prizings as they

---

[38]See ibid., 183–84.

[39]Dewey, *Ethics*, 290–91.

[40]It is often assumed that the practical and moral deal with values and the theoretical with facts. Dewey argues with some justice that a major problem in our culture today is the difficulty of seeing how these matters are related. One

first emerge "problematic goods,"[41] because we do not know what they really have in store for us in the relatively unique circumstances of the particular context, whether they will in fact bring about a restoration of balance. Appraisals arise because we need to judge the worth of these problematic goods. To judge their worth is to judge whether they will in fact function as means for a consummatory conclusion of that particular context.

This distinction is important for understanding the need for thinking about established normative interests in religious traditions. The function of religious norms, among other things, is to give understanding and direction for conduct in the various circumstances of life. Their success in the past is no guarantee, however, that they will continue to be serviceable in the present. Indeed, the problem of religious pluralism, as we have suggested and will discuss in some detail in the next two chapters, helps to expose the normative interests of religious traditions as *problematic goods* for many in the contemporary world. What we need to do, consequently, is to determine whether, in the changed circumstances of human life, these interests are in fact appropriate as they stand, whether they will in fact direct conduct to consummation. In short, they need judgment. The purpose of judgment, however, in this or any other case, is not simply to affirm or negate an end-in-view as it stands but to transform it so that it will be able to guide conduct adequately. What is at issue in judgment, therefore, is the transformation of interests. How

---

way Dewey proposes to establish their continuity is to argue that there is no theoretical thinking, thinking about meanings, that does not involve prizings and their evaluation and no thinking about practical and moral values that does not involve evaluation of prizings with respect to the understanding of the meanings of events as matter of fact connections in interaction. See particularly Dewey, *Quest for Certainty*, 255–56, 261–62, 273–74, 281–82; idem, *Theory of Valuation*, 2–4, 17, 20–25, 29–33, 58, 65–66; and idem, *Logic*, chap. 9, "Judgments of Practice: Evaluation," 159–80. This means that Dewey's value theory and his logic are central to and require one another. The difficulty with many commentators is that they focus upon one side and consider it in relative abstraction from the other. It seems to me that one significant aspect of the concept of "interests" developed in this volume is that it holds together Dewey's theories of value (felt quality) and meaning (understanding of fact) and thus makes it possible to see more easily how he understands value and meaning to develop in relation to one another in the thinking process.

41Dewey, *Quest*, 259.

judgment takes place, however, requires consideration. We turn, then, to Dewey's discussion of the second way to criticize, refine, and test our initial suggestions.

We can begin by noting Dewey's claim that we judge our initial suggested meanings or ends-in-view by "placing the thing judged in its relations and bearings."[42] In order to judge their worth as means, we need to develop our understanding of their meanings, their potential consequences, in order to see what they have in store for us. We develop their meanings, Dewey insists, by tracing their implications:

> This examination consists in noting what the meaning in question implies in relation to other meanings in the system of which it is a member. . . . If such and such a relation of meanings is accepted, then we are committed to such and such other relations of meanings because of their relationship in the same system.[43]

Let us imagine, once again, the hurried parents who want to give medication to their moaning child, believing that the fever indicates the flu. One implication of having fever is that one is ill and that the illness might be appendicitis. Recognition and acceptance of this possible meaning of the fever commits one to a range of other possible meanings having to do with appendicitis: if appendicitis, then acute abdominal pain and an elevated white blood cell count; if left untreated, then the probability of death; if treated by having an appendectomy, then the likelihood of recovery. We can see how this kind of thinking leads to judgment. The worth of the original suggestion of merely giving medication is called into question, for one recognizes that one consequence of giving medication, if the child in fact has appendicitis, is at least the possibility of death.[44]

Complete judgment in this matter, to be sure, would involve further observation. The parents would need to find out, for example, whether the child has an elevated white blood cell count. This illustrates how the two ways of developing the meanings of a context are interdependent. What needs underscoring at this point, however, is the fact that by sim-

---

[42]Dewey, *Ethics*, 290.

[43]Dewey, *Logic*, 111.

[44]For a more extended discussion of this matter, see Gouinlock, *Dewey's Theory of Value*, 140, 199, 207–8, 216–18, 307–10.

ply becoming aware of the possible consequences of a proposed act, the desire to enact it begins to change. One no longer prizes the act in the same way, for the felt qualities of the possible consequences (of the fact, for example, that the child might die if he or she has appendicitis) qualifies how one feels about the end-in-view initially desired.[45] At the same time, one gains direction in observation, and the results of this gain are important for the continued change and development of the initial object of interest.

Reflection upon the implications of meaning, which Dewey also calls reasoning in the narrow sense of the word, can be highly creative. In particular, insight into the possible connections among established meanings allows for the construction of novel possibilities or patterns of meaning. "The development of an idea through reasoning," Dewey writes, "helps supply intervening or intermediate terms which link together into a consistent whole elements that at first seemingly conflict with each other."[46] Reasoning is creative to the extent that it allows us to order conceptually the various elements of a context in a novel patterned series of means-end relations so that the elements are understood to support rather than conflict with one another.

This point is a key element in the argument of this chapter, for it is only as we are able to achieve insight into these novel possibilities as relevant alternatives to established interests (which emerge as suggestions) that those interests are able to be transformed. In order to understand how new patterns of meaning are developed through reasoning, we need to return to the discussion of Dewey's interpretation of meanings.

We have seen that human beings live in the context of qualities which prompt interest. Qualities on the whole are not neutral matters; human beings either like or dislike them. Yet we have also seen that human beings when born have very few instincts to guide their responses to qualities. They need to learn how to do this, and this process happens most effectively as they learn how to participate in cooperative interac-

---

[45]It might be, of course, that one eventually judges the original end-in-view as having worth in that context, but a change in the character of desire takes place here as well, for one has a much better sense of the reliability of the end-in-view, the fact that it is likely to meet the needs of that situation. One no longer simply prizes that object but also understands it and why one prizes it, why it is fitting in that particular situation.

[46]Dewey, *How We Think*, 112.

tion which constitutes language or communication. In particular, they learn how to respond—response is shaped, that is—when they become aware of how to use impulsive energy generated by felt quality for purposes understood and shared by others. We have seen, for example, that a child's spontaneous cry takes on meaning when he or she learns how to use it to draw attention to its discomforting conditions, such as hunger or a damp diaper or loneliness. When children learn to intend consequences in this way, initial qualities and their responses come to mean those consequences.

Meaning, consequently, can be described in various ways. First, it can be understood as awareness of the connections between qualities of initial events and concluding events of an interactive context.[47] Second, as we saw before, it can also be understood as a general "method of action," as Dewey puts it, "a way of using things as means to a shared consummation."[48] To learn a meaning is to learn how to respond intelligently, how to use things as means for accomplishing specific purposes. Third, therefore, meaning can also be understood as a tool or instrument which embodies a means-end relation.[49] To understand the meanings of a shovel or the word "shovel," for example, is to have tools that we can use as means for certain ends. Because it is the means-end relation we understand, our attention is called not only to how we might respond to things but also to the likely consequences of that response. This means, fourth, that meaning also represents possibilities or potentials of a context. As Dewey puts it, "Ideas are largely the obverse side of action; a perception of what might be, but is not, the promise of things hoped for, the symbol of things not seen."[50]

It is helpful to see meanings as abstractions from the full concreteness of any situation. "Every concrete experience in its totality," Dewey writes, "is unique; it is itself, non-reduplicable. . . . What is called abstraction means that some phase of it is selected for the sake of the aid it gives in grasping something else."[51] In this quotation, Dewey is in

---

[47]"In just the degree in which connections are established between what happens to a person and what he does in response, and between what he does to his environment and what it does in response to him, his acts and the things about him acquire meaning" (Dewey, *Democracy and Education*, 274).

[48]Dewey, *Experience and Nature*, 187.

[49]See ibid., 185–86; Dewey, *How We Think*, 146.

[50]Dewey, *Experience and Nature*, 350.

[51]Dewey, *Reconstruction in Philosophy*, 150.

effect describing the emergence of meaning in human life. His claim is that meanings emerge as we select aspects of a context that we take in connection with other aspects for particular purposes.

Abstraction, whatever else it may be, is a creative act. Dewey makes this point when he refers to what he calls its logical value, which "consists in seizing upon some quality or relation not previously grasped at all, making it stand out."[52] When we abstract, we at once distinguish and connect two or more things: we distinguish the elements in and by their connections. These connections, moreover, are not given directly to consciousness. They initially emerge in a constructive, speculative act. We take certain things to be connected with other things.

Any watchful parent, for example, is surprised at how long it takes for his or her children to distinguish colors. It may well be that children feel the colors in certain ways and that their feeling contributes to the overall quality of objects that they like or dislike. Yet it is not until they learn to do something with the colors, using them to pick out their favorite toy or piece of clothing, that they focus upon, attend to, and discriminate one or another color as blue, green, or red.[53] Learning to use the qualities is a creative and constructive act, for it requires the act of conceiving something new for that person, namely, a connection between the qualities and the consequences of their use.

Although the act of abstraction is a creative act of the imagination, what is conceived is not necessarily imaginary. If the conception is reliable, that is, if it adequately anticipates the consequences of certain kinds of interactions, then it becomes embodied in the behavior of the group in the sense that it regulates the way the members of that group interact. Such regulation constitutes the rules for proceeding in conduct. It is not often, however, that we are directly aware of what the rules are. We know how to use a shovel and the word "shovel," but the rules regulating that use often remain implicit.

Because meanings are constituted by abstractions, it is possible to reflect upon them and make the rules explicit. It is possible, for example, to think about what we do with a shovel, what its purposes, functions, and consequences are. This reflection constitutes what might be called a second level of abstraction, for it represents thinking about the implications of our meanings. In particular, it represents another

---

[52]Dewey, *How We Think*, 201.
[53]See ibid., 142–43.

attitude toward meanings, namely, a self-reflective attitude that abstracts from the direct use and enjoyment of meanings, considering them as potentials among potentials.[54]

At least two things happen when we think about the implications of our meanings. First of all, we are in a position to improve their instrumental character. When we understand a shovel, for example, not simply as what we can do with this instrument but more generally—abstracting from our use and enjoyment—as one way things can function in relation to one another, this idea can be used as an explicit ideal, as Dewey says, as something by which to criticize existing shovels and invent new and better shovels.[55] If we see a shovel as a way in which dirt and other matter are dug and removed, for example, we can consider how well our shovels do this job and experiment with different materials and shapes to improve their efficiency.

Second, and more importantly for our purposes, we are in a position to create new ends. Established meanings, Dewey writes,

> may be imaginatively administered and manipulated, experimented with. Just as we overtly manipulate things, making new separations and combinations, thereby introducing things into new contexts and environments, so we bring together logical universals in discourse, where they copulate and breed new meanings. There is nothing surprising in the fact that dialectic. . . generates new objects; that,

[54]This second level of abstraction could also be called "conceptual thinking," thinking with and about our concepts and meanings apart from their direct use and enjoyment in practice. My identification of a "second level of abstraction" or "conceptual thinking" is an interpretation of what Dewey distinguishes as the "task of science" in *Experience and Nature* (see esp. 129–33, 191–94; and idem, *Logic*, 60–80, 114–17). I am hesitant to use the word "science" for this kind of thinking, for although I understand it to go on in the sciences, I also think it occurs as a "moment" in the process of any good piece of thinking, even when one is thinking about highly practical matters. If it did not occur on these and other occasions, we would be limited to capricious and habitual modes of behavior. For a creative interpretation of the significance of reflection upon implications for teaching by someone who has been influenced by Dewey, see Joseph H. Kupfer, *Experience as Art: Aesthetics in Everyday Life* (Albany: State University of New York Press, 1983) 10–17.

[55]Dewey, *Ethics*, 253; Dewey uses the example of a table. See also idem, *Experience and Nature*, 201–2.

in Kantian language, it is "synthetic," instead of merely explicating what is already had.[56]

It is not difficult to see what Dewey has in mind. To understand the way things function in relation to one another is to understand a general potential or capacity that we can bring together with other general capacities. It may be, for example, that we have learned what a shovel means by learning to dig dirt in order to plant flowers and bulbs in the backyard. We can abstract from this particularity and conceive the series of events as the general capacity for things to be dug. We can then relate this to other understood capacities, such as the capacity for the flow of water to be changed or for things, such as trees, to be moved. In the process we can imagine and create new ends-in-view, such as digging trenches to irrigate barren fields or digging up and transplanting wild fruit trees in order to bring home an inexpensive supply of fruit and improve the beauty of the environment.[57]

In this way new possibilities of meaning develop through reasoning. We discussed this construction of new possibilities of meaning more briefly in the last chapter as artistic perception, the capacity to see in ends novel possibilities of meanings. As we saw, to do so is to envision in the present elements of a context new means-end relations, or more particularly, the possibility of using present elements in a new way for new ends. We are in a position now to see readily how this capacity contributes to the transformation of interests.

Let us return one last time to the parents and their moaning child. We might assume that the parents have found the child seriously ill and realize that the child must get to a hospital in a hurry. Imagine, however, that they are on vacation in a mountain cabin that they have rented for the first time, far away from any hospital or neighbor. The sugges-

---

[56]Dewey, *Experience and Nature*, 194.

[57]It should be clear that reasoning in the "narrow sense" has a purpose, namely, the clarification of meanings and their creative development and synthesis. Dewey understands logic to have emerged historically in relation to this purpose. Over time, he claims, human beings have worked out the best means, methods, or tools to accomplish this purpose. The regular use of these tools constitute the rules of logic. The rules of logic, consequently, are understood by Dewey as means-ends matters that are not a priori or metaphysical matters but originate historically in the process of thinking as effective ways of thinking. See Dewey, *Logic*, 1–20.

tion that would most likely occur in this kind of situation is to drive the child to the nearest hospital, for this is the normal and normative way of proceeding in these kinds of situations. Imagine further, however, that one aspect of this relatively unique situation is the fact that their car has not been reliable. Over the last week it has stalled three times in a seemingly unaccountable way. This fact now occurs to the parents and raises serious doubts about driving the child, for they realize that the car might stall on the way, far away from help. We can recognize the result as a conflict of interest, for the parents are pulled in different directions, wanting to get to the hospital in a hurry and not wanting to stall out on the way. As pointed out previously, this conflict sets the original object of desire or end-in-view, embodying the normative interests, on its journey towards transformation. Nevertheless, the transformation can be completed only as alternatives are conceived.

Let us imagine the parents proceeding in reflection by generalizing the act of driving as the capacity of things to transport other things, a concept that connects and thus calls to mind other ways and means of transporting. Let us imagine that this leads to the thought of helicopters, which have the capacity to land in small spaces and transport things quickly by air, and that this thought is related to other capacities, such as the capacity to phone for information, communicate crisis, and urge assistance. Although the parents may never have heard of a helicopter being used to transport sick people from the wilderness to a hospital, it is not inconceivable that they would think of just this possibility, stringing it together in the construction of a concept of continuous means-end relations that might begin with a call to the police to urge assistance in locating a helicopter and end with the flight to the hospital. Such a conceptual possibility would provide a relatively adequate alternative, for it represents a significant way of resolving the conflict.

This novel alternative is not something apart from or unrelated to the previously conflicting interests. It is a resolution of the conflict, occurring by what Dewey calls "sublimation." Interests are sublimated, he claims, when they "become a factor coordinated intelligently with others in a continuing course of action."[58] This means that interests are not denied or suppressed but used positively, taken up into and integrated within the conception of a new form, a new way in which things might proceed in interdependence upon one another. To the extent that this

[58]Dewey, *Human Nature and Conduct*, 146.

constitutes a new form of the old interests, it is not inappropriate to understand the old interests as having been transformed.[59]

One last thing must be said. Criticism of initial suggestions and the construction of alternatives are largely ideational or conceptual matters. What we want to know, however, is whether our ideas will guide conduct to unified consequences. The criterion of judgment for the second way of criticism, refining and testing our ideas, consequently, is whether the different meanings and interests of the context "are coherent with one another."[60] This involves testing in the imagination whether the elements of the context support one another in their functions in such a way that they work together to produce results both unified and continuous.

We need to recall that in testing our ideas in the imagination we are working with abstract possibilities. Consequently, while the worth of our ideas can and should be judged by this coherence criterion, our estimate can never be seen as final, for there is no final guarantee that the abstractions will in fact be relevant to the relatively unique circumstances of a particular context. By using the coherence criterion, we can reconstruct our initial ends-in-view considerably, working out possible ways of making conduct continuous and unified. The emphasis here, however, needs to be placed upon the possible character of these conceptions. Ideas, being abstractions, always constitute hypotheses that may be more or less relevant to any concrete situation.[61]

[59]The word Dewey most often uses for this kind of change in meaning and interests is "reconstruction." This word signifies the reworking of what has already been done or established, certainly one connotation of the meaning Dewey wants to communicate. The word "transformation," however, is more significant, for it implies that established meanings and interests are not only reworked but that they are taken up and integrated in a more comprehensive form. One can, for example, "reconstruct" an existing house simply by taking it apart and putting it back together again. This is not the meaning that Dewey has in mind. The "construction" he takes to be redone or in need of redoing is a design or form; the "redoing," as he understands it, involves a change in the design, a change that utilizes both the advantages and flaws of the existing design to create a new, richer, and more interesting design. The word "transformation" communicates these meanings more clearly and fully than does "reconstruction."

[60]Dewey, *How We Think*, 97.

[61]In the previous chapter it was pointed out that this hypothetical character of our ideas represents a significant implication of what Dewey takes to be the unique and open ended character of contexts.

Two consequences follow from this observation. First, the final test of any conception lies in the actual tasting, so to speak: we need to act upon it in order to see if the consequences we anticipated in fact correspond to what comes about.[62] The final criterion for judgment, as a result, is the correspondence of concrete consequences with anticipated possible consequences. Secondly, the contrast between abstract possibility and concrete reality alerts us to our inability to capture the fullness of reality in and with our ideas. Reality is always more than what we can understand and say, for when we understand and speak we abstract only parts of the fullness of concrete reality. What this means, among other things, is that we should always maintain a vigilant and critical attitude, alert to actual and potential consequences that our abstractions have failed to take into account. Consequently, when we act upon our ideas, no matter how well established they might be, we need to proceed cautiously and critically, with an openness to revision. This attitude towards our constructions is essential if we are to adjust to the continual changes of our contexts in ways that allow for the continual growth and transformation of our interests.

This chapter has been an extended consideration of how thinking, as Dewey understands it, makes possible the transformation of normative interests in and through the discernment of novel possibilities that reconcile conflicting interests. The key to this process, as we have seen, lies in a creative construction of novel meanings that takes up and integrates the established interests in a new form or pattern so that they become mutually supportive rather than conflicting. This is an important point to have established, but more needs to be said, for the interests we have been considering are different at least in degree from what can be called religious interests. The latter, I shall argue, are the most comprehensive normative interests in human life, providing men and women with their understanding of the world and what is of central importance in it. What we need to do now, consequently, is to turn to an examination of the nature and function of religious interests. After we have done that, we can look more carefully at how philosophical thinking—the most comprehensive form of thinking—is able to contribute to the growth and transformation of established religious interests in the context of religious pluralism.

---

[62]Dewey, *How We Think*, 97, 113–14.

5

THE RELIGIOUS FUNCTION OF LIFE AND THE PROBLEM OF RELIGIOUS PLURALISM

W hile religious and theological thinkers have drawn upon the works of Aristotle, Kant, Hegel, Whitehead, and other philosophers, they have not, on the whole, paid much attention to Dewey's philosophy.[1] For

---

[1]The only major theologian I know of to have been significantly influenced by Dewey is Henry Nelson Wieman. See in particular Wieman's *The Source of Human Good*. Today, however, Dewey is beginning to make some impact among those interested in theology and the philosophy of religion. See the work of William Dean, *American Religious Empiricism* (Albany: State University of New York Press, 1986), and idem, *History Making History: The New Historicism in American Religious Thought* (Albany: State University of New York Press, 1988). A more thoroughgoing and comprehensive influence can be seen in Thomas D. Parker, "Immediacy and Interpretation in Religious Experience," in William J. Haynes and William Dean, eds., *American Religious Empiricism: Working Papers* (Denver, CO: Regis College Press, 1988) 1. 5–40 and Steven C. Rockefeller, "John Dewey's Theory of the Religious Quality of Experience," in ibid., 1. 41–

one thing, his writings on religion are slim and frustratingly vague. More seriously, however, Dewey does not have a high regard for institutional religion. Indeed, in his only piece in the philosophy of religion, a short volume he called *A Common Faith*, he rejects traditional religion (1) as hopelessly entangled in mistaken dualistic beliefs about the supernatural and (2) as a source of disintegration in modern culture. On the face of it, consequently, it would seem that Dewey would make a poor resource for thinking about religious problems in general and problems in Christian theology in particular.

This kind of assessment of Dewey's philosophy, I suggest, is premature. In particular, Dewey offers a perspective that focuses upon and helps us to interpret the *function* of religion, making it possible not only to see the continuity among religious traditions but also to evaluate those traditions. This is the positive point to be gleaned from *A Common Faith*, but one that Dewey did not himself see. In *A Common Faith* he contrasts established religious traditions and the religious quality and function of experience, rejecting the former because it inhibits the cultivation of the latter. What Dewey opposes, legitimately, is the reification and hardening of religious doctrine and practices, the routinization of the religious function. It is a mistake to conclude as he does, however, that "the doctrinal or intellectual apparatus and the institutional accretions that grow up are, in a strict sense, adventitious to the intrinsic [religious] quality of such experiences."[2] As Dewey well knows, ideas and practices are not strictly adventitious to but concretely shape how interaction functions, some being more conducive to the acknowledgment, cultivation, and continuity of what he calls the religious function. If this point is recognized, then it is possible not to reject religious traditions outright but to use the interpretation of the religious function of experience to evaluate the extent to which traditions make this function possible and to reconstruct and transform those ideas and practices that fall short of this mark.

Although Dewey did not focus his thought upon religion until late in life and even then only briefly, it is possible to argue that he is funda-

---

74. Interestingly, the school at which Parker teaches, McCormick Theological Seminary in Chicago, has recently reconstructed its Doctor of Ministry program in order to incorporate in a deliberate and self-conscious way Dewey's theory of logic or thinking for dealing with problems in ministry.

[2]Dewey, *A Common Faith*, 17.

mentally a religious thinker, since what informs and motivates all his thinking is his abiding concern for meaningful orientation and human fulfillment. This concern is clearly evident in his anthropology. I have argued above that human beings, according to Dewey, can be distinguished from other creatures by their capacity for a greater number and variety of interests. We have seen, however, that the development of a multitude of diverse interests in any individual or group is capable of resulting in a life that becomes fragmented and unfulfilled. In Dewey's theory of art, however, his interest in the conditions of fulfillment comes most clearly into focus. Art is understood to be the kind of behavior that responds to the fragmented character of life by envisioning and actualizing possibilities capable of rendering conduct unified and continuous. It should come as no surprise, consequently, that Dewey's interpretation of art can be readily understood as continuous with what he calls the religious function of life.[3] Indeed, one can interpret the matter this way: whenever the artistic functions comprehensively, it becomes religious. The result is an ordering and organizing of interests by a normative vision of the whole that provides unity for the self in what is taken to be a unified world of meaning.

Discussion of the religious function of life in this section is not meant to be a strict interpretation of Dewey's position but rather a synthetic development of it. This is due in part to the fact that Dewey did not write extensively upon religious matters or integrate what he did say into his overall philosophy. Nevertheless, what he wrote makes such a promising start, particularly when understood within his general philosophical orientation, that it warrants serious consideration and further development. Indeed, it warrants much further consideration than I provide at this point. My aim is not to present an extensive theory of religion as such but to provide enough understanding of the role and function of religious meanings and interests that we are able to see more clearly the peculiar difficulty addressed in this volume as the problem of religious pluralism.

One final introductory remark is in order. Although Dewey did not use the word "interest" to analyze the religious function of human life, its use in the present interpretation will enable us to see the continuity

---

[3]It is common among commentators to note the continuity between Dewey's aesthetics and his theory of religion. For an illuminating discussion of this continuity, see Alexander, *John Dewey's Theory of Art*, 254–66.

of this position with our earlier discussion. Emergent interests come to function religiously, we shall see, when they take on increased importance in relation to other interests, when their objects become ultimate goods that give meaning and worth to other goods. There are at least three further advantages of using the concept of "interest" for interpreting the religious function of life. First, it brings out the ongoing normative character of the religious function. When experience functions religiously, the unification that occurs is not an isolated event but establishes an ongoing comprehensive tradition of meaning and value that orients and shapes further experience.[4] Second, it helps us to understand Dewey's claim that religious experience is not a separate kind of experience but a function distinguishable yet continuous with other functions.[5] This point can be made more clearly with respect to the function of interests. For example, we can say that aesthetic, moral, scientific, political, economic, and other interests are capable of functioning religiously and that they do so when they gain central importance in life, becoming inclusive and comprehensive. This claim has significance not only for clarifying the religious quality of life amid the secularization of the modern world; it also makes traditional religious interests relative to what is taken religiously or normatively in practice. When men and women adhere to a particular religious tradition and yet place more importance in political, economic and other interests than in their traditional religious interests, then those other interests become their central religious objects of interest. Where their heart lies, there they find their god as well.[6] Finally, it helps us see more clearly the problematic char-

---

[4]This issue is discussed in greater detail below, pp. 135–42.

[5]Dewey, *A Common Faith*, 10.

[6]The understanding of the religious as a function of interests is not foreign to Christian theology. We can trace it back at least as far as Augustine. In his theology, both sin and salvation are understood with respect to human affections, desires, or loves. Sin is understood as desiring material and carnal matters too much, causing a disorder in life; when God becomes the most important love or object of desire, however, the proper order among desires (or loves) is restored. See Augustine, *The Confessions of Saint Augustine* (Edward B. Pusey, trans.; New York: Collier, 1961) 232–33; and Augustine, *Concerning The City of God against the Pagans* (Henry Bettenson, trans.; New York: Penguin, 1972), 556–58. In this century, Paul Tillich, with his notion of "ultimate concern," and H. Richard Niebuhr, with his concept of "centers of value," work out of this same tradition. See Tillich, *Systematic Theology*: (3 vols.; New York: Harper & Row,

acter of religious pluralism. I have suggested that religious pluralism becomes problematic when a conflict among religious interests arises. We can now see that this problem is wider than the problem of pluralism among traditional religious interests; rather, it consists of the conflict among all those human interests that are taken as focal centers around which other interests are organized.

The Context of the Religious Function of Life

The framework for understanding Dewey's interpretation of the religious function of experience, I want to argue, is his understanding of the precariousness or instability of existence. I discussed this issue to some extent in chapter three but need to say something more.

What makes the instability of the world an issue in and for human life is, among other things, the fact that we necessarily rely upon the world for our continued existence. Even what seems to be our own doing, Dewey insists, the goods for which we have labored many hours, days and even years and that now seem to be at our disposal and command, are not in fact a result of our exclusive doing but are actualized in and through the cooperation of "nature, tradition and social organization" which supplement "our own endeavors so petty and so feeble without this extraneous reinforcement."[7] Our dependence upon the world in this and other ways marks the fundamental insecurity and contingency of our lives, for it means that we perforce rely upon powers, energies, and purposes that are not our own, that we cannot fully anticipate, and that can, and often do, surprise us in unexpected and unwelcome ways.

This dependence and contingency of our existence, we have noted before, constitutes the mystery of our lives.[8] What we need to see now is that this mystery is at once the source of tragedy and hope. Its tragic character is the most obvious result. This matter can be illuminated most clearly, I believe, in relation to Dewey's conviction that change is a fundamental and pervasive characteristic of life. As we have seen, Dewey proposes change as a metaphysical trait. His hypothesis is that existence consists of events that undergo change in relation to one another. Things come into being, change, and end. Although Dewey does not himself

---

1963) 1. 11–12; and H. Richard Niebuhr, *Radical Monotheism and Western Culture: With Supplementary Essays* (New York: Harper & Row, 1943).

[7]Dewey, *Experience and Nature*, 43.

[8]See above, pp. 89–91.

discuss the implication of this factor for the tragedy of life, we can note at least two of the more poignant ways in which change can be understood to result in the tragic. First, there is the seemingly inevitable change in all that is achieved by human beings in their individual and collective lives. Nothing they create can stand as an everlasting monument against the ravages of time. Men and women live out of purposes and ideals that give their lives meaning, and recognition that the results of their labor are now lost or will be lost qualifies their efforts with the frustrating sense of futility and tragedy. Second, there is the ultimate finality of death—our own death and the death of those whom we love. Death is not always unwelcome, to be sure. Yet even when we feel relieved and thankful for the death that ends the suffering of an aging parent or seriously ill friend, the feeling of loss and unactualized possibility—of what might have been—is often unexpectedly vivid and disheartening. So much more is this the case when it is a child who has died.

The tragic in life is constituted, I am suggesting, by the actual or potential loss of things we hold precious and dear. To claim change as a metaphysical trait, as Dewey does, is to refuse to deny the reality of this loss. This is to recognize—and Dewey does so unflinchingly, although he rarely puts it in these words—that we do not have final control over the events of our lives.[9] Because of continual change, things that we cannot fully anticipate or prevent befall us. Indeed, however well we plan and labor, however intelligent our conduct becomes, however much we may anticipate change and contingency and strive to secure ourselves against its debilitating effects, we find ourselves in a context that continually surprises us with unwelcome and tragic consequences.

[9]This point is certainly implicit throughout Dewey's *Quest for Certainty*. Dewey argues there that the inability to accept the implications of change is what drove many philosophers to turn away from the world of change they could not control and to create alternative metaphysical visions in which reality is understood to be permanent, eternal, and certain. To be sure, Dewey offers the scientific method as the means of controlling the very changes others denied, but the kind of control that he claims is never absolute or comprehensive but always "by grace not of ourselves," as he puts it in *Experience and Nature* (p. 43). The significance of the scientific method is the capacity it gives us not to achieve final mastery over the mystery of the world but to respond creatively to the inevitable changes of our lives, thereby providing an alternative to the denial of (or resignation to) those changes.

That change results in the tragic, however, is only one side of the story. It also gives rise to hope. That things change means that nothing is just final or permanent but is always turning into something else, something new. We discussed this matter as well in chapter three. We saw there that one implication of Dewey's interpretation of the reality of change is that an indefinite range of novel possibility belongs to and qualifies any particular result of change. Stated more systematically, each change or event is not only the particular or unique change that it is but is also a process which is capable of an indefinite number of qualifications (or unique results), depending upon the kind of events with which it interacts. That a range of novel potentiality belongs to any particular result means that the tragic does not necessarily have the final say in human life, for circumstances that constitute loss are also capable of conditioning new meaning and worth in human life. Again, we explored this point in some detail in our earlier discussion of art. Art, as we saw, is the kind of activity that actualizes possibilities of growth in tensive contexts—including the tragic—by imagining how to use those tensive circumstances in a new way for reestablishing unity and continuity in the interactive context. The point of the present discussion is that this potential for creative growth out of the tragic constitutes the source of hope in human life and is made possible by change, the very thing that also results in the tragic.

The tension between tragedy and hope, I want to argue, is the womb in which the religious function, as Dewey understands it, is nurtured and born. There is no need for the religious function apart from the tragedy of life. On the other hand, the religious function is not possible apart from the potential for growth that grounds the hope that circumstances can change for the better, that fulfillment or satisfaction—salvation, to use the more traditional term—is possible amid the tragedy of life.

The Religious Function as Comprehensive Transformation

Human interaction functions religiously, Dewey argues, when it undergoes a transformation that he calls the comprehensive "adjustment" of the self to its environment. In order to elucidate what he means, he contrasts it with two other modes of resolving tension between the self and its surroundings: "accommodation" and "adaption."[10] "Accommoda-

---

[10]Dewey discusses this matter in *A Common Faith*, 15–16. He is making important distinctions in this discussion, even though his interpretation of the

tion," he suggests, connotes the existence of environmental conditions that block our desires but cannot be changed; we are able to resolve the matter, consequently, only by modifying our desires or interests, "accommodating" ourselves to those conditions. For example, we accommodate ourselves to unexpected inclement weather when we change our plans for a picnic. "Adaption," on the other hand, Dewey suggests, connotes a more active role on our part, modifying environmental conditions to suit our purposes. We adapt lumber, electricity, and water supplies to our desires, for example, when we use them to build homes for comfort and protection from inclement weather throughout the year. The point to note is that the changes involved in accommodation and adaption usually do not affect the full range of one's established interests. In most instances, for example, we change our plans for a picnic and build homes without realigning the other interests that we hold to be important as well.

From time to time, however, we find ourselves in circumstances that call for a different kind of resolution or transformation. In order to see what Dewey has in mind, it is important to recognize that not all interests are of equal worth. Some are so important that they give perspective to other interests, organizing them in a pattern of meaning and thus providing a fundamental orientation in the world.[11] On various occasions these comprehensive interests are called into question; for one reason or another, the circumstances that have supported them change. The resulting loss of a fundamental sense of meaning and worth constitutes the tragic, as discussed above, and requires a resolution more comprehensive than the other two forms of transaction. In particular, Dewey writes, it requires

> changes in ourselves in relation to the world in which we live that are much more inclusive and deep seated. They relate not to this or that want in relation to this or that condition of our surroundings, but pertain to our being in its entirety.[12]

---

meaning of these terms is not as precise in general usage as he seems to indicate.

[11]As suggested earlier, interests that function in this way are religious. See also below, pp. 137–42.

[12]Dewey, *A Common Faith*, 16.

Dewey distinguishes this kind of transformation by the term "adjustment" and identifies it with the religious function of experience. It includes "the idea of a thoroughgoing and deep-seated harmonizing of the self with the Universe (as a name for the totality of conditions with which the self is connected),"[13] and involves a "change *of* will" or a "generic and enduring change in attitude."[14] To interpret the religious function as an adjustment of interests, consequently, is not entirely unwarranted, for it involves a change in what is taken to be the most important and fulfilling—and therefore, normative—modes of interaction between the self and its environment.

Three qualifications of Dewey's position are helpful for our present purposes. First of all, what is important for Dewey religiously is the function of experience, for the "way in which the experience operated, its function, determines its religious value."[15] His claim is that the religious quality or worth of any experience lies in its consequences, in "the *effect* produced,"[16] because the resulting change in interests constitutes "a better, deeper and enduring adjustment in life,"[17] "a sense of security and peace,"[18] a perspective "that lend[s] deep and enduring support to the processes of living."[19] These are all highly significant consequences, to be sure, but the question is why we ought to call them, or the function which produces them, "religious." When Dewey discounts the beliefs and practices of religious traditions as strictly "adventitious" to these results,[20] one is left with the impression that, as far as Dewey is concerned, there is no significant relation between historical religious traditions and his interpretation of the religious quality of experience. Yet there is in fact an implicit connection in Dewey's argument as the following quotation suggests:

> It is the claim of religions that they effect this genuine and enduring change in attitude. I should like to turn the statement around

[13]Ibid., 19.
[14]Ibid., 17.
[15]Ibid., 14.
[16]Ibid.
[17]Ibid.
[18]Ibid., 13.
[19]Ibid., 15.
[20]Ibid., 17.

and say that whenever this change takes place there is a definitely
[sic] religious attitude. It is not *a* religion that brings it about, but
when it occurs, from whatever cause and by whatever means, there
is a religious outlook and function.[21]

Dewey recognizes that people who participate in religious traditions at
least claim that something about those traditions has conditioned the
comprehensive and enduring change in attitude which he wants to call
religious. This is the connection he makes. Why then does he resist
acknowledgment of religious traditions as contributing conditions of this
function? Among other reasons, he wants to emancipate the function
"from dependence upon specific types of beliefs and practices. . . that
constitute a religion."[22] In short, he wants to argue that the religious
function of human life is not dependent upon any particular religious
tradition but can be conditioned by any number of different elements.
This is important, for it helps us to see the continuity in function between what is identified traditionally as religion and the rest of human
life. This point can be maintained, however, only if we acknowledge—
as I think we must—that religious traditions can also be seen as highly
significant resources for religious transformation and that the meaning of
"religiousness," when extended to other contexts, is based upon an examination of what goes on within the traditions we call religious.

The second point is close to the first. By suggesting earlier that Dewey
understands the religious as art functioning comprehensively, I acknowledge that what Dewey takes as the religious function and qualities of
experience is understood by him to be normative for human life and its
transformation. Dewey's aim, it might he said, is not to describe what
goes on in traditional religions but to understand what human interaction
at its best can be. It could be said, in fact, that Dewey aims at a normative position because he finds so little of value in established traditions, filled as they are with what he takes (and therefore describes) as
superstition, intolerance, fanaticism, and the like. Affirmation of the
normative character of Dewey's interpretation, however, is not incompatible with a descriptive examination of traditional religious life. On the
contrary, normative claims depend upon the description of a means-end
relation. Once we understand this relation as it is inherent in religious

---

[21]Ibid., 17; see also 24.
[22]Ibid., 14.

life, we have a normative concept which, among other things, can be used for the criticism and reconstruction of religious traditions. For example, once we see that the aim of religiousness is to find wholeness of meaning amid the tragedy of life, we have a perspective for examining the actual means at work and for criticizing and reconstructing those means in relation to their capacity for making wholeness of meaning possible. It is somewhat surprising that Dewey did not see this point himself, for it is the same argument for the relationship between the descriptive and the normative that he makes in his *Logic*.[23] My point is that Dewey's interpretation of the religious function implicitly relies upon this relation—insofar as he calls it "religious"—and that it clarifies the meaning and worth of what he does to acknowledge it explicitly. As already noted, it helps us to see how Dewey's interpretation of the religious can be used critically.[24]

Third, it is helpful to extend Dewey's interpretation of the function of the religious to include not just the adjustment of interests but the subsequent function of those interests as well. Dewey seems to suggest this himself:

[23]See Dewey, *Logic*, 4–10; see also 12–14, 16–19.

[24]Thomas Parker argues for such a critical use inherent in Dewey's position in *A Common Faith*. He begins by claiming that the worth of Dewey's position does not lie "in giving better descriptions," but in his "novel interpretation of what counts as 'religious,'" an interpretation "which accounts for the ambiguity of religion which both contributes to and undermines human well being" (see Parker, "Immediacy and Interpretation," 27). His argument concludes with the claim that the religious function and quality of experience is at its best—is normative, that is—"when it adheres to the active relation of worthy ideals and actual conditions so that the fullest realization of ideal ends becomes the central value for persons and communities" (p. 35). I think this is an important insight which can be concluded in the context of Dewey's whole program, but I do not see how this can be derived directly from *A Common Faith*, as Parker suggests. In this book, Dewey does not seem to be self-consciously working out a theory of religion that "accounts" for both demonic and genuinely fulfilling forms of religion. On the contrary, he seems to reject all forms of religion as not only irrelevant but as positively detrimental to the cultivation of the religious quality of life. A case needs to be made, consequently, for claiming that what Dewey says is relevant to traditional forms of religion.

Because of their scope, this modification of ourselves is enduring. It lasts through any amount of vicissitude of circumstances, internal and external. There is a composing and harmonizing of the various elements of our being such that, in spite of changes in the special circumstances that surround us, these conditions are also arranged, settled, in relation to us.[25]

The advantage of clearly recognizing the enduring character of adjustment is twofold. On the one hand, it helps us to see that the subsequent interests that result from adjustment function religiously when they provide comprehensive and enduring understanding and orientation. This is important for the discussion of religious pluralism, since what is at issue in this problem is the plurality of normative interests that function in this way. On the other hand, clear acknowledgment of the enduring function of the transformed interests helps us to see how the adjustment of interests provides hope in the midst of tragedy. In particular, to say that they function religiously in the course of life is to recognize that they give continuity of meaning to—or enable us to see possibilities of consummatory meaning in—the continual changes of our lives, so that the changes do not mark mere loss but are qualified by an understanding of continuity.[26]

[25]Dewey, *A Common Faith*, 16.

[26]The traditional Christian notions of providence and immortality are two of the more obvious examples of how a comprehensive vision provides continuity of meaning in the midst of change. Paul's ideas of the resurrection of the dead and of divine governance, as well as the idea that all things work for a good end, for example, qualify the sense of loss due to change with the sense of hope. Dewey, of course, rejected these concepts as unempirical and dualistic; nevertheless, their function is important to identify and then to cultivate by developing ideas more appropriate for the modern context.

On the surface, of course, it might seem as if not all religious orientations seek continuity of meaning in the context of loss due to change. For Hindus and Buddhists, for example, the problem, one might argue, is not change but continuity. For many Hindus, the difficulty of life is the endlessness of the cycles of change, and thus a final release from life itself, an end to continuity, is understood to be the salvific aim of life. On the other hand, many Buddhists would not deny that loss due to change is taken as tragic, but this is because men and women mistakenly presuppose a self that is continuous and that consequently mourns the loss of what is desired and loved. Genuine fulfillment—enlightenment—comes when they understand that the self is not continuous but also changes

Concepts of the Whole: Self and World

I have suggested throughout this volume that the problem of religious pluralism is best understood as a conflict of normative interests. Before we can understand the full significance of this claim, we need to understand more clearly what it means to have a normative interest. Dewey's claim is that the religious function of life establishes normative, ideal interests. Yet it does more, for it also makes a whole out of the parts of the environment. As Dewey puts it in *Human Nature and Conduct*, it creates "the sense of community and one's place in it," "a community of life in which continuities of existence are consummated."[27] To have normative, ideal interests, in short, is to find oneself in a world conceived as a community of parts that support and sustain those ideal interests. In order to understand what it is to have normative interests, consequently, we must also examine what it is to understand the world as a community.

The nature of normative interests and the complementary vision of a supportive world can be understood by considering Dewey's interpretation of the concepts of "self" and "world" as wholes. It should not be surprising to find that Dewey considers these concepts in *A Common Faith* since, as I have been arguing, human life functions religiously

---

in each moment, for this frees them from their attachment to things that inevitably change.

Closer examination of these world views, however, reveals them to be elaborate adjustments of meaning in the face of loss which help the men and women who hold them to endure the changes that they undergo. The problem with the endless cycles of life for many Hindus, for example, is that nothing seems to matter: whatever is achieved will disappear and come back again in endless repetition. The notion of an ultimate release from those cycles qualifies this loss of meaning through change by claiming that what is done now not only will be lost and come back again but also has the capacity of contributing—under special circumstances—to their final release. Consequently, another kind of continuity is established, one in which present activity (which otherwise would seem to be mere loss) takes on the significance of that to which it is understood to contribute. Similarly, the Buddhist vision also establishes another kind of continuity than the one it finds problematic. The tragic sense of loss is taken out of its immediate context and placed in another framework, one in which it is understood as a means for—and thus as connected to or continuous with—the eventual development of enlightenment.

[27]Dewey, *Human Nature and Conduct*, 301.

when it creates wholeness of meaning out of the brokenness of tragedy. By looking at these concepts, consequently, we can see what kind of meaning wholeness has—or can have—in human life.

It is helpful to consider the concept of the self first. We begin by noting Dewey's claim in *Democracy and Education* that "self and interest are two names for the same fact."[28] Our objects of interests—the aims, purpose, and ideals to which we dedicate our lives—give us a sense of identity. If we accept this interpretation of self, then we can understand the condition of the self by the way its interests are related. For example, the self can be described as divided and uncertain when its interests come into conflict or become ambiguous. On the other hand, the self can be described as unified when its central interests are integrated.

There are three things that are useful to note about the concept of the self as a "whole." First, if this concept has reference to the unity of the self, as Dewey presupposes, then it can be said to signify the unification or integration of interests. This integration of interests occurs, Dewey claims, when one's interests are "actuated and supported by ends so inclusive that they unify the self."[29] Inclusive ideal interests, such as justice, peace, and equality, unify and order the interests of the self by their inclusiveness. In and with and through these kinds of interests, consequently, a self becomes a unified self with unified purpose and identity.

Second, the concept of the self as a whole is a construction of the imagination which emerges in history. "The *whole* self," Dewey writes, "is an ideal, an imaginative projection."[30] There is no whole of the self that is complete or actual, for among other things, the self is not a rigid and fixed reality but indeterminate and unfolding in time. Its unification, as a result, is always contingent and anticipatory: it is ideal, not actual. Yet this does not mean that the ideals which unify the self are imaginary or fanciful. On the contrary,

the ideal itself has its roots in natural conditions; it emerges when the imagination idealizes existence. . . . There are values, goods,

[28]Dewey, *Democracy and Education*, 352.
[29]Dewey, *A Common Faith*, 22.
[30]Ibid., 19.

actually realized upon a natural basis—the goods of human association, of art and knowledge. The idealizing imagination seizes upon
the most precious things found in the climacteric moments of experience and projects them.[31]

Third, if an ideal is to become inclusive, then the projection is a
creative process involving the reconstruction and reorganization of existing interests. As Dewey puts it,

> imagination seize[s] hold upon the idea of a rearrangement of ex-
> isting things that would evolve new objects. . . . The new vision
> does not arise out of nothing, but emerges through seeing, in terms
> of possibilities,. . . old things in new relations serving a new end
> which the new end aids in creating.[32]

An ideal interest is made inclusive as we use it imaginatively to recon-
ceive the relations among our interests so that our many aims and purposes become "one in the power of their ideal, or imaginative, quality
to stir and hold us."[33] Justice, for example, becomes inclusive as we
come to understand what it means for all our aims and purposes to be
just. Making an ideal inclusive, consequently, is not a matter of simply
projecting it but of imaginatively reconstructing its meaning in relation
to the simultaneous (and ongoing) reconstruction of all other interests.

Our interests become a unified whole as we envision their intercon-
nections, that is, the ways they can be mutually supportive. This inter-
connected unity is what the concept of the self as a whole means.
Normative ideal interests, I have been arguing, make this unity possible.
As the idealization of particular goods that function normatively, they
provide unity of meaning and purpose among all other objects of interests. This development of unity in meaning and purpose, consequently,
is also what it means to have normative ideal interests.

The meaning of wholeness characteristic of life functioning religiously,
however, is more than personal integration. This point bears underscoring, for the dominant tradition in the West, at least since Descartes, has

[31]Ibid., 48.
[32]Ibid., 49.
[33]Ibid., 43.

claimed that the self is private. Dewey strongly opposes this concept.[34] In defining the self with respect to its interests, he insists that the self is best understood as a public reality, as ways of living *in the world*. Consequently, the meaning of wholeness with respect to interests presupposes something about the world. "The self," as Dewey says, "is always directed toward something beyond itself and so its own unification depends upon the idea of the integration of the shifting scenes of the world into that imaginative totality we call the Universe."[35] What makes the adjustment of interests religious is not only their comprehensive unification but the fact that their integration includes a vision of the world understood as supportive of those interests. This vision of the world therefore provides continuity of meaning as the promise of ongoing consummation.

We come now to the concept of the whole in its reference to the world. The first thing to say about this concept is that it also is a construction of the imagination:

> The idea of the whole, whether of the whole personal being or of the world, is an imaginative, not a literal idea. The limited world of our observation and reflection becomes the Universe only through imaginative extension. It cannot be apprehended in knowledge nor realized in reflection.[36]

It is impossible to conceive in detail the whole of the world, for among other things it extends indefinitely backward into the past, forward, into the future, and outward into space. The idea of the whole world, therefore, is not a concept of something that is fully accessible or even actual, something finished and complete. At most we have bits and fragments before us. If we are to conceive of these bits within a whole, we need to organize them as parts-of-a-whole. Dewey's claim is that we

---

[34]It is quite true, of course, that Dewey recognizes an individualistic and private dimension of selfhood which consists of idiosyncratic impulsive energy. See Dewey, *Experience and Nature*, chap. 6: "Nature, Mind and the Subject," particularly 242–46. While impulse represents the irreducible bias and preference of a self, however, it means nothing unless it is utilized to reconstruct established interests that are public and social.

[35]Dewey, *A Common Faith*, 19.

[36]Ibid., 18–19.

create such organizing concepts through the imaginative generalization of more limited concepts that we project upon whatever occurs. We say, for example, that the world as a whole is like a kingdom, a story, a family household, or a democracy, and in doing so we have a tool for thinking about the many things that go on in the world and for understanding them not as disconnected bits but as interdependent functional pieces of a larger whole.

This kind of conceptualization is not only imaginative but also ideal.[37] In point of fact, it represents the normative character of potentiality. At issue in the religious function, as we saw, is the harmony of self and its environment, the question of whether things work together. To conceive of the world as a whole, consequently, is to conceive of those potential ways of interacting that people believe will result in a consummatory harmony of interacting parts. To envision a particular kind of world, therefore, is to envision the particular capacity that it is believed things have for working together so as to form a continuous and consummatory whole. To liken the world as a whole to a kingdom, for example, allows men and women to understand (1) that, whatever else they mean, the various fragments of the world have the general capacity to work together like the various elements of a kingdom and (2) that their consummatory worth and meaning lies in this potential.

Ideal visions of the world, of course, may be unrelated to the actual course of events. As Dewey writes, "There is idealization [of the world] through purely intellectual and logical processes in which reasoning alone attempts to prove that the world has characters that satisfy our highest aspirations."[38] These are mere projections or "castles in the sky," as Dewey often calls them. They may be of some comfort but only in a piecemeal and private way. Their poignancy for life lies in their inability to provide understanding and direction in the context of change and the loss of meaning that we encounter from time to time.

If the worth of an ideal vision of the world lies in its relevance to the actual world of conduct, that is, in its capacity to provide ongoing continuity of meaning and direction, it would seem that such a vision must be constructed as the ideal generalization and projection of an environment that is *already appropriately relevant* to actual human affairs. Dewey

---

[37]Ibid., 19.
[38]Dewey, *Quest for Certainty*, 302.

suggests this feature when he claims that the "life of the community in which we live and have our being is the fit symbol of this relationship" between human activity and a vision of the whole.[39] This claim is not difficult to understand, since community is an actual environment of mutually sustaining activities held together by means of perceived connections between actual affairs and ideal interests that are taken to be the consummatory potential of those affairs. Even more important, however, is the fact that community is a dynamic reality that is productive of new consummatory meanings. Community, of course, is not a static reality, in part because it is a source of much confusion and hurt as any family, business, educational, or religious institution demonstrates. A community is made up of individuals whose desires and interests change with changing times. A vital community, however, is composed of selves who are loyal to one another in and throughout these changes and are willing to search for new consummatory possibilities of cooperative behavior and to adjust their own purposes and ideals in that light. This dynamic character of community allows individuals to develop confidence and trust that the actual world harbors consummatory possibilities even when they are not perceived and encourages them in their search. A vigorous community, therefore, represents an actual environment in which new ideals emerge over time to restore wholeness to that environment when it begins to break down.

If the concept of the self as a whole provides unity of meaning, the concept of the world as a whole, consequently, provides continuity of meaning over time. It supports the conviction that things change yet fit meaningfully within an ongoing whole. This point does not mean, of course, that men and women who are able to live out of these visions no longer struggle or meet tragedy. It means rather that the tragic is qualified, because it is placed within a meaningful whole. As Dewey puts it, "Even in the midst of conflict, struggle and defeat a consciousness is possible of the enduring and comprehending whole."[40] This sense of the continuity of meaning, in particular, not only gives men and women a meaningful world but also signifies the hope that is the beacon of the religious life.

---

[39]Dewey, *Human Nature and Conduct*, 302.
[40]Ibid., 301.

Community, Communication, and the Problem of Religious Pluralism

We have been discussing the concepts of the self and the world as wholes. When human life functions religiously, it is in terms of imaginative wholes of this sort. Community is vital to the development of both of these concepts of self and world. I have argued, for example, that the concept of the world is best understood as the imaginative extension of community, for what is needed is a vision of the world as supportive of the self's ideals, and community represents a concrete environment in which this is the case. On the other hand, community also makes possible the development of inclusive ideals, since it represents bonds of trust and loyalty that sustain members of a community in the midst of conflict or dissension and encourages the development of new, more inclusive normative ideals that are shared but that also function to unify the self.

The functions of life that Dewey calls religious, as a result, are intimately connected with community, at once presupposing and reconstituting it. In fact, it is possible to claim that men and women, according to Dewey, find the wholeness that marks their deepest fulfillment in the community of shared ideals and cooperative behavior. Dewey argues this point with respect to communication, the means and end of community. "Of all affairs," he writes, "communication is the most wonderful."[41] The significance of this point lies in his further claim that communication is "uniquely instrumental and uniquely final,"[42] at once fructifying means and consummatory end. It functions as unique means in at least two interdependent ways. First, as Dewey puts it, communication is "the only means that makes life rich and varied in meanings."[43] As we have seen, things take on meaning in communication, since this is the process in and through which we learn how to respond to and use things as means for ends. This argument makes communication the means, as it were, for discovering means for ends; it is, as Dewey notes, "the tool of tools,. . . the cherishing mother of all significance."[44] Second, and more importantly, communication is uniquely instrumental for establishing community. As we have seen, communication *is* cooperative behavior, the

---

[41]Dewey, *Experience and Nature*, 166.
[42]Ibid., 204; see also 183–84, 202.
[43]Ibid., 205.
[44]Ibid., 186.

sharing of purposes—doing things together for common ends in such a way that the activity of each supports and reinforces the activity of others. This holding and pursuing of common purposes and ideals constitutes community, and the specific purposes and ideals held in common mark its identity. The unique finality of communication, however, lies in the fact that the establishment of meaning and the establishment of community are accomplished at the same time. We learn the meaning of things as we learn how to respond to them together with others for shared ends. In communication, consequently, we learn that things that lack meaning in their immediacy are capable of meaningful development in relation to human life. In particular, we learn that such things have the potential for working together in interdependence with human beings for consummatory ends enjoyed by the members of the community. Understanding and appreciation of this interdependent harmony—as actualized and as the consummatory potential of an indefinite range of things to the extent that they enter communication—makes communication final. In Dewey's words, communication

> finds in itself all the goods of its possible consequences. For there is no mode of action as fulfilling and as rewarding as is concerted consensus of action. It brings with it the sense of sharing and merging in a whole. . . , a sharing whereby meanings are enhanced, deepened and solidified in the sense of communion.[45]

Dewey is making an extraordinary claim: communication results in wholeness of meaning that exceeds all other modes of human activity in fulfillment. Life becomes a whole, he is suggesting, when men and women live together in community, sharing ideals and supporting one another in their activities. Indeed, it would seem possible to conclude that human life functions religiously, according to Dewey, when men and women communicate.

This assertion may seem an exaggeration. Much passes for communication, after all, which hardly results in the kind of wholeness Dewey ascribes to communication. Often, for example, the interactions in which we engage are routine "communications," ranging from greetings and superficial talk about the weather to the exchanges of information necessary for the maintenance of the household, industry, government, and so on. Often our "communications" are careless, impulsive, and simply

[45]Ibid., 184, 205.

destructive as we talk thoughtlessly or vent our anger and frustration upon one another. Neither routine nor capricious communication creates the wholeness of communion of which Dewey speaks. Lack of communion and community at just these points, however, mark the limits of communication, its failure and breakdown. That this failure occurs all the time does not so much prove Dewey's theory an exaggeration as it serves to underscore the claim that community is not a static but a dynamic, historical reality that continually requires transformation and adjustment of its normative interests. When community fails, new efforts need to be made to reestablish communication, to find new and more inclusive ways of sharing and being significantly with and in support of one another.

This discussion of community and communication helps us identify where the problematic character of religious pluralism lies: in the fact that the world consists of a plurality of communities, the normative interests of which are in significant ways unrelated and which therefore block the communication that is essential for life to function religiously. The difficulty of religious pluralism does not lie in the fact that there are a number of different communities in the world. The number of communities becomes a problem when the normative interests which govern those communities are exclusive and unrelated to one another in meaning and purpose. Again, there would be no problem if the members of different communities did not interact. The existence of a number of communities becomes a problem when their members interact and yet do not share interests, for this means that although they interact, their activities are not interdependent and supportive.

This problem can be understood in three ways. First, it is increasingly rare that anyone belongs to one comprehensive community. Most of us belong to many different communities that have different and often conflicting ideals. This results in a conflict of normative interests which divides the self. Second, it is evident that there are many communities in the world to which one does not belong but which are constituted by members with whom one is increasingly called upon to interact. Not only does the existence of those who are alien and other call into question the extensiveness of meanings about the world as a whole (the otherness refusing to be assimilated); more seriously, the difference in fundamental interests makes communication and the coordination of activities highly problematic. Finally, it is becoming the case for some people that at least some foreign communities—some alternative religious traditions, in particular—are coming to be seen as also having significant worth for human life, even though they are different and alien. The problem is that men and women in these circumstances want to communicate and share interests, but they are uncertain how to proceed, for the normative criteria upon which they proceed—those inclusive interests that give them orientation—are called into question by the appreciation of alternative, alien interests.

This can be called the threefold problem of religious pluralism. What is at stake, as we can see, is a pluralism of normative interests that are unrelated and therefore inhibit life from functioning religiously, from providing comprehensive meaning and orientation.[46] When interests that are unrelated are alien and unappreciated, the most common way men and women attempt to resolve the situation—if they do anything at all—is by dismissing the alien interests as irrelevant or seeking to change them through persuasion or coercion. The history of religious and political life is littered with examples of this behavior. The issue with which this book is concerned, however, is how to resolve tension in a situation where unrelated normative interests are appreciated. To the extent that interests of alternative communities are appreciated, of course, they are no longer simply alien, for the self comes to identify with them as its own. The tension among members of different traditional religious groups in this case, consequently, can be described as a conflict of interests as much internal as external.

Appreciation of alternative religious interests that are unrelated to the normative interests out of which men and women have been living constitutes a form of tragedy that is becoming increasingly pervasive. It arises as a radical change in environment—in particular, as those with whom one interacts come to include men and women from communities other than one's own. The result of the appreciation of alternative norms is deep uncertainty and doubt over the normative character of one's interests that have provided meaning and orientation in the past. This situation is different from most practical and intellectual problems, for when the norms that define the self and the world are in doubt, the very criteria we need to understand, think out, and develop new meanings are called into question. What is required, as a result, is the kind of transformation Dewey specifies as "adjustment." The question of how this transformation comes about is one of how to proceed in the context of religious pluralism. In other words, a methodology for thinking and living in this kind of context is needed. It is to the consideration of this matter, therefore, that I now turn.

---

[46]This lack of relation or communication among interests was described in chap. 3 as the compartmentalization of interests; see above, pp. 74–76.

6

PHILOSOPHY, METAPHYSICS, AND METHOD: TOWARD A THEOLOGICAL METHOD IN THE CONTEXT OF RELIGIOUS PLURALISM

At the end of the last chapter we saw that the problem of religious pluralism consists, among other things, of a conflict among comprehensive normative interests and that this conflict undermines the established norms out of which one lives and thinks, including those norms one would hope to use to think about this problem. I argued, furthermore, that this very peculiar problem calls for a new understanding of how to proceed in reflection, a method for thinking. The thesis of this chapter is that Dewey's theory of philosophical method in fact provides an adequate and significant tool for addressing this problem of religious pluralism. Indeed, I shall finally argue that it is a methodology that can be adopted by theologians as an appropriate *theological* methodology. When analyzed adequately, the concept of God, the central theological concept, can help sharpen and clarify what is important about Dewey's method in and for a context of competing plural interests. Unfortunately, Dewey's theory of philosophical method is not readily accessible. Indeed, his writings on the matter are plagued by obscure language and seeming contradiction. It is appropriate, therefore, not to begin the discussion with Dewey's methodology as such but with his more general interpretation of the nature and function of philosophy, using that as a context for subsequent reflection on method.

Over the course of his long career, Dewey wrote extensively and in various terms on this issue. It is neither possible nor necessary to cover everything he has had to say on the matter. What is important for our purposes is to develop that particular interpretation of the nature and function of philosophy most relevant for the problem of religious pluralism, namely, Dewey's notion of philosophy as the criticism of culture.

Philosophy as the Criticism of Culture and Its Relevance for the Problem of Religious Pluralism

It is helpful to consider Dewey's understanding of the nature and function of philosophical thinking by considering his criticism of alternative views. The view that is most important for our purposes, and the view Dewey himself seems eager to criticize each time he picks up the issue, is the idea that philosophy is the search for knowledge of ultimate being or reality.

It is hard to dispute that this had been the aim of many philosophers in history. The assumption has been that things are often deceptive and that the aim of philosophical thinking is to see through this deception in order to come to true knowledge of what they really are—to see through the seeming chaos, evil, or unreasonableness, for example, in order to understand the real character of reality, its order, goodness, rationality and so on.

This interpretation of the task of philosophy, Dewey argues, rests, among other things, upon what he calls the intellectualist fallacy. By this he means the assumption that "all subject matter, all nature, is, in principle, to be reduced and transformed till it is defined in terms identical with the characteristics presented by refined objects of science as such."[1]

---

[1]Dewey, *Experience and Nature*, 21. Dewey mentions here that this fallacy can also be understood by "the theory that all experiencing is a mode of knowing." Although most commentators discuss this expression of the fallacy, I do not find it as easily understandable. Dewey's claim is that most philosophers

The real traits of things, in short, are identified with traits that are known or knowable. When it is claimed that one seeks knowledge of the really real, of what is ultimately real in existence, this identification of the real with the knowable is *necessarily* presupposed. Dewey criticizes the assumption of this identification, in particular, when he criticizes the notion of philosophy under discussion.

He criticizes the intellectualist fallacy in two ways. First, he argues that the assumption it makes illegitimately strips nature of novel possibility.

> From the standpoint of knowledge, objects must be distinct; their traits must be explicit; the vague and unrevealed is a limitation. Hence whenever the habit of identifying reality with the object of knowledge as such prevails, the obscure and vague are explained away.[2]

In effect, this is to deny reality to the hidden potentiality in what is clear and distinct. Its reality, however, cannot be dismissed so easily. "Strain thought as far as we may," he argues, "and not all consequences can be

---

have equated the concept of experience with knowing. The difficulty with this, he argues, is the accompanying assumption that our interactions are with things as they really are only when we know them. This is not to deny alternative modes of interaction—affectionate, aesthetic, moral, humorous, tragic, and the like— but these are not taken seriously as interaction with things as they really are. At best, they are understood as subjective qualities that we project upon other things. Consequently, our interactions in these ways are not usually taken to be "experience" of these things. In effect, this is to reduce the reality of other things to the traits by which they are known.

It is helpful to note that throughout much of Dewey's later career he attempts to enlarge the philosophical meaning of the concept of experience. Among other things, what he means by this term is what we earlier identified as social or mental interaction, the emergence of an understood connection between a response to qualities and a consequent undergoing of further qualities, resulting in meaning that gives shape to expectation and purpose. Cognition, consequently, is a part of what Dewey takes to be "experience," but it is a phase within a larger context of aesthetic and affectional qualities. These latter qualitites, in fact, are what give meaning and purpose to knowing.

[2]Ibid., 20.

foreseen or made an express or known part of reflection and decision."[3] Inherent in clear and distinct objects of knowledge, *as part of their own reality*, is the vague potential for their unique and novel developments. Consequently, one seriously misunderstands reality when it is identified exclusively with distinct objects of knowledge.[4]

Secondly, this fallacy "ends in making knowledge. . . itself inexplicable."[5] When reality is identified with what is known and knowable, reality is at the same time denied to the large, compulsive, vague, concrete qualities that we suffer, enjoy and respond to. These things are not immediately known but are first "had," as Dewey puts it, felt in their qualitative immediacy. As we have seen, these are the things that matter to us, and it is for the sake of maintaining or avoiding them in further interaction that we then seek to understand them. This qualitative context of human life, consequently, forms the reason for our attempts to know, giving those attempts their meaning and purpose. It is quite true, of course, that we often go on to know (at least something about) the qualities, yet we come to know them not as concrete qualities but as they are connected in various ways with other qualities. Doing so requires selective abstraction from the concrete qualitative context of life. When we go on to identify these selective abstractions in an exclusive way with what is real, then we deny reality to the concrete qualitative context that gives those abstractions their reason to be, making knowledge itself inexplicable.

This second criticism shows that the intellectualist fallacy is in effect a denial of the relevance of context. It is the failure of philosophical thinking to attribute reality to the contextual conditions that give meaning and purpose to that thinking. According to Dewey, this has led to a full range of "pseudo" philosophical problems, including the so-called problem of epistemology.[6] It is not surprising, therefore, to find Dewey

---

[3]Ibid., 21.

[4]This matter can be put another way. What Dewey is claiming, in effect, is that we can never fully understand reality by the very nature of the case, for understanding necessarily involves the clear and distinct and this excludes the vague, novel possibilities hidden in what is clear and distinct. This is an important argument for the claim that all knowledge claims, including this one, are hypothetical, subject to discussion and revision.

[5]Ibid., 22.

[6]Ibid., 23–24. See Dewey, *Quest,* 21–24.

claiming at another point that "neglect of context is the greatest single disaster which philosophic thinking can incur."[7] Dewey's proposal is to turn the matter completely around by making context itself the subject matter of philosophical thinking. We have already seen how the concept of "context" figures in Dewey's philosophy. Not only does it form the central concept of his metaphysics, but it is also pivotal to his interpretation of thinking. Philosophical thinking, of course, is continuous with other forms of thinking. Like other modes of thought, it is prompted by and seeks the resolution of, tension within the contexts of life. Further, all modes of thinking have portions of the context of thought as their subject matter. What is distinctive about philosophical thinking, however, is that its subject matter constitutes a distinctive dimension of the context, namely, the broad, normative interests of culture.

In order to understand this point, we need to return to the claim that philosophy is not the search for knowledge of ultimate reality. This claim does not mean that philosophers should not reflect upon questions of ultimate reality. On the contrary, these are exceedingly important questions, and Dewey reflects upon them all the time. In doing so, however, he does not seek knowledge of what is the case with reality as such, even when he is doing what he identifies as metaphysics.[8] Rather,

---

[7]Dewey, "Context and Thought," 98.

[8]This is a controversial claim on a much debated topic and will be considered in some detail in the next section. Unfortunately, the way Dewey writes lends much confusion to what I understand him to be doing and he therefore misleads even some of his best interpreters. Dewey, for example, is not at all indirect in claiming that "nature is an affair *of* affairs" (*Experience and Nature*, 97) or that experience, in its primary integrity, "denotes," as he puts it, "no division between act and material, subject and object, but contains them in an unanalyzed totality" (p. 8). This kind of reifying language has led an interpreter as astute as Gouinlock to argue for Dewey's positions as if they were direct descriptions of what is the case with reality itself. In defending Dewey's position that there is an organic unity of subject and object in experience, for example, Gouinlock argues as follows (*John Dewey's Philosophy of Value*, 20): "First, experience as experience is found to be that way, and, second, the developments of modern natural science wholly support such a conclusion." I find these arguments troubling for several reasons, but the most pertinent one at this point is that it commits the intellectualist fallacy, for Gouinlock, in effect, is arguing that experience *is* what we *know* it to be. The fault of this misinterpretation, however, does

he seeks to understand the significance various presuppositions and claims about ultimate reality have for men and women—in particular, what they mean for conduct and what their consequences are in and for human life. This kind of reflection is important because one's view of reality or the nature of the world determines how one lives in the world:

> The more sure one is that the world which encompasses human life is of such and such a character (no matter what his definition), the more one is committed to try to direct the conduct of life, that of others as well as of himself, upon the basis of the character assigned to the world.[9]

It is Dewey's conviction that world views are an inherent feature in and of human cultures. They are not always explicit nor are they necessarily coherent. More often they are implicit in or suggested by the many interests shared in a culture. Dewey argues that it is the task of philosophy to reflect upon this tacit sense of the whole:

> There exists at any period a body of beliefs and of institutions and practices allied to them. In these beliefs there are implicit broad interpretations of life and the world. These interpretations have consequences, often profoundly important. . . . The beliefs and their associated practices express attitudes and responses. . . . They constitute, as it seems to me, the *immediate* primary material of philosophical reflection. The aim of the latter is to criticize this material, to clarify it, to organize it, to test its internal coherence, and to make explicit its consequences.[10]

This task is what Dewey means by philosophy as the criticism of culture. He wants to argue that in fact this interpretation of the matter accurately represents what has often gone on in philosophy. For once we see that talk of ultimate reality is actually talk of normative interests,

---

not lie entirely with Gouinlock, for the way Dewey writes has an almost irresistable capacity to deceive us into thinking that he is making stronger and more direct claims than what is warranted on the basis of his own program.

[9]Dewey, *Experience and Nature*, 413–14.
[10]Dewey, "Context and Thought," 106.

that it constitutes "a recommendation of certain types of value as normative in the direction of human conduct" rather than a reflection of what is as such, then we can see that "each philosophy is in effect, if not in avowed intent, an interpretation of man and nature on the basis of some program of comprehensive aims and policies."[11]

This step takes us to a second and related point needing discussion. When we see that philosophy has to do with normative interests of culture, then it follows that philosophy is not a knowing at all. Put more pointedly, philosophy is not after truth. "Truth," Dewey writes, "is a collection of truths; and these constituent truths are in the keeping of. . . science. As to truth, then, philosophy. . . is a recipient, not a donor."[12]

Dewey's claim is that truth is a species of meanings. "Meaning is wider in scope as well as more precious in value than is truth," he writes. "Truths are but one class of meanings, namely, those in which a claim to verifiability by their consequences is an intrinsic part of their meaning."[13] By restricting truth to meanings capable of verification, we can readily see that the issue of truth is irrelevant for a wide range of meanings that we study and enjoy. For example, Dewey writes,

> We do not inquire whether Greek civilization was true or false, but we are immensely concerned to penetrate its meaning. We may indeed ask for the truth of Shakespeare's *Hamlet* or Shelley's *Skylark*, but by truth we now signify something quite different from that of scientific statement and historical record.[14]

Dewey insists that this distinction is evident in the study of the history of philosophy as well: "a student prizes historic systems rather for the meanings and shades of meanings they have brought to light than for the store of ultimate truths they have ascertained."[15]

This last point provides an important clue for understanding Dewey's position. When we study philosophers in history, we do not in practice take their claims to be truth claims that need verification. Rarely, if ever, do we ask how we might verify Plato's forms, Hegel's *Geist* or

---

[11]Dewey, "Philosophy," 25.
[12]Dewey, *Experience and Nature*, 410.
[13]Dewey, "Philosophy and Civilization," 4, 5.
[14]Ibid., 5.
[15]Dewey, *Experience and Nature*, 411.

Whitehead's actual occasions. Rather, we examine the work of philosophers in relation to their cultures. What is important for us is not simply how the great philosophers help to illumine the cultures in which they worked but also how their construals of reality help us think about our own concepts of the world. What we prize, if you will, is the alternative way of putting together a picture of the whole, of integrating the meanings of culture in the construction of normative visions of reality. We prize these visions, in short, as creative and imaginative works of art that we not only admire but that continue to function as a means for us to think more creatively and artistically about our own culture.[16]

This raises an important question. If philosophical thinking is the imaginative construction of a vision of reality rather than the telling of the truth about reality, then what, if anything, makes it trustworthy or reliable? One may grant Dewey his point that the real importance of philosophy lies in its capacity to integrate meanings and direct conduct and yet argue that for just this reason the issue of truth *ought* to be relevant. After all, the importance of truth from Dewey's point of view does not lie in the correspondence of ideas to reality as such but in accurate anticipation of particular consequences of interaction with the environment.

This question is the issue of whether and how a philosophical vision is justified, and it calls for a more careful statement of the relation Dewey understands to exist between philosophy and truth. For one thing, established knowledge and truth are not entirely irrelevant to philosophical thinking. On the contrary, Dewey insists, "Philosophy is thinking what the known demands of us."[17] "Its business," as he puts it at another point, "is to accept and to utilize for a purpose the best available knowledge of its own time and place. And this purpose is criticism of beliefs, institutions, customs, policies with respect to their bearing upon good."[18]

---

[16]To my knowledge, Dewey never explicitly states that the doing of philosophy is artistic behavior, but everything he says about philsophy implies this. The following is especially telling: "In philosophy we are dealing with something comparable to the meaning of Athenian civilization or of a drama or a lyric. Significant history is lived in the imagination of man, and philosophy is a further excursion of the imagination into its own prior achievements" (see Dewey, "Philosophy and Civilization," 5).

[17]Dewey, *Democracy and Education*, 326.

[18]Dewey, *Experience and Nature*, 408.

Men and women have learned highly significant things about themselves and their environment. Among other things, they have learned a good deal about physical, biological, and cultural regularities. These regularities give an indication of what to expect from certain modes of interaction. Knowledge of these matters is exceedingly valuable in regard to the decision of what is important in life and how to live. As a result, it is also significant for considering how to organize and order the interests of culture. A crucial and highly influential piece of knowledge in Dewey's own philosophical thinking, for example, is his understanding that cultural interests that are taken to be important are often reified and absolutized and that one consequence of this is the rigidification and routinization of life that alternates with impulsive behavior that is often destructive and is sometimes expressed in the making of war. To be aware of this, as Dewey was, is to be critical of the tendency to reify interests. Such criticism opens up, as it did in Dewey's case, the possibility of viewing interests in an alternative way, a way more conducive to human well being.

Established knowledge, in short, makes it possible for us to criticize established meanings and interests. Yet this means that the function of truth in philosophical thought, as Dewey says, is "a negative one."[19] What he means is that the criticism of interests on the basis of what is known about them makes it possible for us to know what to exclude from further consideration in the thinking process. While this is important in and for philosophical thinking, it is "far from being identical with a positive test that demands that only what has been scientifically verifiable shall provide the entire content of philosophy."[20]

Dewey is walking a fine line. On the one hand, he claims that established knowledge has an important function in philosophical thinking, making it possible to criticize cultural interests. To this extent, philosophy relies heavily upon what has been verified. On the other hand, he does not see philosophy as a slave to knowledge. On the contrary, part of the function of philosophy is to criticize established patterns of knowledge along with other established interests. This is a positive, creative function consisting of an imaginative and speculative effort to go beyond what is already known in order to construct general novel hypoth-

---

[19]Dewey, "Philosophy and Civilization," 10.
[20]Ibid.

eses that organize those meanings into new patterns. Such ideas, Dewey writes,

> serve an indispensable purpose. They open new points of view; they liberate us from the bondage of habit which is always closing in on us, restricting our vision both of what is and of what the actual may become. They direct operations that reveal new truths and new possibilities. They enable us to escape from. . . provincial boundaries.[21]

It is helpful to see this positive function of philosophical reflection as the third level of abstraction in the reflective process. Dewey distinguishes between "gross, macroscopic, crude subject-matters in primary experience and the refined, derived objects of reflection."[22] The former consists of those common things of daily life that matter to us and to which we respond in various ways. Most of these objects have meanings of some sort, for we often have various ideas of what to expect from them, but these meanings are usually restricted to what is of immediate interest. They are the result of what I called the first level of abstraction. Refined objects, on the other hand, are the result of a reflective process that I identified in the fourth chapter as the second level of abstraction. This kind of thinking, as we saw, consists of reflection upon the implications of our meanings when we abstract from their direct use and enjoyment and consider them merely as general potentials among general potentials. The advantage of this kind of reflection, we saw, is not only that it allows us to improve the instrumental character of our intercourse with things; it also allows us to create new aims or ends-in-view, for it allows us to bring together abstract general potentials of things and to envision their potential for each other, the way they are capable of functioning in relation to one another. Envisioning the mutual relevance of various abstract general potentials, we can see, constitutes a *system of thought*. Refined objects are the result of placing qualitative objects of interests within such a system, since when we take a qualitative particular as an example of one general possibility within this sort of system, we are able quickly to track its implications for a wide range of other possibilities. As Dewey puts it, qualitative particulars "get the meaning

---

[21]Dewey, *Quest*, 310. See also Dewey, *Logic*, 519.
[22]Dewey, *Experience and Nature*, 3–4.

contained in a whole system of related objects. . . and take on the import of the things they are now seen to be continuous with."[23]

It is not difficult to see that these kinds of systems have extensive normative worth within and for human life. By their organization of meanings, they make it possible for us to respond to immediate matters of interest better and more responsibly, for they enable us to compare different possible ways of responding to a qualitative particular and the consequences those responses are likely to produce. The sight of ice cream, for example, may remind us of its taste and prompt the desire to eat it, but our awareness of its potential consequences as understood within the system of biology and our comparison of these with the possible results of eating more nutritious foods, are likely to qualify the initial desire. In effect, therefore, a system of thought is a *method of criticism*, for it is capable of being used to criticize meanings and qualities that attract our immediate interest.

When Dewey calls philosophy "a criticism of criticisms,"[24] what he means is that reflection moves to a third level of abstraction by abstracting various implications from systems of abstract thought that stand in conflict and combining them in different ways until we are able to envision the possible relevance they may have for one another. This task is the highly speculative and imaginative effort of breaking out of the "bondage of habit" that Dewey attributes to the positive function of philosophy. It requires that thought goes beyond established comprehensive patterns of meaning by placing them in relation to one another within the creation of new and even more comprehensive patterns. This process can be understood as the imaginative construction of new normative interests that stand, at one and the same time, as the criticism of what were established norms—exposing their limitations—and as their creative transformation.

Philosophical thinking, consequently, is capable of transforming what have been taken to be reliable meanings, including reliable established knowledge, by setting them in a new theoretical context. This does not answer, of course, the question of whether the resulting general hypotheses, the new theories, can themselves be verified or what other means of justification may be at hand. What are we to make of these ideas? What significance do they have?

[23]Ibid., 5.
[24]Ibid., 398.

We can pursue the issue one step further by focusing upon the *function* of these ideas. That Dewey sometimes calls them "leading" or "guiding" hypotheses[25] tells us what he considers to be central. They have a double function, he argues: they (1) unify meanings and (2) direct operations or conduct.[26] These functions, as we have seen, are complementary. By their novel organization of meanings, they open up novel possibilities of meanings, of what to expect from certain doings, and therefore they "guide" or "lead" attention and conduct. In a significant sense, therefore, these meanings are about the world, about what to expect from various ways of interacting with the environment. What then does Dewey mean when he claims that they are "not themselves verified at the time or indeed verifiable in a strict positivistic sense"?[27] The fact is that they are so general and comprehensive that it is impossible to verify them in a complete way. Take Dewey's claim, for example, that the world consists of events in relation to other events. What would it be like to verify this? We can examine and verify the claim in regard to this or that aspect or part of the world but not in relation to the world as a whole, for as we noted before, we have no access to the whole. Here we need to keep clearly in mind that this and similar ideas are "guiding" hypotheses. What is most important about these concepts, what matters most to us, is their capacity to help us reflect creatively on a range of troubling issues in our lives, including the problems under discussion, religious pluralism and the nature of philosophy. The worth of the ideas, if I may put it this way, lies in their fruitfulness, in the novel possibilities they open up for addressing these matters and for guiding reflection and conduct to consequences that are consummatory. Justification of philosophical visions, therefore, lies at just this point, namely, in the extent to which they fulfill this function. "Thus there is here supplied," Dewey writes,

> a first-rate test of the value of any philosophy that is offered us: Does it end in conclusions which, when they are referred back to ordinary life-experiences and their predicaments, render them more

---

[25]See Dewey, "Philosophy," 33, 36; and idem, "Philosophy and Civilization," 11.

[26]Dewey, "Philosophy," 36.

[27]Ibid.

significant, more luminous to us, and make our dealings with them more fruitful?[28]

Obviously, this means that philosophical visions cannot be justified in advance or in any one or even several cases. Rather, they come to be increasingly justified as reliable visions over the course of time and only as they prove time and again to be rich resources for reflection and conduct.[29]

I have argued that the aim of philosophical thinking is to criticize cultural norms and to integrate them into a unified vision of the whole. This task is neither unimportant nor arbitrary, according to Dewey, but something that needs to be done time and again. We can understand the necessity of philosophical criticism in relation to what Dewey specifies as "the tendency of objects to seek rigid non-communicating compartments."[30] The isolation of interests is a natural development of the grow-

---

[28]Dewey, *Experience and Nature*, 7.

[29]Thomas Kuhn's notion of a scientific paradigm provides a helpful analogy at this point. By this notion he means "some accepted examples of actual scientiful practice. . . [which] provide models from which spring particular coherent traditions of scientific research." See Thomas Kuhn, *The Structure of Scientific Revolutions* (Chicago: University of Chicago Press, 1962; enlarged ed., 1970) 10. He argues that no scientific paradigm and its tradition can ever be completely verified or falsified, for "no theory ever solves all the puzzles with which it is confronted at a given time; nor are the solutions already achieved often perfect. On the contrary, it is just the incompleteness and imperfection of the existing data-theory fit that, at any time, define many of the puzzles that characterize normal science" (p. 146). Kuhn goes on to argue (p. 147), however, that scientists test paradigms only when alternatives emerge that seem to handle problems more adequately . This is not entirely clear, for he argues earlier that scientific traditions enter a state of crisis when seriously anomalous problems are compounded that cannot be resolved within the existing paradigm tradition. Indeed, he seems to suggest that new theories are sought precisely because of such a crisis (see pp. 82–85). This would seem to indicate that there is in fact a cumulative evaluation of a scientific tradition over time and over a spread of issues. It is this nuanced point that I find helpful. Like scientific traditions, philosophical views of the world are never subject to a conclusive test and yet over time they do seem capable of showing their worth or lack thereof by their ability to help men and women to understand and to respond meaningfully to the pressing cultural problems of their time.

[30]Dewey, *Experience and Nature*, 409.

ing complexification of culture that increasingly requires the division of labor and the specialization of institutions and professional disciplines. The interests of culture are developed without reference to one another, and thus they lose their sense of mutual significance. As a result, the normative vision of a culture becomes multiple and often conflicting. This conflict within cultures of different worlds, if you will, of different normative purposes and ideals, makes philosophy necessary. "Philosophic thinking," as Dewey puts it, "has for its differentia the fact that the uncertainties with which it deals are found in widespread social conditions and aims, consisting in a conflict of organized interests and institutional claims."[31]

This kind of problem is the same sort as that which we have identified as the problem of religious pluralism, the only difference being that the conflict of normative interests in the latter case is a result of a convergence of cultures rather than a diversification from within. The result, however, is the same: a lack of communication, community of purpose, and cooperation in conduct. Necessary in both cases, consequently, is "a generalized medium of intercommunication, of mutual criticism through all-around translation from one separated region of experience into another."[32] In other words, what is needed is to envision the meanings that conflicting normative interests are capable of having for one another, so that the pursuit of one interest would reinforce—and would be understood to reinforce—the pursuit and realization of the others.

Philosophical thinking is specifically meant to address this need. Here, therefore, we can begin to see the relevance of Dewey's interpretation of philosophy for the problem of religious pluralism. This is not, of course, to argue that Dewey's interpretation of philosophy is adequate for our problem. The problem that we have already considered to some extent but need to address in more detail is the problem of how to proceed when the most comprehensive norms out of which we think and act are called into question by the fact that they stand in conflict. This is the question of method, or of how to proceed in reflection. My contention is that the adequacy of Dewey's interpretation of philosophical thinking for the problem of religious pluralism lies in his capacity to address this issue of method in a significant way.

---

[31]Dewey, *Democracy and Education*, 331.
[32]Dewey, *Experience and Nature*, 410.

Philosophical Method and Metaphysics

Unfortunately, Dewey is not clear in his writings on the issue of philosophical method. The first chapter of *Experience and Nature*, his major effort to address this issue, is written in such obscure language and in such a confusing way that the criticism it engendered forced Dewey to rewrite it—not entirely for the better. At the very center of this piece lies the argument for what he calls the continuity of nature and experience. He claims that experience is capable of knowing nature, and he presents this point as though it were the linchpin of philosophical method. Unfortunately, in this text Dewey never clarifies what he means by "experience." He writes as though it were something simply there—our experience, as such—that his concept now correctly denotes. If this is what he is doing, there would be serious inconsistencies in his work. For one thing, he would contradict his own argument in that chapter that thinking and its results function by selective abstraction out of the full concreteness of "experience." The force of this argument, as we have seen, is that claims are misunderstood when taken to be of reality as such. Yet in order to make this claim Dewey's argument seems to pre-suppose a correct understanding of reality as such—of what the concrete is, namely, experience in its subject-object integration. Second, at the end of *Experience and Nature*, as we have also seen, Dewey argues that philosophical criticism does not seek truth but meaning in a wider sense, yet in the first chapter he argues that experience, as philosophical method, seeks knowledge of nature in a way similar to that of science:

> the very meaning and purport of empirical method is that things are to be studied on their own account, so as to find out what is re-vealed when they are experienced. The traits possessed by the sub-ject-matters of experience are as genuine as the characteristics of sun and electron. They are *found*, experienced. . . . [T]he theory of empirical method in philosophy does for experienced subject-matter on a liberal scale what it does for special sciences on a technical scale.[33]

If this is not in fact a contradiction, it is at least confusing when placed beside Dewey's later claims about truth.

[33]Ibid., 2.

In his widely read article, "Dewey's Metaphysics,"[34] Richard Rorty discusses similar problems in Dewey's thought. He argues that Dewey has two distinct and contradictory interpretations of the task of philosophy and how to go about it. The first is Dewey's notion of philosophy as the criticism of culture. Like Hegel, Rorty argues, Dewey sees philosophy in a thoroughly historical way as the criticism of ideas in terms of their historical and cultural significance. Its aim is to resolve problems that "philosophical" ideas occasion in contemporary culture by examining the effects of those ideas on culture and by sketching a vision of "culture that would not continually give rise to new versions of the old problems."[35] Yet "never quite content to think of himself as a kibitzer or a therapist or an intellectual historian," Rorty writes, Dewey had another understanding of philosophy that would allow him "to do something serious, systematic, important, and constructive."[36] This second interpretation he called metaphysics, which he took to be the description of the generic traits of existence and different in method, as Rorty puts it, "'no whit' from that employed by the laboratory scientist."[37] Rorty notes that Dewey proceeds in this task by turning to experience to describe it in a nondualistic way, but this is in effect, he claims, a "return to *die Sache selbst*," a move in which Dewey takes "what he himself said about experience. . . [to be] what experience itself looked like."[38] The contradiction in holding these two interpretations of philosophy, Rorty argues, can be summed up best

> by saying that no man can serve both Locke and Hegel. Nobody can claim to offer an "empirical" account of something called "the inclusive integrity of 'experience,'" nor take this "integrated unity as the starting point for philosophic thought," if he also agrees with Hegel that the starting point of philosophic thought is bound to be the dialectical situation in which one finds oneself caught in one's own historical period—the problems of the men of one's time.[39]

---

[34]Richard Rorty, "Dewey's Metaphysics," 72–89.
[35]Ibid., 86; see 81, 87.
[36]Ibid., 73.
[37]Ibid.
[38]Ibid., 80, 79.
[39]Ibid., 81.

My intention is not to defend Rorty's interpretation of Dewey. I think it misleading, however, to dismiss his interpretation, as some of Dewey's best interpreters have, on the assumption that Dewey is perfectly clear and consistent on these matters and that the only problem that exists is Rorty's interpretation.[40] In point of fact, Dewey's discussion of method in the first chapter of *Experience and Nature* is confusing, and we need to admit this. The value of Rorty's essay, for our purposes, is that it helps us to recognize this fact.

The question we need to ask, however, is what we are to make of this confusion. The first thing to be said, I think, is that the kind of issues Dewey is addressing are matters about which we cannot be entirely clear. These are issues, I submit, that lie along what Paul Van Buren has called "the edges of language."[41] When we speak about these matters, this is to say, we speak in a place where the rules that regulate our speaking are neither sharp nor clear, since what we are talking about at this point is the reconstruction and transformation of the very norms out of which we are speaking. By the very nature of the case, therefore, talk about these matters falls somewhere between sense and nonsense. It should not be surprising, therefore, that Dewey's thought is not clear on these issues.

Once we see this point, it is possible to approach Dewey's methodology in a fresh way. In particular, it is possible to step back and ask the more general question about what is going on in his discussion of method. My proposal is that Dewey's discussion of method, as it is developed in *Experience and Nature*, is coordinated with an attempt to work toward a new understanding of metaphysics that will allow him to address the problem of philosophical method in a new and more adequate way.

---

[40]See Alexander, *John Dewey's Theory of Art*, 67, 87; Boisvert, *Dewey's Metaphysics*, 3–5, 192–201; and Sleeper, *The Necessity of Pragmatism*, 107–9. Interestingly enough, Sleeper argues (p. 108) that Dewey proposes a new understanding of and use for the term "metaphysics," and that this is what "Rorty has missed." While I agree that Dewey is working toward a new understanding of metaphysics, my point is that this is not at all clear in Dewey's texts; nor is it clear why he should want to work toward such a metaphysics. It is not mere happenstance that Rorty and numerous other commentators have been deeply puzzled over Dewey's intention in *Experience and Nature*.

[41]Van Buren, *The Edges of Language*, 78–114.

The Need for a New Understanding of Metaphysics

The first thing to note is Dewey's recognition of the dependence of philosophical method upon metaphysics. The first chapter of *Experience and Nature*, which he announces as a discussion of "the method of empirical naturalism,"[42] for example, is not a mere proposal of a philosophical methodology that will be applied to metaphysical questions in later chapters. Rather, it is a consideration of a variety of "metaphysical" issues that are examined in greater detail in later chapters, issues such as the subject-object relation, the function of qualities in thought, the nature, function, and development of meanings, knowledge as a means of intelligent conduct, and the function of contexts and particularly human interest in the thinking process. When, however, Dewey turns in a more formal way to metaphysical questions in subsequent chapters, we do not find what we expect, a detached and merely abstract consideration of the structure of reality. On the contrary, we find a deliberate attempt to sketch a picture of the aspects of the context of human life that give thinking direction and meaning.

The dependence of method upon metaphysics should not be surprising, for method is a *way* of doing things, a path, and unless it is followed blindly and routinely, something about the contextual world in which the path is taken is necessarily presupposed. Such presuppositions focus attention and shape expectation and therefore lead thinking in a particular direction. Consequently, in order to formulate a theory of method, a methodology, it is important to consider metaphysics as a way of making explicit those presuppositions that are at stake in the way philosophical thinking proceeds. It is not unreasonable to suggest, therefore, that *the purpose* of Dewey's metaphysical reflection in *Experience and Nature* is to illumine philosophical method—the way of proceeding that Dewey calls the criticism of culture. Dewey in fact makes this point when he calls metaphysics the "ground-map of the province of criticism,"[43] and the "preliminary outline of the field of criticism, whose chief import is to afford understanding of the necessity and nature of the office of intelligence."[44]

This point is not as simple as it sounds, for what prompts and focuses the discussion of philosophical method is a conflict among the compre-

---

[42]Dewey, *Experience and Nature*, ix.

[43]Ibid., 413.

[44]Ibid., 422.

hensive normative interests of a culture that calls those norms into question, including those norms we use to think about problems. As a result, established metaphysics and established method are called into question at the same time. Metaphysics, consequently, cannot be seen as a neutral and trustworthy framework upon which we can simply rely in order to understand how to proceed philosophically when doing so becomes confusing. Unfortunately, Dewey never explicitly states this serious problem, but his thinking seems to form a direct response to it. An adequate response to this problem, I suggest, would not be the rejection of metaphysics altogether because particular positions prove unreliable, for we still require some metaphysical vision in order to proceed. Nor would it be helpful to insist that any one particular vision is the true one and that conflict among visions exists only because other false ones are around, for this approach does not account for the fact that metaphysical visions have always changed and that the problem of method is addressed because the metaphysical norms out of which one thinks are now called into question. Rather, in order to address this problem it is necessary to develop a metaphysics that can account for the occasional unreliability and historical change of metaphysics and is itself therefore inherently open to criticism and transformation. Indeed the best kind of metaphysics would be one that understands the occasional unreliability of metaphysics as a positive moment in human life, as an opportunity for the growth of metaphysical vision, for this would help give direction to philosophical thinking in the context of the problem we are addressing. This is the kind of metaphysics that Dewey seeks to develop.

At this point Dewey's turn to "experience" takes on significance. It is best understood not as a turn toward a neutral metaphysics as Rorty thought, an effort to capture *die Sache selbst*, but as a turn toward a new understanding of metaphysics, an anthropological and historical interpretation. This metaphysics views all thinking, including metaphysical thinking, as historical, that is, from a human point of view, as a human doing for human purposes within particular historical contexts. This point of view, for Dewey, at least, is based upon earlier anthropological inquiry, particularly the attempt to understand the actual way men and women think as well as the function that meanings, and thinking with and about meanings, have within the wider horizons of human life. We have already examined these matters in some detail. Among other things, we have seen how various normative interests emerge and diversify in human culture and how thinking is the attempt to adjust interests in light of their conflict. When he turns to "experience," Dewey takes up these matters again and tries to show their significance for metaphysics and philosophical method. In order to understand what kind of significance Dewey finds, it is helpful to examine this issue of "experience" by considering again the importance of context in and for thinking. "The significance of 'experience' for philosophic method," Dewey writes, "is, after all, but the acknowledgement of the indispensability of context in thinking when that recognition is carried to its full term."[45]

Metaphysics from a Historicist Perspective

We begin by looking more closely at the subject matter and task of metaphysics. I have suggested that metaphysics is an attempt to articulate our presuppositions about our context that are important in the way thinking proceeds. This interpretation is not immediately evident in many of the claims which Dewey makes in *Experience and Nature*. He proposes, for example, that metaphysics is a "detection and description of the generic traits of existence,"[46] or, alternatively, "a statement of the generic traits manifested by existences of all kinds."[47] The subject matter of metaphysics is described variously as the "ineluctable traits of natural existence," the "common traits of all existence," and "the general traits of nature."[48] One gets the impression that the aim of metaphysics is to describe or denote the common denominator of all things that exist by listing what they have in common, such as precariousness, stability, qualities, ends, histories, and process. If this were what metaphysics really concerns, it would be difficult not to agree with Rorty that conclusions at this level of generality are trivial at best.[49]

An earlier essay, "The Subject Matter of Metaphysical Inquiry" (1915) suggests another interpretation of metaphysics.[50] Here Dewey writes that metaphysics is the attempt to discern those "ultimate, that is, irreducible, traits of the very existences with which scientific reflection is concerned."[51] Like the task Kant sets for himself in the First Critique, for Dewey the task of metaphysics is to state the conditions of the possibil-

[45]Dewey, "Context and Thought," 108.
[46]Dewey, *Experience and Nature*, 54.
[47]Ibid., 412.
[48]Ibid., 413.
[49]Rorty, "Dewey's Metaphysics," 77.
[50]John Dewey, "The Subject Matter of Metaphysical Inquiry," 211–23.
[51]Ibid., 215.

ity of knowledge. Yet unlike Kant, these conditions are not logically necessary conditions and therefore a priori categories but rather the ultimate traits of things that men and women, as a matter of historical fact, do presuppose. This point is evident when Dewey distinguishes what he considers to be the proper task of metaphysics from two other possible tasks with which metaphysics has often been confused. The first is the attempt to discern the ultimate origin or first cause of things. Dewey argues that this is a seriously misleading enterprise. When things are taken *en masse*, such as life, death, sickness, evil or existence in general, the search for the ultimate origin for them is meaningless, since knowledge of origins is and can only be a relative and piecemeal affair consisting of knowledge of the specific causes of this particular effect (a disease, for example). These causes, however, are themselves effects of prior events: "in each case we may trace its history to an earlier state of things. But in each case, *its* history is what we trace, and the history always lands us at some state of things in the past, regarding which the same question can be asked."[52] The task of metaphysics, moreover, is not to be confused with a second task, the legitimate task of science, which is the attempt to understand the relative causes of things.[53] Indeed, metaphysics does not seek to understand the cause of things at all. As Dewey argues the point, metaphysics is not to be explanatory of any particular state of affairs, of what caused it in either a piecemeal or wholesale way. Rather, the task of metaphysics is to reflect upon what our talk about things implies about the kind of world or context in which we live. The theory of evolution, for example, prompts the metaphysical search not for something that caused evolution but for "the irreducible traits of a world in which at least some changes take on an evolutionary form. . . . [This is to] raise the question of the sort of world which *has* such an evolution, not the question of the sort of world which causes it."[54] This attempt to reflect upon the implications of our talk in fact constitutes an effort to discern the comprehensive presuppositions we make about existence.

---

[52]Ibid., 214. This argument can be pushed further. The metaphysical quest for ultimate causes is meaningless, I would suggest, because it represents arbitrary dualism. It presupposes a cause-effect relational continuum as a condition for knowledge while it seeks a cause that is unrelated to anything prior to or contemporary with that cause.

[53]Ibid., 213–15.

[54]Ibid., 213.

This interpretation of the task of metaphysics is more consistent with Dewey's claims in *Experience and Nature* that metaphysics seeks "the traits and characters that are sure to turn up in every universe of discourse," and "the traits [capable of being] discovered in every theme of discourse."[55] The point is that metaphysical reflection does not look out at nature as a scientist does but looks at human life, at what our conversation presupposes about things of the world and the kind of effect these presuppositions have in the way we think and talk.[56] This kind of examination, Dewey argues, is similar enough to "Aristotle's consideration of existence as existence" to receive "the sanction of the historical designation," metaphysics.[57] It is different, of course, in the sense that it is not an examination of existence as such but of what we presuppose about existence. This difference, however, makes Dewey's interpretation of metaphysics a historical one. As Dewey understands it, to think about our meanings is to think about the way we use them, about their effects and the circumstances of their use. It is to recognize, at least implicitly, that meanings, including metaphysical meanings, are not ahistorical but bound to the specific contexts of their use, and that meanings, therefore, not only come to be but develop in such contexts.

Key Metaphysical Ideas Inherent in the Use of Meanings within Historical Contexts

The significance of "contexts" warrants special note. Dewey's theory of metaphysics is historical because of his understanding that our mean-

---

[55]Dewey, *Experience and Nature*, 413.

[56]In *Theory and Valuation*, Dewey explicitly acknowledges the cultural significance of metaphysical positions. After claiming that the idea of metaphysical individualism joined with the metaphysical belief in a mentalistic realm undermines the possibility of criticizing tradition, he criticizes the positivists who dismiss these metaphysical ideas as not worthy of note on the grounds that metaphysical claims are simply meaningless: "the statement, sometimes made, that metaphysical sentences are 'meaningless' usually fails to take account of the fact that culturally speaking they are very far from being devoid of meaning, in the sense of having significant cultural effects. . . . Interpreted as symptoms or signs of actually existent conditions, they may be and usually are highly significant, and the most effective criticism of them is disclosure of the conditions of which they are evidential" (p. 64 n. 2).

[57]Dewey, "The Subject Matter of Metaphysical Inquiry," 215 n. 4.

ings have emerged as meanings within particular historical contexts. This view has a crucial metaphysical implication: that things develop meanings in the way men and women use them within particular contexts implies that the world—the contexts of human life—includes human life as a constitutive element, as contributing significantly, that is, to what the world is at any particular time. Our creation and use of meanings within contexts, consequently, presupposes that *an important connection exists between human life and its contexts* that makes meanings possible and significant. This presupposition in turn implies that the study of human meanings is not simply a study of human life but of the kind of connection between human life and its contexts that our use of meanings presupposes.[58]

Dewey's interpretation of this connection and its significance can be developed by considering two interrelated fallacies that result from the denial of the role of context in the process of thinking. Dewey addresses them in one of his most important essays, "Context and Thought." These fallacies, which he calls "the analytic fallacy" and "the fallacy of unlimited extension," represent the respective philosophical mistakes of empirical realism and idealism.

The analytic fallacy, according to Dewey, occurs whenever analysis results in a reification of what is discriminated, that is, whenever the constituents emphasized in analysis are taken to be concrete realities complete in themselves apart from their context.[59] This fallacy involves two misleading assumptions: first, that the discrete meanings that emerge in analysis correspond to what exists in nature itself, and second, that these meanings are simply given to experience and directly apprehended—a position taken with respect to sensations, for example, by Locke, Hume, and the logical positivists.[60] In his *Logic*, Dewey identifies these as-

---

[58]When Dewey claims that the task of metaphysics is the effort to describe the generic traits of nature or existence, he presupposes this connection which makes it possible to speak about things in and of the world in general. Again, this is not to be mistaken as the "neutral" task of describing the generic traits of things as such. Rather, it is the effort to imagine the kind of connections that pertain in the world and can be inferred from our meaningful use of language within historical contexts and in turn can be understood to make possible and support that use.

[59]Dewey, "Context and Thought," 93.

[60]Whitehead describes this same fallacy as the "fallacy of misplaced concreteness." See Albert North Whitehead, *Science and the Modern World* (New York: Free Press, 1925) 51–55, 58–59.

sumptions as inherent in the position of epistemolgical realism, which he criticizes for its failure to note two important things about the way the context of thought functions in the thinking process:

> (1) That qualities as. . . signifying are deliberately selected for the purpose of inquiry out of a complex that is directly had in experience; and (2) that the existence of the problematic situation to be resolved exercises control over the selective discrimination of relevant and effective evidential qualities as means.[61]

The act of thinking as we have seen, involves human choice, selective interest, as a constitutive part of an inclusive context. This interest results in the abstraction of some features of the context for the purpose of addressing the particular tension inherent in that context. What this means, Dewey claims, is that meaning "is not inherent but accrues to natural qualities in virtue of the special function they perform in inquiry."[62]

What is significant about this fallacy is that, in reifying meanings, it restricts the human imagination so that thinking is confined to the habits of the past. This feature can be seen in Dewey's discussion in *Experience and Nature* of a more general form of this fallacy that he identifies as the "fallacy of selective emphasis." He does not mean that selective abstraction is itself a fallacy. On the contrary, "selective emphasis, with accompanying omission and rejection, is the heart-beat of mental life."[63] When we think, we selectively emphasize things for a purpose, for the *value* they have within a context. The fallacy, however, arises when we "take that which is of chief value. . . at the time as *the* real."[64] It is helpful to see that we commit this fallacy all the time simply by identifying things by their most useful traits, calling them bottles or cars, for example, because we use them to bottle up liquids or to drive about. By doing this, however, it often becomes difficult to envision alternative ways of using or responding to these things, so that when we use up the liquid in a bottle or our car no longer works, we believe we have no further use for them and throw them away. In reifying the meanings of

---

[61]Dewey, *Logic,* 528.
[62]Ibid.
[63]Dewey, *Experience and Nature,* 25.
[64]Ibid.

things, taking them to be in reality simply what they mean for us within certain contexts, consequently, we severely restrict our capacity to imagine novel alternative possibilities for understanding and responding to them. Indeed it becomes difficult to imagine that there even are possible alternatives.

This fallacy is problematic enough when it comes to bottles and cars but it is even more harmful in relation to the comprehensive claims of philosophical and religious thought. By taking claims that were meaningful and useful in one historical situation as directly corresponding to reality itself, men and women become closed to possible alternative reconstructions that may be more meaningful within their present historical context. Alternatively, to state the positive side of the case, if we can see our claims as human meanings that do not directly correspond with reality itself but that we have developed for our purposes within particular contexts, our imagination becomes freed to criticize those meanings and to reconstruct and develop them in new and more meaningful ways. Certainly, this freedom of the imagination is one crucial condition for the transformation of established religious normative interests when those interests come into conflict.

There is significant danger, of course, in acknowledging the role of selective interest in the construction of philosophical and religious claims. Such claims, after all, may seem arbitrary, constructed according to human purpose and not about the world at all—"useful fictions," to use a phrase popular not long ago. Interestingly enough, Dewey addresses this problem of "subjectivism" by criticizing the second fallacy that results from neglecting the context of thought, the fallacy of unlimited extension or generalization. This represents the failure of men and women to see that generalizations are meanings made in and of a context. "When context is taken into account," Dewey writes, "it is seen that every generalization occurs under limiting conditions set by the contextual situation. When this fact is passed over or thrown out of court, a principle valid under specifiable conditions is perforce extended without limit."[65]

Dewey aims this kind of criticism at what he elsewhere identifies as idealism. He does not object to the notion that thinking has a constructively instrumental office. To this extent, he believes that the idealists are correct in their interpretation of thinking. What they ignore, however, is the one aspect of the realist position that Dewey appreciates,

[65]Dewey, "Context and Thought," 95.

namely, the notion that thinking, in order to be responsible, must be responsive to something beyond the self. When Dewey claims that idealism fails to understand that thinking actually is a history,[66] what he has in mind is that the work of thinking is not simply a construction—as an all-at-once occurrence—but an evaluation and therefore a reconstruction of meaning over time in relation to a context. To put the matter another way, all thinking involves judgment, criticism, discrimination of what is better in the way of meanings within a particular context. As we have seen, meanings, as they first occur, need to be weighed, and doing so is a developmental or historical process. Because they are meanings of particular circumstances, evaluation involves not simply examination of logical consistency but also careful consideration of the circumstances of use and a comparison with the possible consequences of different possible alternative meanings in and of a particular context. If an established meaning or a new idea is to have meaning or significance within a new situation, therefore, it must be weighed and reconstructed in relation to that context. The reconstruction of meaning which takes place, consequently, is contingent upon the specific events that constitute the given context. This is what Dewey means by the claim that the context constitutes the specific limitations that give thinking its relevance, plausibility, and worth. Thinking, in fact, becomes arbitrary at just that point when it is thought that this temporal or historical contingency can be avoided, namely, when the ideas of the subject, which are taken to reflect the truly real, are imposed and extended arbitrarily upon the world irrespective of what occurs in daily life.

The significance of recognizing this fallacy is that it encourages the criticism of established meanings as an opportunity for the growth of meanings and interests in life. That the meaning and usefulness of claims is contingent upon particular historical circumstances means that established meanings, including metaphysical meanings, have the status of hypotheses subject to further criticism. On the one hand, such contingency means that we seriously misunderstand our meanings when we take them as dogmatically absolute and final and simply extend them to new circumstances with the assumption of their reliability. To do so

---

[66]Dewey, *Experience and Nature*, 158. For Dewey's criticism of idealism, see also idem, *Quest*, 166–67; idem, *Logic*, 529–34. See Boisvert, *Dewey's Metaphysics*, 70–85, for a first-rate account of Dewey's discussion of idealism and realism and his alternative to these positions.

would mean that they would likely lose their capacity to provide under-standing and orientation in that new context. On the other hand, recog-nizing the contingency is not to dismiss the generalization of meanings altogether but to recognize that the generalization and extension of meanings from one context to the next has significance and worth if we are willing to criticize and reconstruct them with respect to their rel-evance to the new historical context. It does not mean, of course, that it is impossible to use established meanings without criticizing them. On the contrary, we rely upon a wide range of meanings in everything we do, and this usually seems to work well. Hence, there is often no need for criticism. Yet from time to time, our use of meanings involves us in conflicting and ambiguous circumstances. At such times it is important to examine and criticize the meanings involved. Recognition of the fal-lacy of unlimited extension fosters creative uncertainty about established meanings which opens us to such criticism, allowing us to take seriously the distinctive and novel elements of the present context and explore novel possibilities for the reconstruction and growth of established mean-ings and interests.

I suggested above that Dewey's investigation of meanings, as they function within contexts, has certain metaphysical implications about the sort of world in which we live that are important for understanding how our meanings—and also our thinking with and about our meanings—are significant. The most important implication is the one already mentioned, the notion that the world includes human life as a constitutive element. We can now say three other things about this connection between human life and the world of which it is a part. The first idea is the most general one; the following two qualify it in different ways.

First of all, Dewey's interpretation of meanings implies that the world yields to and supports human purposes. Our use of meanings, as Dewey understands it, presupposes human interests that selectively abstract parts of the context and use those abstractions as means for the fulfillment of the interests. That such use often involves changes in the world that satisfies our purposes implies that the world is capable of being used as a means for our ends and that it consequently is a productive and sus-taining source of our enjoyment. Dewey expresses this point metaphysi-cally by the principle of continuity between nature and human experi-ence.[67] He means that nature is not an alien and separate kind of being;

---

[67]See above, pp. 5–9.

rather, nature not only includes human life as its own product but also yields, from time to time, to the fulfillment of human dreams, aspirations, and ideals that give human life its purpose and meaning.

Second, Dewey's interpretation of meanings implies that the world is not simply the same thing as human life or experience, for while it often supports human interests it also, from time to time, stands over against them as a relativizing force. Meanings, we have seen, neither directly correspond to reality nor are they simply constructions of a subject. They are means, and their use as means often entails surprising consequences that prove the instruments unreliable, placing us in circumstances that we are unable to understand or respond to with our established store of meanings. The ecological problems that beset our lives today are some of the most conspicuous examples of the surprising consequences resulting from the indiscriminate way we use things as means to fulfill our purposes. In a similar way, the problem of religious pluralism is a surprising and unanticipated result of using established views of the world for understanding and orientation. Dewey expresses the metaphysical implications of this observation with the notion that nature is constituted by events in relation to other events, each with its own unique quality.[68] This notion reminds us of the irreducible and often unyielding and implacable forces of nature that qualify our capacity to use the world simply as a means to our ends. We have previously identified this idea of the relativizing side of the world as the mystery that characterizes the context of our lives. This idea has an important function in life, for it calls into question the certainty and finality of our claims, opening us to the possibility of criticizing and developing them in various ways.

Third, Dewey's interpretation of meanings implies that the world is rife with a plethora of unexplored possibilities for understanding and responding to matters of concern. As a hypothesis that has been selectively abstracted from the concrete qualitative context of life, a meaning represents a possible means or way for understanding and responding to that particular context, anticipating a particular result, and acting accordingly. That such a meaning does not directly correspond to the full reality of that context implies that there are alternative possible conceptions. Indeed, once one sees that the development and result of a context is in part a function of how one understands and responds to its initial

[68]We have examined this claim in some detail above, pp. 6–8; 53–59.

qualities—the meaning taken—and once one sees that an indeterminate number of responses are possible, then one can readily see that any context harbors an indeterminate array of unexplored possibilities. Dewey expresses this matter metaphysically by claiming that there are no fixed ends in nature; each event, rather, is capable of interacting with other events in an indeterminate number of ways.[69] This interpretation sees the world not simply as a relativizing force but as an occasion, in the context of relativization, for the reconstruction of meanings, for considering alternative, previously unexplored possibilities. This idea has a positive force and function in human life. Whereas the idea of the world as a relativizing power restricts our pretentions toward dogmatism, the idea of pluralistic possibilities of the world draws us out with the hope and promise of fulfillment, encouraging imaginative speculation. This represents the other side of the meaning of the world, as Dewey understands it. It imbues our understanding of the mystery of the world with a humanizing quality. This perspective allows us to see the conflict and confusion of normative interests in human life not simply as a failure of meanings but as an opportunity for their growth.

Several important things need to be said about these and other metaphysical meanings that follow from our discussion. First, like other meanings, they do not correspond directly to concrete realities, but neither are they simply constructions of a subject. Rather, they are best understood as imaginative hypotheses, as selective abstractions from the multiplicity of inclusive historical contexts made for the purpose of better orientation for philosophical thinking. They are ideas that have meaning and significance, therefore, to the extent that they fulfill this purpose. To the extent that they fall short, they are subject to criticism and development. Second, these ideas constitute a view of the world that can account for itself. Among other things, it is one in which meanings are understood to emerge in the thinking process for the purpose of understanding and direction within particular historical contexts. This view, as a set of meanings, is no exception; in particular, we have tried to show that it has emerged as a result of an effort to find understanding and direction for philosophical reflection when established norms for guiding reflection become confused and confusing. Finally, this view is also able

[69]See above, pp. 60–64.

to account for other views. What is valuable about this particular view, however, is that it does not dismiss alternative views as flatly wrong or simply mistaken but takes them seriously as views that have also emerged in particular historical contexts and have provided meaning within those contexts. The presumption toward alternative views, moreover, is in favor of their continued worth as means for understanding and orientation, although they are now seen as hypotheses that may require development and transformation so that they are able to orient life in the present context more adequately. This concern for their development is concern for their growth, not their replacement.

This interest in growth, including the growth of world views, is an integral element of Dewey's historical perspective of the world, constituting its central normative interest, as we saw in chapter three. What is significant about it is its self-correcting character which conditions interest in its own growth. This feature allows one to be prepared, and indeed eager, to learn from those who hold alternative views. Consequently, the normative interest in growth is part of a view of the world that sees value in mutual criticism and in the alternatives that those with different interests provide.

This perspective is exceedingly important for addressing the problem of religious pluralism. It makes it possible to view this problem as an opportunity for mutual growth. In particular, it allows those with different views to view each other not merely as different or other but as mutual resources for the enhancement of meaning in life that can be shared and enjoyed by all. This perspective does not solve the problem of religious pluralism, to be sure, but it does provide the kind of context in which discussion of, and reflection upon, this problem can be creative and mutually beneficial.

The Significance of Dewey's Metaphysics for Philosophical Method

I have argued in the previous section that *Experience and Nature* represents a new understanding of the task and function of metaphysics, one I have called historical because it understands meanings, including metaphysical meanings, from a human point of view as having been developed within historical contexts for human purposes. The task of metaphysics, we have seen, is to state the conditions for the possibility of meanings and for thinking with and about meanings by examining the way meanings function within the contexts of human life and by sketching the sort of world ("the generic traits of existence" as Dewey often puts it) presupposed.[70] Doing so is not an arbitrary task, as Dewey understands it, an entertaining diversion for intellectuals who have nothing better to do. On the contrary, its purpose and function is to give orientation to philosophical reflection when the established norms that have guided such reflection in the past become confused and confusing.

The discussion in this section, consequently, has been more than a discussion of metaphysics; rather, it has been about the relationship between philosophical method and metaphysics. My claim has been that Dewey's historical metaphysics provides significant orientation for philosophical reflection when the norms out of which one reflects are called into question. At this point it is possible to state three important ways in which this is the case. First, Dewey's metaphysics provides a starting point for philosophical reflection. We have seen that meanings, includ-

[70]It may be important at this point to clarify the relation between metaphysics and philosophy as the criticism of culture. Dewey tends to draw a rather sharp distinction. Whereas philosophy as criticism is concerned with value and the judgment and reconstruction of value, metaphysics aims at "analysis and definition. . . [of] the traits and characters that are sure to turn up in every universe of discourse" (Dewey, *Experience and Nature*, 413). Explicit statement of these traits makes metaphysics the "ground-map of the province of criticism" (p. 413). The distinction Dewey makes, consequently, appears to be a difference of kind. Metaphysics is depicted as a neutral, analytical enterprise that functions as the foundation for judgment of value. I have tried to argue, however, that this understanding of metaphysics is a misleading aspect of Dewey's writing and illustrates some of the confusion of his thinking on these exceedingly difficult matters. It would be more appropriate, I suggest, to distinguish between metaphysics and philosophy as the criticism of culture as a difference of degree rather than kind, by arguing, as I have, that metaphysics is judgment upon and reconstruction of established normative meanings of the world; this makes it an instance of the criticism of culture. It is clear throughout Dewey's text on metaphysics, for example, that he is engaged in the criticism and reconstruction of established metaphysical meanings, not in an attempt simply to denote the generic traits of existence as such. In what sense, then, can it be said that metaphysics is the ground-map for criticism? My suggestion is that metaphysics is the aspect of the criticism of culture that is most fully *self*-critical, constituting the examination of its own presuppositions. All criticism, of course, is self-critical, but metaphysics is the kind of thinking that looks at the possibility of criticism as an enterprise and at what this means for its continued possibility and direction. This is why I take metaphysics to be closely connected to philosophical methodology.

ing comprehensive normative meanings, emerge in history as means for human purposes. This means, among other things, that meanings are neither fixed absolutes nor simply arbitrary; they have their meaning in the way they are used within particular contexts. As contexts shift and purposes change, therefore, the emergence of conflict among comprehensive normative interests and meanings is something to be expected. The previous discussion of metaphysics allows us to see this conflict as a starting point for philosophical reflection. It is a starting point not just because established normative interests conflict, for this kind of conflict has often been taken to mean other things, such as the need to assert one interest as the truth or as the right one, not as an occasion for reflection. Rather, it is Dewey's metaphysical notion that a range of novel potentialities are inherent in any tensive context and that they can be discovered and used for the transformation of interests that makes this conflict the starting point for philosophical reflection, since it allows men and women to see that this conflict is not the end of the matter but forms an opportunity for the growth of interests in and through the reflective process.

Second, Dewey's historical metaphysics also provides direction for philosophical reflection. In particular, it provides an intellectual context that gives meaning to the aim of philosophical reflection. At the end of his chapter on philosophical method in *Experience and Nature*, Dewey writes that the serious problem of most other philosophies is that they "have denied that common experience is capable of developing from within itself methods which will secure direction for itself and will create inherent standards of judgment and value."[71] In attempting to provide an alternative to this way of viewing things, Dewey needs to do more than show how it is possible for new standards of judgment and value to emerge in the midst of the breakdown of established standards. We have seen how he understands this to occur for many levels of meanings, including the philosophical criticism of culture. The latter, that is of particular interest, is the effort to explore the implications of normative systems of thought that stand in conflict and to speculate imaginatively about the possible relevance they may have for one another. The aim of speculation, we have seen, is to construct more comprehensive normative patterns of meaning which, in turn, reconstruct and transform established normative systems of thought so that they are now

[71]Dewey, *Experience and Nature*, 38.

understood to be mutually supportive and to reinforce one another. This aim, however, would be meaningless in a world understood to consist of mere flux or static substances or to be ruled by fixed absolutes. How one views the world makes a considerable difference for how one understands the origins, nature, and function of norms. It is to metaphysics to which Dewey must turn, consequently, in order to provide an intellectual context to give meaning to his interpretation of philosophical reasoning.

The most crucial aspect of Dewey's metaphysics for this purpose is his understanding of the emergence and evolution of order within tensive contexts in which established order has been disrupted. As we saw in chapters two and three, order or form in nature is constituted by the way events sustain each other in their activities.[72] Because order is the order of change, it is subject to change itself, to a disruption in the way events have interacted. Order, of course, can break down altogether, but it can also increase or develop. It develops, as we saw, when events of a context become coordinated in a new and more complex form of interdependence, releasing novel potentialities that enhance the functioning of each event of that context. This is the metaphysical meaning, if you will, for what it means for things to develop or grow. It provides significance for the emergence of standards of judgment and value as soon as we connect it with Dewey's interpretation of meanings which presupposes the continuity of nature and human life. Meanings, as we have seen on numerous occasions, are meanings of forms of change, of the conditions and consequences of change, but they function as meanings in the way we use them to anticipate various consequences and to respond knowingly and in ways that seem best. The emergence of meanings in human life, consequently, constitutes the emergence of standards of judgment and value (of what seems best) which are in effect more complex forms of the way nature functions, taking up and utilizing less complex forms.

I am arguing that Dewey's metaphysics provides the intellectual context that gives meaning and direction to the aim of philosophical criticism. As we have seen, the aim is the development of comprehensive normative interests that constitute the transformation of established and conflicting interests. Dewey's metaphysics shows the continuity between this aim and the functions of other types of order and their development in nature; it therefore makes the aim understandable and meaningful.

---

[72]See above, pp. 7–9; 58–61.

More importantly, his metaphysics shows why this aim at the growth of interests is important and therefore why it is normative in a context in which comprehensive normative interests come into conflict. In particular, the reconstruction of normative interests, if successful, makes possible the development of forms of human interaction toward fuller cooperation in which the activities of each sustain and enhance the activities of others. As we have seen, this process increases unity and continuity in human experience and makes conduct art.

Dewey's historical metaphysical perspective provides orientation for philosophical reflection in a third way, for it shows the latter to be a cooperative and ongoing enterprise. The key lies in the understanding that growth is finally not in our control. If growth is to occur, it is something in which we can only participate in cooperation with others. That we do not have final mastery over this matter is to recognize, again, the mystery of the world in which we live. I have argued that although Dewey rarely uses the word "mystery," "mystery" in fact connotes a metaphysical claim that Dewey makes about the world. Again, it is most evident in the tragic circumstances of life. In spite of our best efforts to reflect upon, strive for, and preserve our aims and purposes, including our aim at growth, we find that we are often subject to frustrating powers beyond ourselves that we cannot simply control. To be sure, from time to time we are able to achieve our purposes, but the result is not our own doing in the sense that we did not have complete control over the matter. At most, we can say, there existed a fortuitous combination of circumstances in which we participated and to which we added a voice. At times, our voice may have been crucial and even decisive, making it appear as though we were in control. Yet when we see this as an event within a history of events, then we must also see it as something conditioned by a range of gratuitous past events over which we had little to say, as requiring the cooperation of many contemporary events upon which we must rely, and as subject to future changes that we cannot fully anticipate. Whatever control we may possess when we lend a decisive voice, consequently, is by no means comprehensive.[73]

---

[73]We should add that it is precisely when we emphasize our control over things in the midst of conflict that we are likely to lose our capacity to respond creatively to changes in our environment, to be willing to adjust to those changes, to search out novel mediating possibilities, and to listen to and cooperate with others in this search.

That we do not have full control over our lives does not mean, of course, that we must simply resign ourselves to the changes, tensions, and problems of life. To do so would be to give up thoughtful and intelligent response that we call "responsibility." What it means is that we cannot find intelligence simply within ourselves, in the isolation of the individual, but in that kind of interaction called "communication" and "cooperation." Philosophical reflection, Dewey writes, is "a free messenger of communication," "a liason [*sic*] officer, making reciprocally intelligible voices speaking provincial tongues, and thereby enlarging as well as rectifying the meanings with which they are charged."[74] The result of philosophical reflection is the transformation of interests that once stood as a conflict of voices speaking provincial tongues. Yet this result does not happen by magic or in an instant but emerges, if it emerges at all, as a result of the effort of various provincial tongues to communicate.

The point of importance is that Dewey's metaphysical understanding of the mystery of the world provides direction for philosophical reflection in the context of conflicting interests, for it helps us to see that the growth and transformation of interests will not occur simply by turning inward to consider the matter but by engaging in communication with those who hold alternative interests. This point should not be surprising. For one thing, philosophical reflection can proceed in its aim at the growth of conflicting interests only as it comes to a fuller, critical understanding of existing interests. Only as men and women increase their understanding of what those interests mean, of what their consequences in the lives of one another in fact are, is it possible for them to imagine their possible connections and transformation. This increase of understanding requires critical dialogue, a willingness to criticize and to be criticized and to explore possible alternatives together. Yet the significance of critical dialogue lies beyond this increase of understanding, for when men and women engage in dialogue, they are already communicating, since they are participating in a cooperative interaction held together by the shared purpose of making their provincial tongues reciprocally intelligible. This interaction provides the existential context that gives meaning to mutual criticism and the exploration of alternatives and

---

[74]Dewey, *Experience and Nature*, 410.

also allows men and women to work together, that is, to continue to cooperate in the shared effort to make the conflicting interests reciprocally intelligible and mutually supportive.

In other words, Dewey's metaphysics helps us to see that philosophical reflection not only aims at communication among conflicting normative interests, but also constitutes community in the making. Philosophy is not viewed as something done by disengaged scholars who want to understand the truth about reality or by refined intellectuals who are interested only in explaining away the problems with which traditional philosophy has grappled—"to kibitz," as Rorty might put it. Rather, philosophy is best understood as a social process of mutual criticism, a process that is the communication of partners aiming at deeper and more extensive communication. In practice, of course, philosophical reflection often occurs in a private study, in the writing of papers and dissertations and books. Yet if this work is to be communication that makes provincial tongues reciprocally intelligible, it needs to be a critical response to the criticisms of others and itself open to further criticism in ongoing dialogue. Moreover, philosophical reflection, like the world it presupposes, is not only an interactive exchange but something that is never finished once for all, something that requires continuous ongoing adjustment as contexts shift and purposes change.

The Problem of Religious Pluralism and Theological Method

The Adequacy of Dewey's Philosophical Method for the Problem

It is now possible to see the significance of Dewey's historical philosophical method for the problem of religious pluralism. This problem, as discussed in the previous chapter, can be described not only as a conflict among the comprehensive, normative interests of religious traditions but also as a lack of communication and community. Dewey's method provides orientation in the context of this kind of problem. First, it helps us see the problem as an opportunity for the growth of interests and therefore as a starting point for reflection. Second, it provides direction for reflection, clarifying what it means for interests to grow and why this is important. Finally, it encourages men and women from different religious traditions that now conflict to recognize their common aim and therefore to enter into communication as the cooperative means of reflection and as the condition for the development of a richer communication among the normative interests of the different traditions.

The problem of religious pluralism, as I mentioned before, is not an issue Dewey addresses specifically, but it is similar to other problems that he interprets as conflicts among normative cultural interests and understands to be the task of philosophical reflection to address. The discussion in the previous section has been an attempt to show how Dewey's historical perspective allows for a significant and adequate way to respond to these kinds of problems and therefore to the problem of religious pluralism as well.

It is important to add two points to forestall misinterpretation. First of all, it may appear as though I am suggesting that the mutual criticism of established religious interests is an easy thing to do. On the contrary, religious interests give human beings their world and provide them with the normative ideals on the basis of which they think and act. Religious interests, in short, make human beings who they are. Therefore, it is exceedingly difficult to take criticism of these interests seriously. Indeed, most men and women throughout most of history have taken religious interests as absolute, as the unquestioned and unquestionable foundation upon that they live. As a result, when conflict among the interests of different religious traditions has emerged in the past, the most frequent way of dealing with it has been to reject the alternatives as wrong or false or at least as less worthy than one's own. In other words, men and women have used their own interests as the norm for judging the alternatives. In principle, therefore, these interests have been closed to criticism.

If this were how everyone took their religious interests, the proposal in this volume would be meaningless. It has significance, I suggest, to the extent that the historical context constituting the relationship among people from different traditions has begun to change. In particular, there is something new or unique in the way at least some men and women are viewing the interests of alternative religious traditions. For these people, the alternatives are no longer taken to be simply alien. As long as they still see the alternatives not only as different than, but often as conflicting with, the religious interests that have been established in their own tradition, they have yet to understand the alternatives to be worthy of (other people's) serious consideration and loyalty. In short, some men and women have begun to appreciate the worth of some alternative religious interests. The effect of this, as we have seen, is to call the certainty, finality, and normativeness of their own established interests into question. When this question arises, it is no longer possible simply to live out of the established interests of their tradition. The vision of how they are to live, in fact, is no longer clear. It is not even clear how they are to think about the tension occasioned by the conflict among established religious interests.

The philosophical method offered in this volume is addressed to people who live with this particular problem. These are men and women who already suspect that their inherited religious interests are not absolute. More importantly, they are no longer interested simply in defending those interests but in finding some way to reconcile the conflict among the alternative interests. Consequently, the criticism of established interests, for such people, need not be seen as an attack upon what is taken as unquestionable; rather, it is quite possible to understand it as an important means for the reconciliation of conflict.

Second, it may seem that the proposal offered here is a call for some kind of syncretism or reduction of diversity to a unifying, single religion for all humanity, a religion held together by one comprehensive religious interest that does away with pluralism altogether. This is not what is intended. For one thing, I have defined human beings as distinct from other animals by their capacity for a greater number and diversity of interests. It should be evident, therefore, that pluralism of interests in human life, according to this perspective, is natural and inevitable. More significantly, it is possible to argue that such pluralism is healthy, for it makes human life rich and diverse and protects it from the dullness of mere routine.

There is, of course, a price to pay for this pluralism, for it means that as our interests diversify, they often come into conflict, and this requires their adjustment to one another. Adjustment, however, does not mean picking out the parts that are compatible and thus reducing the interests to a common denominator. Nor does it mean the creation of an entirely new third interest in which the diversity is eliminated altogether. To be sure, I have argued that the aim of philosophical reflection is to create a more comprehensive norm that takes up the conflicting norms and transforms them. This transformation is best understood, however, not as a reduction of the diversity but as an elimination of their conflict. The construction of a more comprehensive interest, in effect, is the construction of a more complex system of meanings in which established interests are developed so that they come to qualify, support, and reinforce one another. This means, for example, that Buddhists in dialogue with Christians do not have to become Christian or something in between. They can remain Buddhists but Buddhists who now see their interests as qualified by and as supporting the central interests of their Christian friends. The same thing, of course, must be said of Christians as partners in the dialogue process.[75]

[75]For a helpful example of what I have in mind, see John B. Cobb, Jr., *Beyond Dialogue: Toward a Mutual Transformation of Christianity and Buddhism* (Philadelphia: Fortress, 1982). This book has been an important inspiration for my own position. Cobb's claim is that men and women from different religious traditions need to carry on dialogue, but they also must move beyond it in the effort to transform one another. The significance of this book lies in Cobb's effort (pp. 97–143) to propose what he believes the Christian and Buddhist traditions have to offer one another to their mutual benefit. In other words, he shows how some of their central interests might be developed and transformed. Of special interest is Cobb's discussion of the way his understanding of Whitehead has been transformed in dialogue with Buddhists (p. 146).

One difference between Cobb's position and my own is that he is much more willing to talk about the "universal truths" of different religious traditions. What allows him to do this is his presupposition that there is one multifaceted reality viewed in many different yet true ways; the contradictions that exist among perspectives, consequently, exist because the perspectives themselves are diverse. See David Ray Griffin and Thomas J.J. Altizer, eds., *John Cobb's Theology in Process* (Philadelphia: Westminster, 1977) 162–64. This means that people entering dialogue each come with their perspectival truths, and thus the task of dialogue is twofold: (1) to listen as carefully as one can to what others are saying in order to see things from their perspectives, and (2) to use those interpretations of reality to enlarge and transform their own truths so that what once appeared as contradictions are now seen as complementary contrasts. My own position understands the human relation to the world in a more participatory way, at least in this sense, that how men and women understand (or take) the world makes a difference (sometimes a considerable difference) in what the world is at the time, for how they understand the world determines how they live in or interact with the world. This means that I am more prepared to look at the function of ideas in life and to engage in dialogue as a way of acting in the world intended to open up novel ways of understanding the potential relevance that different functions of religious interests have for one another. What is at stake in religious dialogue, I think, is changing the world, building community, and fostering reconciliation. This is one reason I have placed so much emphasis on Dewey's understanding of the function of meanings and interests in life. When we look at and reflect upon our interests with respect to their function rather than simply their truth value, then we are in a better position to criticize and reconstruct them with respect to their worth for promoting human well-being in the world. I do not for one mo-

I have argued that philosophical method is best understood as a process of communication that aims at the creation of community. Community, of course, is held together by shared common interests. It is helpful to recall a point made earlier, that to share interests is not necessarily to have identical interests or to be equally committed to the same interests.[76] If this were the case, community would be oppressively monolithic and routine. That I like to listen to Beethoven, for example, does not mean that my oldest son has to listen to or even like listening to Beethoven in order to share my interest. It may be that he prefers Michael Jackson instead, not one of my favorites. Sharing an interest, rather, requires that we see means-end connections among our interests. For example, my son may see that my interest has led me to purchase a disc player and that this act has allowed him to play and enjoy his Michael Jackson recordings. More significantly, he may come to understand Beethoven's work as contributing in various ways—culturally, economically, technically—to what Michael Jackson is doing today. I, on the other hand, may see my son's interest in Michael Jackson as contributing to the development of an independent and creative character that will eventually allow my son to do the same kind of thing as Beethoven did, namely, to question, protest, and reconstruct the established social norms of his generation—although, perhaps, on a more modest scale. When we are able to see these and other kinds of means-end connections among our divergent interests, our appreciation of the interests of one another is increased. We begin to take interest in them, and thus to share them as integral elements of our interest systems. Clearly, this does not mean that our own interests are reduced to the interests of others or replaced by some third interest. Rather, both sets of interests, while remaining

---

ment want to deny that Cobb is not also interested in reconciliation and community or even in the consequences of various religious meanings; nor do I want to leave the impression that I think it unimportant to learn to see matters from the perspectives of other people. The difference between Cobb's position and my own, therefore, might be best described as one of emphasis rather than kind. I think the emphasis on the criticism and reconstruction of religious interests in relation to their functions rather than to what is "seen" from alternative perspectives, however, is somewhat more conducive to the promotion of reconciliation and human well-being, for it explicitly focuses upon issues of good and bad, better and worse.

[76]See above, pp. 87–89.

distinct, are developed and transformed by the connections between the interests that we have come to see. Consequently, while sharing interests with others, we are still able to remain committed to our own interests and to pursue them. Indeed, our commitment to our own transformed interests is enhanced in part because they are now understood to support and to be supported by the interests of others.

In this book, I have proposed a method for reflection based upon Dewey's thought that is meant to be helpful in the context of religious pluralism. I have called it a historical method, for it is developed out of a historical interpretation of human nature and the function of meanings as well as of thinking with and about meanings in human life. To propose a method for reflection in the context of a particular problem, of course, is not to solve that problem but to point out a direction for further reflection. The problem of religious pluralism, in particular, will be solved, if it is solved at all, in critical communication among members of various religious traditions. Yet our interpretation of human nature upon which this method is based indicates that this kind of problem will never be solved once for all, because it represents a fundamental and recurring problem in and of human life. To be sure, from time to time men and women have responded and will continue to respond adequately to a particular instance of this problem by appropriately transforming their interests and reestablishing communication and community. Still, the harmony of interests established at that point can never stay put, for we live in a changing world. Consequently, we need to address this kind of problem again and again.

It may be tempting to compare this unending cycle to Sisyphus and his stone and conclude that the orientation presented here is nihilistic. Such might well be the case if we were to presuppose that the end of human life is fixed and static, something that can be achieved once for all, something, therefore, that should stay put. There can be no doubt that this conception of eschatological perfection has deeply affected Western consciousness. It is a Greek conception, for it is based on the Greek idea that there are fixed and final ends for all things, ends, that is, which are not also conditions for further change. When this concept is replaced by Dewey's notion that ends in nature are also beginnings, then the fact that men and women face the same kind of problems time and again does not seem nihilistic. In particular, this idea allows men and women to transfer their interests from fixed goals to the process of adjusting meaningfully to change in the present. "Perfection means perfecting, fulfillment, fulfilling," writes Dewey, "and the good is now or never."[77] The good life, as Dewey puts it, does not lie in some "fixed ideal of a remote good" but in present activity, in the attempt "to convert strife into harmony, monotony into a variegated scene, and limitation into expansion."[78] This perspective sees the end of human life as the process of growing, of "present reconstruction[,] adding fullness and distinctness of meaning."[79]

I argued at the end of chapter three and elsewhere that this interest in the process of growing is a comprehensive, normative interest within Dewey's philosophy. Among other things, it allows us to see that when our achievements (and even our aim at growth) are frustrated by powers beyond us, not all is lost, for it is still possible to understand and use these tragic circumstances as an opportunity for growth. To claim that growth is normative for life, consequently, is to claim that what matters most is not our achievements as such—performing well in school, establishing supportive friendships, maintaining an enriching marriage, advancing in our chosen profession, even communicating and reconciling ourselves with those who hold alternative religious interests. These accomplishments, of course, are all wonderful and good and ought to be supported, but we also need to recognize that they often cannot be achieved when we want or in the way we want them, and that even when they are they cannot be everlastingly maintained in our world of change. To place our trust and sense of worth in these kinds of achievements, consequently, is to place our faith in the golden calf that promises abundance and yet is sure to let us down. What matters most, according to Dewey, is not the achievement of this or that end but the effort and attempt to grow in each moment, to respond imaginatively and creatively to whatever circumstances we face. This outlook casts an entirely different light on the frustration and failure that often befall us. When we take this interest in growth as normative, the frustrations and failures of our lives become qualified in an important way. While the tragedy remains, these circumstances are now also seen as occasions for growth, harboring possibilities for their meaningful development and thus for creative reflection, decision, and response.

When the growth of interests becomes normative for other interests, therefore, the fact that men and women have to address the problem of

---

[77]Dewey, *Human Nature and Conduct*, 267.
[78]Ibid., 260.
[79]Ibid., 259.

religious pluralism time and again is placed in a new context. While it does not eliminate the pain of loss that this problem often occasions, it nonetheless qualifies that loss with hope, allowing men and women to see that loss as also an opportunity for growth, for increasing meaning and fulfillment in life. I have tried in this volume to present an understanding of human life that supports this hope and a method of reflection by which that hope can give way to the reconciling transformation of concrete reality in human affairs.

Toward a Theological Method

In the preface I noted that there is a good deal of confusion on the theological scene. No longer are we able to talk of there being a theological consensus about the nature and function of theology. Today there are many different kinds of proposals called "theological." Anyone just beginning to study theology must wonder what is occurring. What is it that holds this pluralistic and dissonant array of voices and interests together? What, if anything, makes these pieces of reflection theological? Are there any norms that are appropriate for sorting out various positions and distinguishing between the better and the worse? Finally, what difference do these positions make? Why ought we to take one or another seriously?

These questions occur not only to the theological novice but to the seasoned theologian as well. The problem we all face is the seeming disarray among the various options offered in the theological marketplace. With all of these different and conflicting views, we are bound to ask whether there is anything any longer that can be identified as distinctively theological. More significantly, we are forced to ask how is it that we can do theology at all. How are we to think about this confusion, and how do we move on in our reflection from that point?

These questions, of course, have to do with theological method; they are questions, in particular, that have distinctive relevance in the context of a pluralism of contemporary opinion. I suggested that we may gain some perspective on this issue by examining the problem of pluralism among religious traditions, for this is a more comprehensive instance of the same kind of problem. The result of this inquiry has been the proposal of a historical philosophical methodology based upon a historical interpretation of human nature that attempts to account for the pluralism of interests in human culture. My suggestion at this point is that theologians can find meaningful direction for their reflection in the context of the pluralism of normative interests, both within the Christian community and between that community and persons of other traditions, by adopting the philosophical method discussed and developed in these pages.

This philosophical method, as we have seen, is a proposal for how to proceed in thinking about the most comprehensive and important interests in life when those interests stand in conflict. What are taken to be the most important interests in life are best understood as religious interests, for they have a religious function by helping us to adjust to our changing world and providing us with comprehensive and ongoing meaning and orientation. What I have argued so far is that the philosophical method proposed here is an adequate and significant method for reflecting upon religious matters in the context of religious pluralism. What I now propose is that it can be understood as an appropriate theological method as soon as we see that the idea of God is the normative idea of what ought to constitute the most important interest in life. Indeed, when we properly understand this idea, we can see that it in fact helps to give focus and clarity to what we have called the method of philosophical reflection.

Etymologically, "theology" means thinking or reasoning about "*theos*" or "God." The concept of God, therefore, is central to any theological effort. There are, of course, many different ideas and images of who or what God is within the Western religious traditions. However, when we approach this concept with respect to its functions, as Gordon Kaufman has pointed out, these images and ideas tend to fall into two sorts. First of all, there are images of God as Creator, Lord and Judge of the universe and more abstract ideas like the Almighty, the Absolute, the Infinite and the Ground of Being. These images and ideas of God take God, Kaufman argues, as "the relativizer of everything human and finite."[80] The images of God as Creator, Lord, and Judge of the world, for example, combine to convey the idea of God standing outside of and over against the world as the one who has called it into being, who holds all power, and who sits in judgment upon it. These images are built up out of the tragic elements of the world and the resulting realization that we are not in final control of our lives but are subject to powers and forces that restrict and relativize us in various ways. In the idea of God, this aspect of our lives is extended without limit. God, consequently, is taken to be that ultimate power that stands beyond all finite powers, beyond all finite things, and therefore beyond all our own ideas and interests,

[80]Kaufman, *Theological Imagination*, 35.

including this idea about God. Consequently, the idea of God has a very peculiar self-referential function. As Kaufman puts it,

> It instructs us never to stop with any proximate or penultimate reality—anything in the world—regarding that as God. To do so would be idolatry, for God is the ultimate—i.e., the final or last— reality, beyond which there is nothing more. But how are we to know when we have reached final reality? The answer can only be that we never do. In the search for God we must always press on, never resting content with what we have discovered or expressed.[81]

When we flatly identify any of our ideas or interests with God, consequently, we are no longer talking about God but about some idol. The first function of the idea of God, therefore, is to relativize human life by calling into question the finality of all our interests.

There are also images of God as Father, Savior, and Friend and more abstract notions such as Light, Teacher, the Good, and Truth. These images and ideas represent God as "a humanizing center of orientation."[82] As Kaufman puts it, they represent God as

> a focus for orientation which will bring true fulfillment and meaning to human life. . . [personifying] what are taken to be the highest and most indispensable human ideals and values, making them a visible standard for measuring human realization, and simultaneously enabling them to be attractive of loyalty and devotion which can order and continuously transform individuals and societies toward fulfillment (i.e., bring "salvation").[83]

These sorts of images are material images constructed out of goods of human experience that are idealized and projected as positive ideals of and for human life. As a result, they are meant to provide orientation toward genuine human fulfillment and to function, therefore, as a humanizing power in human life. The second function of the idea of God, consequently, is to humanize our lives by showing what is the most

---

[81]Kaufman, *Essay on Theological Method*, 51.
[82]Kaufman, *Theological Imagination*, 35.
[83]Ibid., 32.

important interest in life, the commitment to which will bring fulfillment.

The importance of the concept of God lies in the fact that it holds
these relativizing and humanizing functions together in creative and dialectical tension. "Thus," writes Kaufman, "that which serves to call into
question everything we do and are and experience is at the same time
apprehended as ultimately humane and beneficent, that which fulfils and
completes our humanity."[84] On the one hand, this is to see the tragedy
and mystery of our lives in a new way as also the source of our hope
and fulfillment and therefore worthy of our trust and loyalty. On the
other hand, it means we can never rest content with what we take to be
our most important interests in life; we are discouraged, that is, from
directly identifying what we take to be most important with what in fact
is, and therefore ought to be taken as, the most important interest. When
the concept of God is functioning as it should, consequently, we at once
embrace our understanding of God as the most important focus of interest and orientation, and we become critical of how we understand that
focus, thereby opening ourselves to its development and transformation.

It is important to carry the argument one step further. The concept of
God, I suggest, is in fact a complex way of conceiving the world. Initially, this may not seem to be the case at all. After all, the concept of
God is constructed out of images that portray a reality that is, among
other things, absolute and completely independent, standing beyond and
over against the finite world as an entirely different sort of reality. To
this extent, of course, the concept of God is a concept of a relation
between the reality of God and the reality of the world, but the relation
is one of disjunction and separation. This disjunction has from time to
time been proclaimed as the whole meaning of the concept of God.[85]
Yet there are serious problems with this claim. For one thing, there are

---

[84]Kaufman, *Essay on Theological Method*, 56.

[85]This was the central position, for example, of the so-called dialectical theology
in Germany following World War I. The clearest expression of this comes from
Karl Barth in his preface to the second edition of *The Epistle to the Romans*
(Edwin C. Hoskyns, trans.; New York: Oxford University Press, 1977) 10: "If I
have a system, it is limited to a recognition of what Kierkegaard called the
'infinite qualitative distinction' between time and eternity, and to my regarding
this as possessing negative as well as positive significance: 'God is in heaven,
and thou art on earth.'"

certain logical difficulties. For example, the concept of the world, as we have seen, is a concept of reality as a whole. If God as another reality is introduced, then either that reality is a part of the whole, in which case it is not an independent and entirely other sort of reality, or there is "a whole" of reality plus one other thing, in which case we are making logical nonsense out of the meaning of "the whole." More significantly, however, when God is understood simply as a reality different from the reality of the world, God is conceived as a mere "X." There is no positive or material content in this conception that could possibly attract our attention and interest. One is left wondering why anyone would bother with this concept at all.

Fortunately, there is another side to the concept of God. This concept is of interest to men and women because it also represents the source of fulfillment in their lives, holding together those comprehensive ideals that make a difference to them and organizing their other interests. This side of the concept of God portrays a positive relation between the realities of God and the world, for it takes God to be the fulfilling potentiality in and of the world. As we saw before, however, the concept of the world is a concept of this very thing. I argued earlier that it represents the normative character of potentiality, those potential ways of interacting that are believed to result in a consummation of interacting parts. Consequently, the concept of God is best understood not as a concept of an entirely different sort of reality than the world but as a particular way of conceiving the world. Once it is evident that talk about God as another sort of reality does not describe or denote that other reality but relativizes our talk about all matters of ultimate interest, then it is clear that the concept of God is not only a concept of the world but one more complex than most, for it includes its own relativization.

It should be evident how this idea is helpful for the method of philosophical reflection. For one thing, it helps to clarify the fact that this kind of reflection is about a normative and humanizing vision of reality. As we saw before, philosophers have often taken their concepts of reality to be descriptions of what reality is as such and have thus failed to see that what they in fact offer is a normative program that organizes other interests and orients conduct in the world. The concept of God, on the other hand, is above all a normative concept. In particular, it is a concept of what *ought* to be taken as the most important interest in life. When we identify the concept of God with a particular way of conceiving the world, consequently, then it becomes clearer that what is at stake in philosophical reflection upon the concept of the world is the discovery of what constitutes the potentials for fulfillment in and of the world.[86]

[86]It is possible to object, of course, that most theologians throughout history and many even today have taken and continue to take talk about God as a direct description of that reality we call God. One may agree that God constitutes the most important object of interest in life but still claim that God is really and truly *there*, an objective reality that can be denoted and described not unlike other objective realities. Yet talk about God is not easily reduced to talk about an object in and of the world like other objects, for part of the very meaning of the word "God"—when we talk about God as "Creator," "Lord," "the beginning and the end," "the Almighty"—is that what it is we are talking about is beyond us and our capacity to describe it or to speak of it directly. Recognition of this is inherent throughout the tradition. Paul expressed it with his eschatological notion that matters having to do with God are matters that are not clear to us now but will be at some point when we will see them "face to face" (1 Cor 13:12). Anselm, as well, refused to identify God with this or that thing but spoke of God as "that, than that nothing greater can be conceived" (Anselm, *Saint Anselm: Basic Writings*, trans. S. N. Deane [La Salle, IL: Open Court, 1962] 8). Aquinas agreed that we can talk about God only with analogies, not directly. "[I]n this life," he writes, "we cannot see God in his essence. But we do know God through creatures. . . . We can accordingly apply to God names which are derived from creatures. Such a name, however, does not express what the divine essence is in itself" (Aquinas, *Aquinas on Nature and Grace: Selections from the Summa Theologia of Thomas Aquinas* [trans. and ed. A. M. Fairweather; Philadelphia: Westminster, 1964] 76). This relativizing dimension of our talk about God, when it is functioning properly, appropriately restricts us from identifying our talk with an existing object as such. This makes it possible for us to see that the normative (or humanizing) dimension of our talk about God is not a description of what is as such as much as a projection of ideal interests—constituting what is potential about the world for fulfillment in it.

Interestingly enough, this last point characterizes what Dewey himself wants to identify as the meaning of "God" in the contemporary world. This word, he suggests (*A Common Faith*, 42), "denotes the unity of all ideal ends arousing us to desire and actions" rather than "some kind of Being having prior and therefore non-ideal existence." It is crucial to see, however, that Dewey understands "God" to be more than human ideals: "this idea of God. . . is also connected with all the natural forces and conditions. . . that promote the growth of the ideal and that further its realization. We are in the presence neither of ideals completely embodied in existence nor yet ideals that are mere rootless ideals, fantasies. . . . For there are forces in nature and society that generate and support the ideals. They are further united by the action that gives them coherence and solidarity. It is this

This is a creative and speculative task that requires a good deal of vision and imagination to go beyond established patterns of thought in order to transform them. The advantage of this concept of God, with its emphasis upon normative potential, is that it helps to free thinking from its past, from feeling the need to assert and defend established positions as "the truth," as the way things are as such, in the context of alternative normative claims. Positively stated, this concept of God helps to focus attention on the present and its particular pluralistic demands and therefore liberates human imagination and thinking to reconstruct established positions in ways that will meet those demands.[87]

Even more significant is the fact that the concept of God helps to underscore the self-critical and relativizing nature of the method of philosophical reflection. When understood with respect to its functions rather than as a reified object, it reminds us that the conclusions we make are always open to question, review, and reconstruction. The advantage of this reminder is that it helps to break down the walls that separate people and opens them to critical dialogue with those who hold alternative normative interests by encouraging communication and the development of community.[88] As we have seen, this openness to and

---

active relation between ideal and actual to which I would give the name 'God' " (pp. 50–51).

I find Dewey's position an important suggestion for developing a contemporary interpretation of the meaning "God." Among other things, it suggests that "God" might be understood as a particular ideal type of process of the world, that process which we have called growth. This would be a "humanizing" image of God. If appropriately developed, it would relativize the overtly anthropocentric tendencies of the constructivist position offered here, for it could help men and women see that they are participating in a long evolutionary and historical development of which they are a part but certainly not the whole. For theological proposals developed along these lines, see Gordon D. Kaufman, *Theology for a Nuclear Age* (Philadelphia: Westminster, 1985) 30–46, esp. 41–42; and Wieman, *The Source of Human Good*, 54–83.

[87]When the relativizing function of the concept of God is not recognized and the concept is therefore reified, it tends to have the opposite effect, closing the imagination to novel alternatives.

[88]Again, it is important to note that historically the concept of God has often separated people, closing them off from those holding alternative normative interests. This is because they have taken the images and ideas about God as directly corresponding to a reality as such. That men and women have often

communication with others are vital conditions for the development of reflection that aims at the transformation of interests in a pluralistic context.

A final advantage of this concept of God for philosophical reflection is that it unites more tightly these humanizing and relativizing functions of our reflection than does the concept of the world by itself, for it brings these functions together in a single and sharp focus of attention. In particular, it makes two things clear in a way that almost no other concept can. First, it indicates that what relativizes us also humanizes us; therefore it gives us hope by encouraging us—in the midst of relativization that we undergo from time to time—to search for healing and reconciling possibilities. Second, it cautions us that what we take as normative, humanizing potentials may be mistaken, and therefore it encourages us at the same time to be alert and sensitive to the actual consequences of our ideals and to be prepared to reconstruct them if need be. In this way, the concept of God helps to clarify the crucially important historical dynamic inherent in what we have proposed as the method of philosophical reflection within a pluralistic context, namely, the ongoing and creative movement and exchange between claim and question and counterclaim that keeps the human spirit alive and developing.

I am not proposing that philosophy is simply disguised theology or that philosophers ought to adopt the concept of God for their reflection.

---

made this move should not be surprising, for the scriptures and traditions in the West are full of stories depicting God as a person who speaks to and interacts with human beings in a number of ways. Nevertheless, this way of taking the meanings of the word "God," as I have tried to argue, is seriously mistaken, for to identify its meanings directly with our understanding of any reality constitutes what the Western traditions have called idolatry, the confusion of Creator and creation. This is an exceedingly hard point to see clearly, for it constitutes an affirmation, that God is Creator of the world, and its own negation. To say this is to say that all claims about God, *including this one*, are open to question, for they are claims made by creatures and thus part of creation. The advantages of using the concept of God for directing reflection in the context of religious pluralism presuppose that this point is understood and utilized in the process of reflection.

Some philosophers, to be sure, have found this concept useful, but many in this century have not. Nor am I suggesting that men and women from other religious traditions adopt this concept for the purposes of reflection. This would imply that communication is possible only if others embrace the concept most central to Western religious traditions. My proposal is more modest. What I am suggesting is that theologians can use the philosophical method discussed in this volume as a method for theological reflection as well. What theologians bring to that method— the concept of God—constitutes a significant development of that method itself, since it brings into sharper focus what is important about that method within the context of a pluralism of interests.

This work is, of course, simply one more proposal for understanding what theology is about and how to proceed with theological reflection. Nevertheless, it has at least three distinctive advantages for theological reflection within a pluralistic context. We can conclude our discussion by taking note of these advantages. First, it allows us to recognize a pluralism of normative interests as a natural and healthy development of human nature and as capable of enriching human life in the modern world. Second, and at the same time, it offers criteria for judging the relative worth of different normative interests. As we have seen, interests, according to this perspective, are to be judged by their capacity to grow and to promote growth. To put it in the terms discussed in chapter three, interests are to be judged by the extent to which they make it possible for conduct to become art, to develop unity and continuity of meaning within the shifting contexts of life. To put it in yet a third way, interests are to be judged by their capacity to develop a rich and dynamic community of individuals who are capable of developing their own interests and qualifying them in relation to others so that the interests and activities of each reinforce and support the interests and activities of the others in an ongoing and developing way. Finally, to put it in terms of the theological concept of God that we have just been discussing, normative interests are to be judged by their capacity to relativize and humanize human life at one and the same time.

All of these criteria are important for theologians in their evaluation of normative interests in a pluralistic context. I have examined in some detail in chapter three how the first three criteria are connected; in this chapter I have suggested how they are related to the final set of criteria. Particularly worthy of note is the relation between growth and the final set of criteria since both are self-correcting, regulative norms. There is, therefore, a third advantage of this particular theological method. As self-correcting notions, the criteria inherent in the proposal are intrinsically open to their own criticism, development, and transformation. This is thoroughly consistent with the historical perspective developed in these pages. As historical criteria that have emerged in human life and been developed and used for human purposes, it would be a mistake to take them as final or absolute, incapable of question and reconstruction. Nevertheless, it is important to see that they are not simply arbitrary criteria. One of the central aims of this work has been to show their appropriateness and plausibility for philosophical, religious, and theological reflection in the context of plural and conflicting normative interests.